HONFB

D0866958

A Voice of the Warm

A Voice *of the* Warm

The Life of Rod McKuen

Barry Alfonso

GUILFORD, CONNECTICUT

Published by Backbeat Books
An imprint of The Rowman & Littlefield Publishing Group, Inc.
4501 Forbes Boulevard, Suite 200, Lanham, Maryland 20706
www.rowman.com

Distributed by NATIONAL BOOK NETWORK

Copyright © 2019 by Barry Alfonso

All rights reserved. No part of this book may be reproduced in any form or
by any electronic or mechanical means, including information storage and
retrieval systems, without written permission from the publisher, except by
a reviewer who may quote passages in a review.

Book design and composition by Michael Kellner

Library of Congress Cataloging-in-Publication Data is available

ISBN 978-1-61713-709-9

The paper used in this publication meets the minimum requirements of
American National Standard for Information Sciences—Permanence
of Paper for Printed Library Materials, ANSI/NISO Z39.48-1992.

Printed in the United States of America

To Sylvia Franklin and Janet Ingram—with gratitude, warmly . . .

CONTENTS

FOREWORD

By Michael Feinstein

I FIRST MET Rod McKuen at a party in Los Angeles's Los Feliz neighborhood in the late 1970s. I was playing piano, and he came over and we
tossed tunes back and forth. He asked me to play "Over the Rainbow," and
then he sang his own song "The Beautiful Strangers" in counterpoint. I said,
"That's lovely." He told me that he'd always loved "Over the Rainbow" and
that he'd written "The Beautiful Strangers" as another way of expressing that
same emotion. Years later, I performed at Carnegie Hall with Cheyenne Jack-
son and we did those two songs in counterpoint the same way. Though Rod
had written it secretly as a contrafact, it had never been publicly heard that
way, and it was a thrill to present the two songs in tandem, especially on the
Carnegie Hall stage, the setting of his previous triumphs.

In a real sense, Rod was the archetypal Beautiful Stranger. He was warm,
amiable, and considerate of others. Yet he was also very controlled and self-
protective—I felt he hid a lot. He had so many friends, but I wonder how
many of them really got close to him. It was confounding. He was a paradox,
very open and closed-off at the same time.

Firsthand, I can say that he was incredibly generous. Rod was the greatest
fan of other artists and was a champion of so many of them. I have always

had a particular affection for Rosemary Clooney, and I casually mentioned to Rod that I was looking for a master tape of hers that had disappeared. Out of the blue about two weeks later, he sent by messenger a digital dub of the very tape I had been searching for, which he'd had professionally copied at his own expense. He wouldn't take a penny for it. That's the kind of guy he was.

Rod had a real love for the singers and songwriters of the Great American Songbook era. In some ways, his industry might be compared to Johnny Mercer, with his desire and ability to write in so many different styles. Rod was prolific as a songwriter and poet—he seemed to want to prove he could do anything he chose. It may be that if he'd had a smaller output, he'd be regarded differently now. That's not his fault—I think he felt it was necessary to be constantly producing, because the demand was there.

Rod was very much ahead of his time in making a cottage industry out of who he was and what he created. Other songwriters had done something roughly similar in the past. Richard Rodgers and Oscar Hammerstein became hard-boiled businessmen who were ruthless in protecting their assets as a writing team. They knew how they were perceived by the public, and they made sure they were marketed in a certain way, with the business unseen so as not to sully the benevolent image. There are many other examples. Polar opposites from Noël Coward to Duke Ellington were all astute with their creative output. But Rod went beyond all of them with his tremendous ability to understand pop culture and appeal to public taste on a whole other level. I can't think of another example of someone as industrious as this until you get to Madonna—but the difference is that from the outset, Madonna was marketed for mass culture, with talent being secondary, whereas Rod's trajectory evolved from his creativity coupled with an undaunted work ethic.

How did Rod do it? He clearly understood the essence of human nature. He knew how to create something that made a reader or listener say, "That's me." Like Gershwin's, his work is a document of the time in which it was created. But what he did also transcends that time and still speaks fundamentally to the things that matter to people: romance, relationships, the human condition. Those things don't change. He used the vernacular of his time to reach the widest audience. But at its essence, his work is still valid and, I think, timeless.

Rod McKuen's life and career were remarkable in many ways. His contributions to popular culture have been overlooked for too long. Strip away the accrued soil of judgment and misunderstanding, and underneath you will find a pure and shiny patina. It's time for a reintroduction to this beautiful stranger.

INTRODUCTION

S INGER-SONGWRITER-POET Rodney "Rod" Marvin McKuen (1933–2015) is arguably the most successful popular artist of his time who has never had a biography written about him. Why?

The past half century has seen a host of million-selling songwriters, certified-gold recording artists, and authors who stormed up the best-seller lists. Rod McKuen was all three of these things. He was constantly on American television, profiled in newspapers and magazines around the world, a top draw in concert halls from Cincinnati to Sydney, Edinburgh to Johannesburg. People embraced him as a sort of personal savior and excoriated him as a harbinger of cultural decadence. You could love Rod or loathe him, but you could hardly avoid him.

Rod McKuen made history in a big way. The media stood in awe of how many books and records he sold. While you can quibble about the exact figures, the numbers were undeniably record-breaking. The jacket copy for his 1972 poetry book *And to Each Season* . . . proclaimed him not only the best-selling author in America, but the best-selling poet in history. He received upward of sixty gold and platinum records and had songs recorded by legendary artists like Frank Sinatra, Johnny Cash, Nina Simone, and Dusty

Springfield. In 1971, his annual income was "conservatively estimated" at $3 million.

So, with all of the above in mind, why is this the first full-length book about McKuen? There are two main reasons: First, Rod never wanted anyone to write his biography. And second, the literary establishment didn't think he deserved one.

McKuen is the odd man out in the history of American pop culture. Music encyclopedias almost never included him, even though he released albums for over forty years. Surveys of contemporary literature overlooked him despite (or perhaps because of) his enormous sales. Rod's work as a musician and poet didn't lend themselves to easy categorization. Over the decades, he was associated with the San Francisco Beat poet scene, the twist dance craze of the early sixties, the folk revival, the Great American Songbook school of pop, the early days of New Age environmental recordings, and twentieth-century classical music. Yet none of these genres or movements claim him as even an adjunct member. He remains sui generis, by his own choice or otherwise.

His fans didn't care. Try to see him as they saw him at the height of his fame: a rumpled, slightly stooped thirtysomething man with lemon-frosting-colored hair ambling into the spotlight to the sound of orchestral fanfare. Inevitably, he is dressed in a sweater, jeans (or chinos), and high-top sneakers—no amount of success could change his outfit. There's a laid-back cowboy charm about him, as well as the romantic melancholy of a French cabaret singer. He laughs bashfully, gives wistful sideways glances, rises from quiet murmurs to emotional crescendos. Now close your eyes and hear his voice—hoarse, pitted, compelling in its imperfection. It adds to his pathos and his sexiness.

That voice could be heard clearly on the printed page, as well as live and on record. He wrote about commonplace things, ordinary scenes, passing incidents and moods. However you took in his words, McKuen seemed to be whispering in your ear. His unabashed nostalgia for old-fashioned pleasures like butterflies in the summertime and snowy Christmas mornings contrasted with his frank celebrations of a lover's thighs or the soft glow of a postcoital reverie. On albums like *Lonesome Cities* and in books like *Listen to the Warm*, Rod found a way to make an erotic encounter in a steamy back room seem as wholesome as a basket of puppies or flying a kite on a windy hillside.

McKuen's critics—and they were legion—wouldn't have any of it. They refused to concede that this "King of Kitsch" had an outstanding talent for anything except fleecing his customers. When TV host Dick Cavett cracked that Rod was "America's most understood poet," he was voicing the agreed-upon opinion of the cultural tastemakers of the time. To the likes of poet/teacher Karl Shapiro and journalist Nora Ephron, Rod was a clever hack, who cranked out treacly songs and superficial poems as if they were Hostess cupcakes, with utter cynicism. His sensitive-poet act was a con, a snare for the mentally lazy and the aesthetically stunted. This last line of thinking is impor-tant to note, because these critics looked down upon not only McKuen but his audience as well. That anyone would lap up such cloying pap was prima facie evidence of Middle American mediocrity. That these fans seemed to worship Rod as something more than an entertainer and writer of greeting-card verse only reinforced their indictment.

Rod just didn't smell right to press pundits and academic arbiters of good writing. There was something less than legitimate about him—it was as if he'd snuck into respectable circles by slipping past the guard at the gate (which, according to McKuen, is in fact how he got a screen test at Universal Pic-tures as a young man). He was a feral sort of talent—ill-bred, wily, and look-ing for the main chance. Big record companies and major publishing houses embraced him for a quick buck, betraying their responsibility to maintain high standards. They delegitimized themselves by promoting his products and spreading his fame.

His defenders were many as well—they just weren't part of the cultural establishment. To them, Rod McKuen was a hardworking, kindhearted voice of the people, a dedicated artist who rose from poverty without forgetting his roots in unglamorous everyday America. He learned the trades of radio broadcaster, songwriter, movie actor, and nightclub performer—but what set him apart was his willingness to share his desires, fears, and often painful memories through his songs and poems. Rod was not the mouthpiece of the cultural elite or the fashionably hip. He wrote and sang about love, loss, momentary daydreams, and longings for the past in ways anyone could grasp. "I don't think someone should have to have a twelve-foot bookshelf to understand a poem I've written," he said. His work offered an outstretched hand to the lonely and brokenhearted, to anyone in need of comfort and healing.

Those were the polarities in the debate over the merits of McKuen's work a half century ago. Issues of culture and class swirled around this slouching figure in cashmere and denim, and continued to swirl long after he left the spotlight. Rod spoke for a vast constituency with a directness and sincerity millions responded to. He embodied shifting attitudes about sexuality, personal freedom, and humanity's connection with nature. As much as Bob Dylan, Allen Ginsberg, Timothy Leary, and other voices of the counterculture, Rod McKuen spoke for his times.

More than that, his life and work anticipated changes to come. McKuen presented himself as sexually fluid many years before the term came into vogue. At a time when male and female identities were still rigidly defined, he was a man willing to confess weakness and vulnerability without shame. As an entrepreneur, he innovated forms of personal branding and self-promotion that would be imitated decades later. His diary-like poetry resembled blogging in its free-flowing commentary on life lived moment by moment. (Rupi Kaur and other members of the currently popular Instapoet movement owe something to Rod's brevity and simplicity of expression as well.) A born loner and outsider, he figured out ways to bring far-flung readers and listeners into a greater community that resembled the social networks of today. Rod did all of this after surviving a harrowing childhood, a stretch in reform school, and intermittent years of poverty. He was a damaged, street-savvy kid who grew up to be something of a visionary.

McKuen's place in twentieth-century pop culture deserves a reassessment. "Rod is an important, significant part of musical history because of the way he touched the hearts of so many people," says artist and Great American Songbook scholar Michael Feinstein. "Spiritually and emotionally, he had a tremendous effect upon the planet. He clearly understood the human condition. It was almost a divine gift, even though people had various assessments of his talent. There's no question that his achievements were remarkable."

You can't help but respect McKuen and what he accomplished once you know more of his story. I was drawn to write about him both because I've long admired his best songs ("Jean," "If You Go Away," and "Love's Been Good to Me" among them) and because so many "smart" people found him objectionable. Anyone who provoked that strong a reaction, pro or con, was worth investigating. Looking at his life and work was a way of understanding the craft of writing, the nature of fame, and the great American myth of the self-made man. Rod's sheer tenacity and chutzpah impressed me—and his last years struck me as deeply poignant.

Countless public figures have lied or exaggerated about themselves. Robert Frost is an outstanding example of a poet who stretched the truth as he presented himself to the world. But Rod McKuen made it especially hard for a biographer to tell his story. Fact and fabulation are often inseparable in the accounts he gave of his life. For whatever reason, Rod couldn't help salting his interviews with a generous seasoning of wishful thinking, fantasized incidents, or outright untruths. Sifting them out from the verifiable information has been difficult. In many cases, Rod was the sole recorded witness to events in his life. I've looked for consistency in his accounts and weighed the probability of the more unlikely claims. Some stories must be taken on faith.

McKuen's apocryphal claims include writing a newspaper column called

"Scribbling on My Shirt Cuff" for the *San Francisco Examiner* during his teens (no such column has turned up in the paper's files); acting in several Japanese movies made by Toho Films while serving in the U. S. Army (his name isn't found in any database for the studio); singing with Lionel Hampton's band sometime in the 1950s (possible, but not verifiable); performing for a state dinner at the Kennedy White House (the JFK presidential library has no record of this—although it is true Rod had at least passing contact with Robert F. Kennedy around 1968); and receiving a nomination for a 1973 Pulitzer Prize in Music (the Pulitzer Prize board did not announce finalists in the 1970s and has never announced nominations).

Many more examples could be added to this list. These include novels, screenplays, records, stage musicals, feature films, and various business ventures that were announced as completed or in the works but never actually saw the light of day. In some cases, they may have been wholly imaginary.

Three and a half years of research has led me to believe that Rod told many white lies and some real whoppers about his life and career. A constant need to legitimize himself and prove his worth drove him to exaggerate his actual accomplishments, which were truly formidable. His deceptions were mostly benign; he probably came to believe many of them were true. In the end, they invoke more sympathy than outrage. No amount of recognition could still the nagging inner voice that he just wasn't quite good enough.

At this writing, I've interviewed close to one hundred people who knew Rod McKuen as a friend, creative partner, or employer. Almost to an individual, they described him as charming, thoughtful, kind, and generous. Conversations and email exchanges with these men and women reinforced my belief that Rod was essentially sincere as an artist. The tolerance and compassion found in his work—as well as its pervasive melancholy—reflected who he really was. This was the opinion both of people who were close to him when he was young and those who spent time with him in old age. Rod left many fond memories behind him when he died.

Beyond his own personal circle of close and casual friends, Rod touched countless lives through his words and music. Fans came to consider him a confidant they could turn to in times of loneliness or sorrow. He didn't just inspire devotion from afar—he made himself unusually accessible for a celebrity, spending hours with fans after shows and corresponding with admirers, sometimes over decades. McKuen gave his listeners and readers comfort and inspiration—and, not incidentally, motivated many to explore the larger world of poetry.

A current Facebook page dedicated to McKuen's memory confirms that his presence lingers on in the lives of many. Their loyalty to the artist and his work remains unshaken and vital. A longtime fan from Illinois spoke for many when he wrote, "Over the years I found many McKuen songs to describe my life. His music said I wasn't alone and my joys and despair were part of being alive. I also think [his work] made me a deeper man and a better person 'in touch with my feelings,' as they used to say . . . "

We live in a time drenched in irony and fearful of expressing genuine sentiment. Rod tried to touch the chords of emotion directly, without apology. His aesthetic choices and merchandizing excesses might be questioned, but what he meant and still means to people should not be. He wasn't fooling when he famously wrote, "It's not who you love or how you love but that you love." That was his core message, pure and simple—too simple for the critics to believe.

Yet that simplicity concealed something deeper about the man. Those who knew Rod often found him to be "enigmatic," a "chameleon" who "juggled personalities." As his former assistant Rose Adkins put it, "There was a mystery to who he really was as a person, and I don't think anybody will be able to solve it. I don't think he himself could solve it."

"Everybody knows my name . . . but no one knows me," McKuen wrote in "Solitude's My Home." Rod was ambivalent about revealing all that he was. He would not have chosen to have his biography written without his control and approval. But somehow I think he'd appreciate this attempt to uncover something of his inner identity and explore what he meant to his times.

In 1967, Rod invited the world to *Listen to the Warm*. All these years later, maybe it's time to lean in and listen a little closer . . .

A Voice of the Warm

One

~

The Wandering Soul

A MIRROR BALL throws flickering shards of light across a crowded taxi dance hall in downtown Oakland, California. Couples move to music churned out by a weary jazz combo—you can smell the sweat and feel the erotic tension. At the edge of the dance floor, sellers rip off tickets for a dime and hand them to anxious male customers as each song ends. The women on the dance floor take tickets from the men and stuff them under the hem of their stockings; some carry a bulge the size of a goiter. The band strikes up the inevitable "Baby Face" as the floor comes alive.

Some of the partners are grotesquely mismatched in size, age, and dancing ability—they slide and shimmy and avoid injuring each other's feet. Others genuinely seem drawn to each other. They slowly move toward a darkened corner, dancing slow and close . . .

A young woman and a somewhat older man are swaying to the music at the edge of the floor. The taxi dancer is a saucy bleached blonde, but she lacks the hard edge of some of the girls—there's a sweetness and vulnerability in her wistful eyes and soft lips. Her partner is taller, handsome, immaculately groomed, a man from the mountain West very different from the citified sheikhs prowling the hall tonight. For a moment, the dance these two share is more than a commercial transaction. They continue to cling to each other as the song ends and the ticket sellers hustle the leering, nervous men for one more dime.

Outside, the Great Depression grinds on. It is August 1932 and hard-pressed working people are scrounging for any dollar they can cadge. They are also looking for escape in the cheap dance halls, the movie theaters and amusement parks, anywhere they can find company. Men and women are wandering the country looking for work, uprooted from family, morally adrift. There are plenty of men on the make and good girls gone bad (or at least teetering on the brink). In spite of it all, love can still survive, even in times as bleak as this . . .

It sounds like a scene from a pre–Hays Code Hollywood film. The scenario is at once tawdry, dreamy, poignant, and painful. It all depends upon how you tell it.

Rod McKuen told it like a tragic love story. The couple in this scene are his mother and father. They came together fleetingly, conceived a son in a night of passion, and went their separate ways soon after. The son would carry his father's name, even though he would never meet him . . .

Though all of this took place before he could remember, the scene above lies at the heart of Rod's work as a writer. The story of his mother, Clarice Woolever, and her brief connection with Rodney Marion McKune touches upon all of his major obsessions: transitory happiness, illicit sex, abandonment, nostalgia, wanderlust, the search for identity. He returned to these themes throughout his career as a songwriter and poet. If the characters and settings changed, the same yearnings were expressed over and over, with no final resolution.

Rod's work wrapped core personal truths in gauzy fantasies about beautiful strangers, lonesome cities, and soft places to land. First among these were the circumstances of his birth at the Salvation Army home for unwed mothers on April 29, 1933. Examining nearly every aspect of McKuen's life involves peeling back layers of fact, semi-truth, and sheer fabulation. But the basic outline of his family history appears to be solid enough.

Clarice Isabel Woolever was the youngest of five siblings born in Union, Oregon, a small town on the thinly populated eastern end of the state. Her parents, Charles W. and Jessie M. Woolever, were a working-class couple in an area dominated by farming, logging, and cattle ranching. Jessie had an artistic streak—Rod discovered snatches of poetry in old notebooks that showed a real if unrefined gift for writing. Her husband seemed to have been a sturdy, hardworking man with a gruff streak who provided for his family. Little apparently distinguishes them from other families in that place at that time.

There are shadows in the Woolever family story. According to his daughter-in-law Marion, Charles was "very hard to please" when he was drinking. Sometime later in life, he began to show signs of dementia, leading to his commitment at Oregon State Hospital. Marion Woolever wrote to the hospital superintendent that Charles was prone to delusional behavior like attempting to harness imaginary horses in the family barn. "I was real glad to care of him (sic) until he would threaten the children with the long stove poker," she wrote. Charles died not long after being admitted to the hospital in January 1936.

Does Charles's behavior help explain why all but one of his children moved away from Union? Certainly there was far more opportunity and stimulation to be found elsewhere. Ted became a merchant seaman, while Ruth, Fern, and Clarice made their way to the San Francisco Bay Area. 1932 found the sisters living together at the Abbey Apartments in downtown Oakland. As Rod tells it, the eldest reinvented herself as Madame Ruth, a crystal-ball-gazing fortune-teller. Fern engaged in bootlegging and eventually saved enough to buy a dry-cleaning business. As for Clarice, she worked as a waitress and long-distance operator, moving from job to job around the area.

At some point, Clarice went to work as a taxi dancer at various Oakland dance halls, most notably the Rose Room on Twelfth Avenue. In *Finding My Father: One Man's Search for Identity*, Rod quotes an old friend of Clarice's who claims his mother was coerced into taking the job to support her sisters. Whatever the truth of this assertion, there were good financial reasons to become a dime-a-dance girl. According to a 1932 study of Chicago taxi dance halls, even an unskilled dancer could earn up to $35 or $40 a week—decent money in the Great Depression. The rewards from the job went beyond the commission from each dance, of course. As the Chicago study drily points out, "The economic interest is paralleled by an interest in the 'thrill' and excitement of the dance hall."

Though Rod looked back on the taxi dance halls with a certain romantic nostalgia, that scene was a tough racket with disreputable roots. Dime-a-dance ticket palaces originated in San Francisco around 1913 and were well established around the country by the time Clarice became involved with them. They were part of an entire subculture dominated by uprooted, economically marginal men and women. Taxi dance halls were generally near rooming houses and residential hotels favored by struggling working-class people like the Woolever sisters. The women who worked there were rarely over thirty; many were underage. "Nice girls"—fresh faces and peppy dancers not yet hardened by the taxi dancer life—were the most sought-after.

The game was about more than selling ten-cent tickets. In dance hall argot, the customer was a "fish" who could be "fished" by dancers for favors and presents after hours. Such gold-digging often more or less descended into outright prostitution. Still, the "romantic impulse" could override the mutually exploitive rules of "the sex game." Dancer and customer sometimes fell in love.

The idealized taxi dancer looked and talked like Joan Blondell, the plucky blonde who played the wisecracking gold digger in Hollywood comedies and musicals throughout the 1930s. Blondell was sexy and playful, but nobody's fool—the perfect role model for tough yet tenderhearted young women loose in the big city. In *Finding My Father*, Rod noted how much Blondell reminded him of his mother. Photographs of Clarice from the thirties bear this out—she has the same blonde good looks, bright eyes, and expressive mouth as Joan did in those days. Thinking about the two of them caused Rod to blend them in his imagination, stimulating visions of Clarice flashing a warm smile at a passing "sheikh" beneath the Japanese lanterns lighting up the dance hall.

There is one scene starring his mother that Rod replayed over and over in his mind: A handsome stranger steps out of the crowd and falls for her inviting smile, takes her in his arms, and gazes deep into her eyes. There was no famous actor he could cast in the role of this dashing sheikh. Rod could not write a Hollywood happy ending to the story of their brief time together. Even after McKuen discovered the rough details of his father's life after the older man's death, Rodney Marion McKune remained fundamentally a mystery to his son.

A few basic facts can be established. McKune—called "Mack" by friends—was born in Blue Creek Park, Utah, in 1900. He served in the U. S. Army in 1923–26, and then headed south to work in the oil fields of Texas and Oklahoma, before returning to Utah. He was married twice, both times to older women—first to Charlotte Wallace in 1921, and then to Maude McNabb nine years later. According to Rod, his father's friends remembered his marriage to Maude as a happy one. By the late thirties, McKune was running a lumber mill in Altonah, Utah, he'd inherited from his father. In 1943, he sold the mill and moved to California with Maude. He settled in the Los Angeles area, worked for the Union Ice Company, apparently lived an uneventful life, and died in 1963.

Rod came to believe Mack McKune was his father. He based this belief on information dug up by a private detective agency and follow-up interviews he conducted with McKune's surviving relatives. The physical proof linking Clarice and Mack is scanty, however. A photo of the two of them turned up in Clarice's papers. Beyond that is a loosely strung web of conflicting memories, likely inferences, and poetic logic. As in McKuen's writing, there's a mixture of knowable fact and wishful fantasy in the story he told about his parents.

The narrative presented by Rod in *Finding My Father* goes something like this: Sometime early in 1932, Mack and a friend traveled to the Bay Area. There, he worked as a refrigerator salesman and began visiting the Rose Room, where he met Clarice. (The two may also have met at a sales convention in a hotel where Clarice worked as a waitress.) They began a monthlong affair that took them to the Alpine Hotel in East Oakland, the place Rod believed he was conceived. Not long after that, Mack left town, possibly driven off by Clarice's sisters, who resented his presence. It is unclear if he knew Clarice was pregnant. She never heard from him again.

Clarice was admitted to the Salvation Army Home for Women a week before she gave birth. A staff member recalled that she was extremely nervous and possibly suicidal at the time she was admitted. Clarice was adamant about not contacting the father of her child. She misspelled his last name on the birth certificate as "McKuen," complicating her son's attempts to find him in later years. She left the home about six weeks after her son was born, asking that all contact with the hospital be ended after she was discharged.

According to an interview with its superintendent, the Salvation Army home offered "rehabilitation" for the unfortunate women who came there for help. Adjutant May Wilber claimed that unmarried mothers often chose to marry their child's father right there at the hospital chapel. If this wasn't possible, there were other ways the Army tried to promote "the physical, moral, and cultural uplift of motherhood." Apparently, Clarice wasn't interested in any of the organization's advice and guidance. She and her baby went to live with a friend from her waitressing job, and she applied for assistance from the local charity commission.

Though Rod claimed he was certain Clarice didn't tell Mack about her pregnancy, there is no way to verify this. Some of Clarice's old friends told him she had been raped. Rod rejected this and added that it didn't matter even if his father had raped his mother. "It doesn't matter to me whether or not my mother was taken against her will or whether she gave herself to my father in an act of love," he wrote in *Finding My Father*. "I would prefer to think that my mother and father knew and loved each other even for a night or a week." Did Clarice love Mack, even though she never wanted him to know she'd had his child? Rod took the fact that she named him after his father (substituting Marvin for Marion) as evidence she did. Other than that, there is no record of how his mother felt. When Rod asked her about Mack in later years, she grew visibly upset and refused to talk about him.

Clarice's whereabouts are hard to track for the next few years. She left Rod with her brother Ted and his wife, Frieda, for six months to a year while she looked for work as a waitress or taxi dancer. There were fears she had abandoned her son. When Clarice returned to reclaim him, she and Frieda fought over who was fit to take care of Rod. His mother won the argument and took him to live in Nevada, where she had recently married a man named Bill Hooper.

Rod described his stepfather as a dark, good-looking man of two-thirds Native American ancestry—Hooper reminded him of the actor Charles Bronson. According to Hooper, he had met Rod's mother in an Austin, Nevada saloon sometime in 1935. Clarice told him she had been lured from the Bay Area by a man promising her a job at an Austin dance hall. The place turned out to be a brothel. She took a job at a nearby bar instead and was probably happy to be rescued by a handsome stranger, one willing to take care of another man's child. (Rod would be known as Rodney Hooper during his childhood, though he was never formally adopted.)

Hooper worked for the Works Progress Administration on road crews in Nevada's vast backcountry, a sought-after relief job during the Depression. When Clarice married him in 1936, she must have hoped for a better shake than the heartache and shame she'd found in Oakland.

What she got was a stretch of ten years filled with poverty, rootlessness, and physical abuse. Rod spent his childhood watching his mother being ground down by life with a violent, hard-drinking husband in a series of isolated small towns strewn along the highways of the West. Surrounded by strangers and Bill's no-account family, she doggedly worked menial jobs in kitchens and bars while trying to raise first one and then two children. Rod's accounts of these years read like a Dickensian retelling of *The Grapes of Wrath*. The emotional scars of his childhood never truly healed.

As he recalled, Rod lived with his mother and stepfather in six different Nevada towns in 1938. The one he liked best was Alamo, a tiny community along Highway 93 known for its tall cottonwood and poplar trees. The Hoopers lived there in a weathered two-story house with a leaky tar-paper roof and a big backyard. Rod savored the taste of homegrown tomatoes and melons from the family garden. He cared for a pet rabbit (unfortunately sacrificed to the dinner table) and caught crawdads in a nearby creek. Each night, step-grandfather George Hooper (with whom he shared a bedroom) gave him a nickel to keep quiet for five minutes—after the time was up, Rod would run barefoot to the local grocery store to buy candy.

Rod claimed he taught himself to read by peeling back the wallpaper in his bedroom and studying the layer of newspapers revealed underneath. He wrote down words he wanted to remember, and then covered up the holes with pictures drawn on butcher paper. George helped him learn and framed the drawings Rod made.

The boy needed an ally in the increasingly dysfunctional Hooper family. His stepfather wanted Clarice to bear him a child and resented having another man's son around. When he drank, Bill would let Rod know how he felt about him. "I could always tell whether I was going to be beat up by the heavy footfall on the stairs," Rod said at a conference on child victimization in 1982. "If my stepfather had been drinking, I would be beat up. If not, he would go to bed. I had both arms broken and my ribs caved in several times." Bill's mother, Miranda (who lived with the family off and on), would also beat Rod on occasion.

When he was barely five, Rod began first grade at Alamo's three-room schoolhouse. Already able to read, he considered the lessons too easy and his teacher too strict. She finally kicked him out of her class, after he called her an old cow. Rod hid out by the creek for the rest of the day, afraid of punishment waiting him at home. When he finally did come home, he overheard a drunken argument in the kitchen between Bill, Clarice, and Miranda over what to do about him. Bill told Clarice he'd never wanted Rod around in the first place. His step-grandfather hid him in his room and brought him supper.

By 1939, the Hoopers had left Alamo (and, sadly, step-grandad George) behind and moved to a WPA work camp in Pioche, another small desert town about eighty miles north. Conditions there were primitive—families lived in tents lit by kerosene lamps. The tents were prone to being blown down by the wind and could catch fire from a stray spark. Bill worked on the state construction crew while drinking up more and more of his paychecks. Clarice took jobs as a waitress and short-order cook and fed her family on beans, macaroni, and a homemade fried-dough concoction called "whanniker." (Rod insisted as an adult that he preferred such humble grub to more elegant cuisine.)

In this hardscrabble environment, it's easy to see how Rod fell desperately in love with the movies. The extravagant visions of Hollywood were projected into a flimsy tent theater every night, feeding the imagination of a lonely kid stuck in the middle of nowhere. Rod drank in the dash and suavity of Clark Gable and thrilled to Johnny Weissmuller's jungle adventures as Tarzan. He began to imagine his missing father living out one of these heroic roles. Someday, he dreamed, his real dad would find him, beat up Bill Hooper, and reclaim him as his son.

In a real sense, Rod's career as a mythmaker began in Pioche. He began to make up stories about his father to the older boys in town. He told them his dad was a World War flying ace who took out enemy pilots before being shot down and killed. It was an innocent lie that gave a small, vulnerable boy a sense of stature, even if nobody believed him. Wishful thinking shaded over into casual fibbing, not so different from the skills needed to write songs and poems. What began as childhood fantasizing would grow into a formidable, highly marketable talent that would make Rod wealthy and famous. It all began with a longing for a father he could be proud of.

As it was, Rod's bond with his mother was about the only thing he could count on. He lived in a world of uncertainty, filled with constant threats of violence. Moving from town to town in the late thirties, he received minimal schooling and formed no lasting attachments. His almost feral upbringing marked him as an outsider for the rest of his life—but it also sharpened his wits in dealing with adults and left him with a faith in his own imagination.

Looking back, Rod would emphasize the freedom and good times of life in Great Depression–era Nevada more than the poverty and abuse he endured. "There was a certain camaraderie between all of the families in the thirties that were traveling around from job to job," he wrote in *Finding My Father.* "Nobody really went hungry, especially the kids. Booze was really plentiful . . . While the kids played night games outside around the tents, the adults were always laughing and drinking and making a rumpus inside." Rod never seemed to regret not having a stereotypical middle-class home life as a boy— he was an unashamed product of a wandering childhood lived out in the vast Western outback.

After a life-threatening pregnancy, Clarice gave birth to Rod's stepbrother, William Hooper Jr., in October 1938. Rod hoped Bill Sr.'s violent temper would ease now that he finally had a son of his own. At this point, though, the hated Miranda returned to the household and took to walloping her step-grandson when he tried to keep her from gambling away the pension checks she was supposed to share with the family. Rod decided to run away—not surprisingly, he didn't get far as a five-year-old. This was the first of many attempts to escape.

In 1939, the Hoopers left Nevada for the Pacific Northwest. They stayed with Rod's uncle Wesley and his family in Bay City, Oregon, for a time, and then headed northeast to Skamania, Washington, a small logging town near the Columbia River. There, they moved into an abandoned dirt-floor log cabin. It seems likely that Bill brought his family to the area in hopes of finding a job at nearby Bonneville Dam. Rod put a mostly positive spin on his year or so in Skamania, noting that his mother made the primitive cabin feel homey and comfortable.

In *Finding My Father*, Rod tells a couple of stories from this time that foreshadow later themes in his writing. In one, he befriends a mountain lion who watches him walk through the woods to and from school. Eventually, the lion grows tame enough to eat out of Rod's hand and allows Bill Jr. to pet it. This vision of peace is shattered when a horrified Clarice discovers the boys and the beast communing together. It sounds like an incident from the life of St. Francis, or maybe Thoreau. Whatever the facts are, the story does reflect Rod's love for and identification with the natural world.

The other story is a bit darker in tone. Rod encounters two male hitchhikers while hunting for interesting trash along the highway. The men ask him about his schooling and words he has learned. One of them asks Rod if he's ever heard the word *fuck* before. Rod says he hasn't. The story ends with Rod going home and repeating his new word to his mother, who washes his mouth out with soap. Considering Rod's involvements with adult men a few years later, the incident seems significant. Were the hitchhikers just bored drifters or sexual predators trolling for victims? Rod plays the run-in as just another funny anecdote from his hardscrabble childhood. But it can also be seen as a small violation of a boy's innocence that anticipated far worse breaches to come.

Leaving Skamania in early 1940, the vehicle-less Hoopers hitched rides on cars, trucks, and a tractor as they slowly traveled down the back roads of the Pacific Northwest. Rod recalled his mother catching the eye of motorists as they hitchhiked on their long trek back to Nevada. The family's wanderings were starting to get more aimless and desperate. America was changing around them—the camaraderie among the rootless job-seekers of the late

Depression years would soon give way to the more settled and purposeful era of World War II. More and more men would be claimed by the military as the WPA began to wind down. The Hoopers weren't among those who benefited from the economic boom stimulated by the war. As far as they were concerned, the Depression never ended.

Bill had a sister and brother-in-law in North Las Vegas who were willing to put up his family until the Hoopers found a place of their own. Clarice looked for work in a local bar or café, leaving Rod in the care of his step-aunt. On at least one occasion, she sexually molested him. "She began to sort of fondle me, and I said, 'Don't do that. I don't like that,'" he said in a 1982 interview with *People* magazine. "I finally started getting a bit hysterical and started screaming . . . she stopped and left before my mother got home."

About two weeks later, Rod went on a hunting trip near Hoover Dam with his step-uncle. Rod recalled him as kind, affectionate, a great storyteller— the sort of substitute father a lonely boy longed for. Rod described him as someone he loved and trusted, the only member of the Hooper clan he ever characterized in such terms.

That trust was shattered around a campfire in the woods: "I got in my sleeping bag, and he got in his. Then he said, 'Rodney . . . are you asleep?' I said, 'No, I'm not. I don't know why.' . . . We were out in the wilds, and it was a little bit scary, because there were a lot of animals and night sounds I was unfamiliar with. He said, 'I bet you're scared . . . Why don't you just come over and get in my sleeping bag?' . . . So I got into his sleeping bag and we each talked . . . And then things started happening. He ended up raping me."

"I didn't cry until I got back in my own sleeping bag," Rod recalled to *People*. "He had been satisfied and was just as glad to get rid of me. He certainly didn't want to wake up with a child whom he had sodomized. In the morning I couldn't look at him. Then I started getting really mad. I said, 'Listen, your wife did something like this too. I'm not going to tell my mother about this, but if you ever come near me again, if you do anything at all, I'm not only going to tell my mother, I'm going to run down the street and tell everybody on the block.'" As it turned out, Rod would keep silent about the abuse for over forty years.

It's tempting to see this deep psychic wound as the key to Rod's life and career. The ambivalence and melancholy that color the scenes of physical contact in his work can easily be traced back to the childhood abuse he suffered. Rod's songs and poems take on darker meaning with this in mind—all those accounts of thwarted intimacy, misplaced affection, and chronic wanderlust lose some of their romantic appeal when you consider the emotional damage he endured. Rod's own reflections upon his abuse explain why he was so driven to succeed, to write and perform and release product to an almost manic degree. Working served to cover up his gnawing sense of shame and worthlessness.

Rod often told interviewers that the need for "communication" between people was a basic theme in his work. Considering this, it seems ironic—and tragic—that Rod and his mother each had a secret they could not share with the other. Clarice could not bring herself to tell her son who his father was. Rod could not tell his mother that her husband's sister and brother-in-law had sexually abused him. The bond between mother and son was strong. But the secrets still went unrevealed.

All of this doesn't explain how Rod achieved so much and why his work connected with such a vast public. You can only go so far in linking the need "to be as good as everybody else" to the ability to become a cultural icon. Rod McKuen can't be reduced to an abused child who transformed his pain into popular art. But it's also clear he felt that the abuse profoundly affected the sort of man—and artist—he would become.

Life continued to be brutal as Rod approached his tenth birthday. Clarice's waitressing jobs barely kept the family afloat as Bill's drinking made him less employable. Rod and Bill Jr. were reduced to asking the local grocery store for bones—supposedly for the family dog, but actually for the family soup. When not scrounging for pop bottles to return for deposit money, the two boys foraged for treasures in the city dump. Rod tells an O. Henry–like story in *Finding My Father* about replacing the furniture in his mother's house with even worse discards rescued from the trash on Christmas Eve. Clarice's kitchen table, dresser, and other hard-earned possessions were left out on the lawn and sold as rummage sale items for a total of $71.30. When she got home from work, she screamed and cried over what her kids had done. But when Rod handed her the money they'd made, what could his mom say but "merry Christmas"?

Such sentimental moments weren't enough to relieve the ongoing misery, however. The reappearance of Rod's hated step-grandmother Miranda made things even worse. He recalled her as a truly heartless woman, capable of egging on the bullies who beat him up on the way to school. Life with the Hoopers was nothing less than horrible. Though he never wavered in his love for her, Rod makes it clear that Clarice could not protect him from her husband or his family.

Movies offered Rod a temporary escape from the hunger and abuse. He took to building model theaters out of cardboard, complete with marquees made from the covers of discarded restaurant menus. Nickels and dimes earned from shining shoes and selling newspapers bought tickets to matinees at local film palaces like the El Portal and the Princess. Rod felt Hollywood calling to him, so he stole money from his mother's purse, bought a ticket on a Greyhound bus to Los Angeles, and then rode the streetcars out to the movie studios in the San Fernando Valley. After failing to get into the Universal Pictures lot. he headed back to downtown L. A. and went to a screening of *Dixie*, a biopic about the nineteenth-century songwriter Dan Emmett starring Bing Crosby. (Rod had fantasized about Bing being his father.) His adventure ended when he was nabbed by a policeman after he fell asleep at another theater. Rod was packed onto a return bus to his family.

Rod hoped his stepfather would get drafted after America entered World

War II. No such luck—Bill Hooper was declared 4-F. There seemed no hope of escaping the drunken beatings but to run away again. This time, Rod headed north to Elko, Nevada, where ranches needed men—or even eleven-year-old boys—to work in the fields. His jobs as an underage hired hand included carrying milk pails, putting up hay, and tending cattle. The money he sent home no doubt helped his struggling mother—in any case, his family seems to have let him fend for himself for the next two years.

The cowboy culture of northeastern Nevada was welcoming to migrants and runaways willing to work hard under often harsh conditions. Elko summers were scorching hot and the winters bitterly cold. The countryside, though, was stunningly beautiful, with clear streams running through green valleys surrounded by snowcapped mountains. A budding poet would find much inspiration in the scenery in between sweating and freezing on the job.

As he tells it, Rod grew up fast once he was on his own. Fighting wildfires and digging ditches in blizzards proved he could hold his own with the older ranch hands. He began to keep a journal while minding the cows and started to make up his own lyrics to the songs he heard on the bunkhouse radio. Along the way, he acquired a faithful dog who had lost a leg to a hay mower. And he met a young man named Leonard.

Tall, blond, and husky, Leonard steps into Rod's life at a crucial moment. Up until then, McKuen's story is devoid of role models or close friends. Other than his step-grandfather, no one encouraged him to better himself. There were no nurturing teachers who recognized a bright child from a dysfunctional home, no kindly librarians who encouraged his love for books. If Rod had the potential to be anything, no one noticed it. He needed a guiding hand—but even more, he needed someone to look up to.

Leonard checked off every box on the list of qualities Rod was looking for in a companion. Five or ten years older, he was both athletic enough to walk on his hands for long distances and spiritual enough to quote Thomas Aquinas while philosophizing about God. Leonard was tough enough to defend Rod against bullies at the ranch, yet displayed an uncommon gentleness toward wild animals. Playmate, teacher, protector, confidant, and more, he took on truly heroic proportions in Rod's eyes. More than just be close to him, Rod wanted to *be* Leonard.

About a year after they met, Leonard was killed while crossing the highway. Rod went to see his body at the Elko morgue—it was unscarred but ghostly white, the empty shell of someone no longer there. Leonard had meant everything to him. "We were friends, yes. He was my father, yes," Rod said. "We even experimented with sex together . . . I'm not ashamed to admit I must have loved him."

Looking back forty years later, Rod was aware he offered up something precious in exchange for what Leonard gave him. "Innocence is not too much to give to one who gave you back the world," he wrote in *Finding My Father*. (Of course, the laws of society say that a twelve-year-old cannot and should not make bargains like this.)

The Leonard story—told in *Finding My Father* and nowhere else—has an idealized glow about it. Its details sound reminiscent of boy-man relationships found in classical Greece. So do Leonard's heroic, Adonis-like qualities—he seems like a finely chiseled statue come to life and given a cowboy hat. In the largely male culture of the Western ranch hand, it's easy to imagine a close bond between a vulnerable kid and a protective father figure. Beyond that, it's easy to imagine Rod turning the real-life Leonard into a mythic figure— McKuen was a poet, after all.

Embellished or not, the story foreshadows themes Rod would return to again and again in his writing. As a mature artist, he blurred the lines in his work between chaste friendship and erotic love, childhood need and adult desire, the binary choice between male and female—as he put it, "It doesn't matter who you love or how you love but that you love." The beginnings of this signature McKuen maxim can be found in his relationship with Leonard—or at least the Leonard of his dreams.

Rod found another job after the death of his friend. Back in Las Vegas, Miranda Hooper learned of his whereabouts by reading his letters to Clarice and alerted the juvenile authorities about her runaway step-grandson. Rod was brought before a judge, who took a look at his disordered home life and decided to send him to the Nevada School of Industry, a juvenile detention facility on the outskirts of Elko.

At thirteen, Rod McKuen was a lonely, introspective kid with big ears and sweet smile, physically slight but surprisingly tough, a survivor of beatings, rape, and emotional abuse, largely unschooled and far from home. He was about to be locked up with older juvenile offenders for three years. The future promised more struggle, heartache, and bad luck. Really, everything had pointed toward failure from the moment of his birth. At this point in his life, anyone thinking Rod could grow up to become rich, famous, and beloved by millions would seem more deluded than those romantic fools looking for love in a cheap taxi dance hall.

Two

~

The Lonesome Boy

R OD'S THREE YEARS at the Nevada School of Industry were filled with physical labor, boredom, and terror, punctuated with occasional Saturday nights at the movies. By his account, he was the youngest ward at the minimum-security facility, a withdrawn kid barely in his teens who made no friends and didn't want any.

Built in 1913 and largely unchanged since then, NSI was a brutal place where rehabilitation of its wards was only a negligible concern. Local courts sent minors there for nonviolent offenses as well as serious criminal acts. Confirmed delinquents regularly beat up and sexually assaulted kids who had done nothing worse than skip school too often. That Rod was sent there says a good deal about the dysfunction of Nevada's juvenile justice system in the 1940s. He gave up the life of an unsupervised ranch laborer for the life of an imprisoned one.

A 1958 investigation of NSI by the Nevada Legislative Counsel Bureau squares with Rod's description of how the place was a decade earlier. Accountable only to a distracted supervisor, the poorly trained, sometimes sadistic staff veered between neglecting and brutalizing the inmates. Rule breakers could be sent to the Doghouse, a concrete isolation cell in the main building's basement without plumbing or heat. Boys were regularly locked in the filthy, urine-scented dormitories all night without staff supervision. Teaching by non-accredited instructors brought in from Elko was sporadic and indifferent. Boys as young as eight were vulnerable to be preyed upon by wards in their late teens and older. Being "punked"—raped—was a real fear among new arrivals.

Rod was vague about any abuse he suffered at NSI. As he recalled, he mostly kept to himself and took low-profile work assignments where he wouldn't be noticed. Still, he couldn't hide from the constant threat of violence that pervaded the place. He recalled being unjustly blamed for various offenses by older boys "who were more experienced at lying." Punishment was meted out by a tall, thin, and sinister "instructor" who didn't hesitate to whip a boy for an imagined offense on the theory that the child had "probably gone unpunished too long for something else he did." Rod shut down emotionally and started to disassociate from daily life—"At times it was as though I could stand outside myself and watch growing but not changing in any way, unable to alter what was happening."

Not all of his memories from this time were unhappy ones. Boys were hired out at bargain rates by NSI to relieve the wartime labor shortage in Nevada and neighboring states. Among those who benefited from this program was Bing Crosby, who owned several cattle and horse ranches in the Elko area. Rod spent a couple of weeks clearing brush on one of Crosby's properties for a couple of weeks—but the real thrill came from meeting a Hollywood star whom he'd fantasized about for years. (Bing probably never expected to see the towheaded reform-school kid again after their brief encounter on his ranch. In 1974, the two ran into each other again in San Francisco; Rod didn't mention their earlier encounter.)

Sometime in 1948 or 1949, Rod completed his sentence at NSI and was released. Most likely, he received no follow-up counselling from the juvenile authorities. His three years under the care of the state had been a sustained stretch of misery that further eroded whatever trust he might have had in the adult world. Apparently, no one was waiting to receive him when he left the school. In any case, he had no intention of returning home.

The next several years of Rod's life are especially hard to document. His own accounts of where he went and what he did don't quite hold together chronologically, especially when you consider his age (fifteen to sixteen). Still, it seems likely his tales of working as a cowboy and rodeo rider after his stay at NSI are largely true—the West was an accepting place for boys who wanted to take on men's jobs in those days.

After leaving NSI, Rod wound up on the rodeo circuit. The cowboys he met there impressed him as tough, stoic daredevils willing to take it face (or ass) first in the mud for the reward of hanging onto a bull or a horse for a few more precious seconds. Though not one of the best competitors, Rod said he'd win enough to pay for the entrance fee to the next rodeo down the line.

The rough-and-tumble camaraderie of this hyper-masculine world helped give Rod a sense of identity at a crucial age. It also became a key element in his personal mythology—as an adult, he would temper his sensitive poetic persona with a hint of the cowboy's stolid nonchalance. But even as he lived out a boy's Wild West fantasies, part of Rod was only playacting: "I was just pretending . . . Filling up days and nights until something *happened* . . . "

What Rod was listening to was much more important than his cowpunching and bulldogging. A love of popular music continued to develop alongside his fascination with the movies. He'd stay awake in the ranch bunkhouse on Saturday nights to catch *Your Hit Parade*, a weekly rundown of America's top tunes. His efforts to remember what Frank Sinatra or Joan Edwards had sung led to him making up lyrics of his own. Rod also recalled learning cowboy songs and folk ballads during his days as a ranch hand. It's easy to imagine this teenage cowboy wannabe singing to himself while working the rodeo circuit, playing with words and perhaps learning a guitar chord or two. His childhood dreams of breaking into show business started to gain more form and direction—maybe as a singer instead of an actor, or maybe as both . . .

A freak riding accident that broke both of Rod's legs cut short his rodeo career and convinced him to seek employment elsewhere. He took a bus to Portland and eventually found work in a series of lumber camps around Oregon and Washington. At fifteen, he was apparently considered mature and skilled enough to take on a series of dangerous jobs there, including shimmying up tall trees and breaking up logjams on rivers. It was hard work, but, as with his time on the Nevada ranches, he enjoyed the physical challenges as well as the companionship of the older men who seemed to accept him as one of them. Looking back as an adult, he felt a twinge of nostalgia for the cast-off furnishings in the camp barracks and the awe-inspiring timber that surrounded them.

Sex flowed along with the pine sap in those all-male encampments. An entry in Rod's journal from this time mentioned a certain "Dave" who broke his foot "horsing around" while "bunkhopping in the middle of the night." While it's not clear if Rod was wrestling in the sheets when the lights went out, he did recall erotic adventures beyond the camps: "I had a chance to hustle in the towns and I probably did a few times. In fact, I know I did, but if it wasn't worth remembering in detail, it hardly seems worth mentioning." (Despite the vagueness, Rod still found this detail important enough to include in *Finding My Father*.)

Stints as a ranch hand, rodeo rider, lumberjack, and teenage sex worker had given Rod an education beyond his years. Now he was ready to try living with family again. His mother had written to tell him she was leaving Bill Hooper and moving from Las Vegas back to Oakland with Bill Jr. Rod was supposed to go there in advance and find a home for the three of them. When he got to town, he moved in with Aunt Ruth, who was still working as a fortune-teller while getting by on public assistance and money sent by her twin sons. Rod got along poorly with his aunt, who may still have resented Clarice for getting pregnant and dropping out of the taxi dancer game.

One day at the dinner table Ruth told her nephew he was a bastard—not a figurative one, but a real one. She added that he probably would never know who his father was. The news came as a shock—Rod's mother had allowed him to assume that she had divorced his dad when he was very young. Now he'd learned the truth from someone who hated him and took delight in causing him pain. "I felt unhappy, betrayed, cheated, empty, lied to, all at once," he recalled.

With a few cruel words, Rod's dreams of an idealized father who would someday reenter his life were taken away. His fragile sense of identity was further undermined—a complete sense of who he was would remain beyond his grasp. More than just an outsider from a broken home, he was marked as *illegitimate*, a word that carried deep meaning for him. It's worth noting that Rod's efforts to make a mark in the world begin after he was told about the status of his birth. From age fifteen onward, he struggled to prove his legitimacy as an artist and human being. Winning acceptance and recognition in as many areas of life as possible became his all-consuming mission. "It was almost as though I was trying to prove to myself that I could be just as good as anybody else by doing a number of things," he wrote at the peak of his fame in the 1970s. "So what if I was illegitimate?"

Rod's reunion with his mother was bittersweet. He recognized that he had changed since he last saw her—and that she had changed as well. Years of hard work, poverty, and drunken arguments with a no-account husband made Clarice seem "beaten by life," though still beautiful in her son's eyes. Still, she was tough and resilient enough to come back to Oakland to raise her children on her own. Rod loved his mother and forgave her for not telling him the truth about his father. But he was no longer a brutalized little boy in need of her protection. He was a road-hardened young man who supported his family, kept his own hours, and had dreams he could hardly explain to her or even himself.

After living on a rat-infested houseboat for a short time, Rod, his mother, and half-brother moved to more suitable quarters on dry land. (Depending on which differing account you accept, this was either a flat above Aunt Fern's place or an apartment above a grocery store on 17th Street.) Rod had a room of his own for the first time, which he proceeded to fill with books and records. He was reading omnivorously, sampling contemporary fiction (Norman Mailer's *The Naked and the Dead*, Thomas Wolfe's *You Can't Go Home Again*, Truman Capote's *Other Voices, Other Rooms*), and dipping into the canon of modern poetry (everyone from Baudelaire and Rimbaud to Whitman and Sandburg). His listening habits veered from the commercial pop singers of the era into jazz and classical music. As with most things in his life, Rod's tastes in literature and music were self-cultivated. No one schooled him about what a budding poet/songwriter ought to absorb.

He drew particular inspiration from Walter Benton, whose poetry collections *This Is My Beloved* and *Never a Greater Need* were hugely popular in the 1940s. The Austrian-born American writer's free verse was highly visual and achingly passionate, mixing paeans to sunsets, flowers, and favorite meals with dreamy erotic imagery—all hallmarks of the poetic style Rod was beginning to cultivate. Benton offered his odes to desire in the form of diary entries—"I took your body like a glass of sweet milk at bedtime. / And my eyelids let go at the hinges when I entered you," he wrote in a typical passage from *This Is My Beloved*. Rod was deeply influenced by Benton's work and acknowledged his debt in interviews years later.

There wasn't much that school could offer Rod at this point. He spent a few months attending Westlake Junior High, and then left home again to seek work in Nevada and Wyoming. He came back to enroll in Oakland Technical High School, where he daydreamed his way through classes and sang in the choir (though he was finally asked to leave for "singing too loud"). He must have seemed out of place among conventional teenagers at the dawn of the fifties. Looking back fifty years later, Rod described himself as "somewhat of a misfit (who) enjoyed faking my way through school by pretending to be an extrovert." Already, he was learning how to move among circles and cliques, charming yet slightly distant, an all-American kid with a toothy smile and a sketchy past.

Rod's stories about his Oakland Tech days are of a piece with the accounts of innocent love and illicit lust that recur in his writings. In one, he uses poetry to beguile a gorgeous "goddess" in the senior class into being his prom date. Another more sordid anecdote finds him in a sexual relationship with a female teacher "who possessed him physically and, for a while, mentally as well." Rod tired of the affair and broke it off. The teacher called up Clarice, confessed her love for the boy, and asked for help in winning him back. Rod's mother was said to be "stunned, then angry and finally most of all confused" by this conversation—suggesting she had little idea of the life her son had been leading since he'd left home.

Bored and alienated, Rod dropped out of Oakland Tech in his sophomore year and took on a series of ill-fitting jobs. These included brief stretches as a shoe salesman (he got fired for putting shoes back in the wrong boxes) and bagging machine supervisor in a cookie factory (he grew absent-minded and let cookies pile up on the floor). It all felt absurd and pointless. At sixteen, he was full of ambition but lacking direction, wasting his time with dead-end jobs while filling notebooks with poems and dreaming about show business.

His first real break came when he was hired as a doorman at the T&D Theatre on 11th Street in downtown Oakland. Manager Hugh Jones took a liking to the personable teenager, who obviously loved movies, and started to teach him the arts of publicity. Part of Rod's duties included dressing up in costumes and performing stunts to plug the latest feature at the T&D. He put on a rabbit costume to promote *Harvey*, led a mule through town on behalf of *Francis*, and walked around in a space suit to drum up interest in *Destination Moon*. It was all in the name of grabbing attention and selling tickets, a lesson Rod took to heart and would apply to his own career.

Early in 1950, Rod got the idea of hosting his own radio show. With no broadcast experience but plenty of enthusiasm, he approached Oakland's

KROW and pitched himself as a disc jockey/radio host. He came armed with promises of sponsorship from Blumenfeld Theaters (owners of the T&D), as well as the formidable East Bay Council of Milk. That was enough to launch Rod McKuen onto the high road to fame.

According to its former newsman Gordon Greb, KROW was "a leader" among Bay Area stations, "the kind of place that produced all kinds of successful broadcasters." Like McKuen, Ralph Edwards—future creator of TV's *Truth or Consequences* and *This Is Your Life*—began his career there as a teenage writer-announcer in the 1920s. Everyone from DJs Don Sherwood and "Sweet" Dick Whittington to Jack "Joe Friday" Webb got their start at the station. Giving an untested seventeen-year-old his own show was risky but still in keeping with KROW's innovative spirit.

The *Rhonda Vu with Rod* program debuted on Saturday, August 5, 1950 at 10 p.m. Surviving scripts from the show indicate that Rod got significant help from some of the older hands at KROW. Especially important was Bruce Sedley, an experienced broadcaster with a background in comedy. He served as Rod's straight man in the rather groan-inducing skits that dominated the first four months of the show. Sedley took on the role of Professor B. Fuddle, who engaged McKuen in dialogues like the following:

Rod: Professor, will you change the water on the fish?
Professor: Why? They haven't drank what I gave them yesterday!

Also pitching in to help make the new kid a success was Phyllis Diller, KROW's copywriter, publicity flack, and "continuity gal." The future comedy star wrote Rod's commercials and bonded with him as a fellow outsider trying to break into show business. Rod later recalled that he gave her a speaking part in a Christmas episode of his show—Diller's debut as a performer.

Adjusting the format, Rod toned down the corny gags and boosted the music quotient starting with his December 9, 1950 show. "Let me explain my reasons for switching from stale jokes and equally stale situations to straight music," he said. "Lately I haven't been getting too much response from you listeners out there . . . So I thought if all of a sudden I did something drastic, from comedy to records, you might write in and tell me what you think of the change. Remember, the decision is up to you." Rod was still looking for direction, eager to please and discover what his audience wanted.

By February 1951, Rod was introducing himself on the air as "that madcap meddler of modern music," still serving up goofy routines with the Professor in between spinning platters. Sometime later that year, though, his program tossed out the jokes completely and veered in a more overtly romantic direction. For the first time, Rod stepped out as a poet, framing the lovelorn hits of the day with yearning verse straight out of his notebooks. He reined in his boisterous side in favor of an intimate, caressing delivery that spoke directly to the listener: "Hello . . . it's raining now / and there's nowhere to go / no one to go to / On rainy nights / a man needs a woman / and I want you . . . "

Rod's new approach set him apart from other local broadcasters, but it was not completely original. Radio shows like *Words with Music* (featuring stars like Agnes Moorehead, Mary Astor, and Raymond Burr reading verse over ethereal organ music) and *Moon River* (a late-night program out of Cincinnati that paired a "hypnotic" narrator with soothing live accompaniment) had found a niche by combining poetry and music. Unquestionably, though, the most direct inspiration for the retooled *Rendezvous with Rod* (note the more serious spelling) was a mysterious lady who called herself the Lonesome Gal.

Launched in the mid-forties on a Dayton, Ohio station, *Lonesome Gal* was syndicated across the country by the end of the decade. Host Jean King's sultry voice purred its way into the hearts of male listeners as she mixed promises of love with pitches for Bond Street pipe tobacco and Red Top beer. "Sweetie, no matter what anybody says, I love you better than anybody in the whole world," the Lonesome Gal would coo as she segued into a lush, string-draped ballad. Tender and vulnerable while teasingly erotic, King (who wore a mask for public appearances) proved there was a huge audience for the right kind of aural seduction.

At nineteen going on twenty, Rod didn't try to play the sophisticated gentleman wooing the ladies with suave bedroom talk. His boyish earnestness and up-front need was his selling point—here was a gentle young man who came across as much as a playmate as a seducer. Rod's scripted dialogue was more poetic and nuanced than what the Lonesome Gal offered. He invited women to step into his recollections of shared intimacies at a picnic in the park or a dance under the stars—he spoke as if they remembered these things too.

During his "enchanted hour," Rod conducted a kind of guided visualization session for the lovelorn, blurring the lines between storyteller, poet, confessor, and therapist. Speaking in subdued yet eager tones as sweet string music played behind him, he leaned in toward the listener . . .

"You're very close to me. Your chest cradles my head. Your breath comes up slowly through your body and yet is very fast, loud, and wonderful. You're breathing as only a woman in love breathes. What do you love? I wish it were me. I wish I could be the man you are in love with. When you're here, pretending you love me is easy. But sometimes you're far away and I walk alone, silently alone, through a city that without you seems empty . . . a city where only the chill of winter and reality is left. A city that once was ours. Yours and mine . . . "

Rendezvous with Rod found a wide audience around the Bay Area during its three and a half years on the air . Local critics took notice. "This kid fascinates me," wrote columnist Dwight Newton in the *San Francisco Examiner.* "He grapples with the microphone like it was a long lost lover. He plays slow beat, sad songs with intimate 'intros' unlike anyone except maybe 'Lonesome Gal' . . . His is the most original and unstereotyped voice to hit this area in a long time." *Oakland Tribune* critic Marjorie Larmour had a different opinion: "Oldsters who haven't heard this 19-year-old 'junior Charles Boyer' should tune in also for the sheer incredulity of it all. (Unbelievers describe his whispered endearments as 'nearest thing to a sick cat.')"

Even at the start of his career, Rod had a way of inspiring extreme reactions. And, as would be true in later years, he wasn't content to stick to one creative medium at a time. He'd dabbled in acting as a member of the San Francisco Young Players prior to joining KROW. Roles in community productions and volunteer work at hospitals broadened his contacts and got his name in the papers. As a cast member in an Oakland pageant celebrating the life of Joaquin Miller ("the Poet of the Sierras"), he wore a special wig woven by Miller's daughter from the hair of her long-dead dad. If nothing else, gigs like this proved that young Rod was a trooper.

Rod was testing his wings as a singer around this time as well. In September 1950, he entered a local studio and laid down a sincere if somewhat wobbly rendition of "Some Enchanted Evening," the first of at least two dozen tracks recorded over a two-year period. Rod croons his way through the tune over a prerecorded orchestra, showing none of the he-man verve he would display in his performances of folk material a few years later. Further versions of popular hits followed, ranging from "Blue Moon" and "The Trolley Song" to "Thou Swell" and "Cincinnati Dancing Pig." These recordings appeared on acetates and probably had a small circulation. The sketchy label copy on the discs indicates that local musicians and talent agents used them to promote Rod in some way.

It would be a few years before Rod got a serious shot as a recording artist. In the meantime, he continued to explore his possibilities as a poet. On his January 10, 1953 show, he announced that he was "quitting radio for a while" and let it be known that first collection of poems would be available in July. He ended the program with an expansive Whitmanesque salute to Americans of all stripes:

"This is for the poor like me and the rich, those that cling to life because they want it . . . this is for the Greek and the Italian and the Negro, this is for the Indian and the Chinaman, this is for everyone, this is for the beloved, this is for the banished, the victor and the beaten and the homo, the second-story man, the mother-in-law and her daughter, the girl I held in my arms last night, this is for the wishless . . . "

(As it turned out, this grand farewell turned out to be temporary; Rod's show was part of KROW's weekend programming through the end of 1953.)

Clearly, Rod saw himself as more than a radio Romeo. The solidarity he expressed with the poor and downtrodden in the poem above came naturally from his experiences—he knew he was an outsider no matter how charming he might be. As such, he might have been expected to find fellowship among the artists and dropouts of Sausalito, a Bay Area bohemian enclave referenced in one of his early poems. But if Rod wasn't quite the clean-cut all-American boy, he wasn't a brooding rebel either. He was fine-tuning his persona in a way that allowed him to travel among different social circles without surrendering his loner status. By the time he wrapped up his stint on KROW, he had begun to learn how to reach a diverse public on his own terms.

If Rod was serious about developing as a poet, it would have been only natural for him to become involved with the burgeoning local poetry scene of the early 1950s. The Berkeley Renaissance poets—Jack Spicer, Robert Duncan, and Robin Blaser—were changing the cultural landscape with public readings of their mythic, technically innovative works. They were building upon a long-standing Bay Area poetic tradition that extended through Kenneth Rexroth's quirky, erudite brand of modernism back to the playful verse of George Sterling. New recruits kept that tradition vital. Rod combination of boyish sensitivity and street-kid confidence would have appealed to the older poets, even if they felt his work needed refinement.

It's unclear if Rod had any dealings with the Berkeley Renaissance poets on a literary level. There *is*, however, a significant connection between McKuen, Jack Spicer, and Robin Blaser that went beyond poetry. All three were both early members of the San Francisco chapter of the Mattachine Society, the first sustained gay-rights organization in America.

Being a part of a pro-homosexual organization in the early 1950s took courage. The "Lavender Scare" was raging full force in those days—according to politicians and the press, dangerous sexual deviants had invaded the federal government, academia, and private industry, infecting the unwary with their perverse desires. "Sexual misfits" were easily blackmailed and ripe for recruitment by the Communists. In fact, homosexuality was held by some to be a tool used by the Reds to break down America's moral order—as one commentator put it, same-sex love was "Stalin's atomic bomb." Talk of secret government lists and investigations kept the paranoia level high. According to historian David K. Johnson, "Even a rumor of homosexuality was often considered a graver transgression in 1950s America than an admission of former membership in the Communist party."

The relatively tolerant Bay Area was not immune to the Lavender Scare. Gays lived under constant risk of arrest, physical violence, and loss of employment. In 1947, California became the first state in the union to create a sex offender registry, one that that included those convicted of committing homosexual acts. Section 647.5 of the California Penal Code (directed against "idle, lewd, and dissolute persons") could be used to arrest two men dancing together in public or private. Police had carte blanche to harass and entrap anyone suspected of "crimes against nature."

It was in response to this atmosphere of fear and repression that Los Angeles–based activist Harry Hay and seven of his friends organized the Mattachine Foundation in 1950. The group took its name from the Société Mattachine, a troupe of French medieval players who wore masks while criticizing the rich and powerful. Disguise and discretion were necessary to protect homosexuals from the world at large as they campaigned for better treatment. Toward that end, Hay drew upon his background in the Communist Party to set up Mattachine chapters as separate cells requiring oaths of secrecy to join. In a sense, the group lived up to the conspiratorial fantasies of the rabid homophobes, although its goal was self-protection rather than subversion.

In early 1953, a young librarian at UC Berkeley named Gerard Brissette contacted the Mattachine in L. A. about starting a local branch. By March he had visited the foundation's leadership and was actively seeking recruits. Brissette's network of contacts spread the word from friend to friend and beyond. Among those who heeded the call was the Lonesome Boy of KROW.

Exactly how Rod became part of the Mattachine Society's vanguard in the Bay Area is unclear. Though he was open about many parts of his life in later years, he never mentioned the group in any of his published writings. The important thing is that he was there at the dawn of the modern gay-rights movement at a time when even sympathizing with such a cause was profoundly dangerous. Rod was a rising star on the local entertainment scene who had built his heartthrob persona around his yearning for young women. He dreamed of success that went far beyond a weekend radio show. To get caught in a police raid of a homosexual cell would label him a criminal, a pervert, and a subversive. Why risk all that for some undercover organization founded by a Communist?

Rod doesn't seem to have worried about any of that. In the minutes to the meeting of a Mattachine "group discussion" held April 8, 1953, he comes across as fully engaged and committed to the cause. When the talk turns to the "fun" side of the group's mission, he jumps in with a plan to buy or rent a five-hundred-seat theater for parties and movie showings—perfect for "a bunch of homosexuals having fun together." "Everyone agrees (Mattachine) meetings are wonderful places for cruising—better than bars," he points out. (At nineteen, Rod was still under the legal drinking age in California. He was over the age of consent, however.)

When the agenda moved on to political involvement, Rod became serious, suggesting that members lobby and submit petitions to candidates as both representatives of Mattachine and as individuals. It is telling that most of the participants in this discussion are listed as "anonymous" in the minutes. Rod is second only to Gerry (Brissette) in the number of times a member is identified by name. He is present until the close of the meeting at 11 p.m., when he collects donations from the group totaling $5.10.

Jack Spicer was present for the April 20 meeting of Mattachine's Oakland cell. Like Rod, he came to these meetings to socialize as well as brainstorm about the group's collective goals. Members shared their stories, confessed their desires and fears, and engaged in epic bull sessions thrashing out their shared identity against a hostile world. When asked about his "interests," Spicer said they included "homosexual integration into the major culture, social action, personal adjustment, psychological research into cause and effects." Rod's list of likes was less cerebral, more geared to action: "singing, theatrics, radio, recording, young boys, anything."

The Mattachine Society soon became split between conservative and radical factions. Fear of infiltration by government informers raised the paranoia level—at one point, Spicer accused a fellow member of being a "crypto-Fascist" FBI informer. These tensions cropped up when delegates from various Mattachine groups came to Los Angeles for a convention in May 1953. Sexual conflicts added to the strained feelings at the gathering—and Rod was at the center of it all.

"Rod McKuen set the whole thing on fire," Brissette recalled. "He was immediately gobbled up by a group of people who just thought he was just a honey of a guy, and I don't know what the hell happened . . . [Rod] had gotten into a twosome from a triad that someone was being cut out of and was threatening suicide. I was supposed to get a hold of McKuen to get him out of this dyad and was far more concerned with him than this other character that no one seemed to like . . . "

It's unclear what the outcome of these erotic crises was. In any case, the L.

A. Mattachine convention appears to have been the climax of Rod's involvement in the organization. Though he is listed as an East Bay member of the group in October 1953, there is no specific mention of him in any of the surviving minutes after April of that year. Rod had a good reason for his absence—he had been drafted into the United States Army.

Rod reported for basic training as part of Company D, 63rd Infantry Regiment at Fort Ord on June 12. He entered the service a successful local entertainer, a budding poet, a covert human-rights activist, and something of a heartbreaker. People in the Bay Area didn't forget about the Lonesome Boy after Uncle Sam claimed him—in fact, newspaper listings show that *Rendezvous with Rod* continued to be aired on KROW through the end of the year. (Electrical transcription technology available in 1953 would have allowed Rod to prerecord shows for broadcast after he was in the army.)

From reform school to the rodeo circuit, from the broadcasting booth to boot camp—Rod's life thus far had the makings of a classic American story of tough times, lucky breaks, and hard-won maturity. His glory days were far ahead of him, but at age twenty the questions he would deal with as a pop culture icon had already emerged. Was he the painfully honest Lonesome Boy or a facile young man desperately on the make? Was he a legitimate poet, singer, actor—*anything*? Could he tell the world what he really thought and felt, what and whom he really loved? Talented and ambitious but deeply unsure of his identity, Rod was already a master of self-promotion who did not know or understand the person he was selling. Maybe a two-year tour of duty would tell him more about the man and artist he was meant to become.

Three

~

Happy Is a Boy Named Me

T HE INK WAS barely dry on the U. S.–North Korean armistice when Rod
    McKuen reported for duty as part of the army's 63rd Infantry Regiment
at Fort Ord, California. The shooting was over, but Uncle Sam still needed
young men to help hold the line against Communism in the Far East. Rod
was just another draftee, although one with specific skills valuable to the military. His background as a radio personality and singer made him a prime
candidate for a Special Services job entertaining the troops. Or his writing
skills could be tapped to help fight the Reds from behind a typewriter. Rod
preferred the latter assignment, and that was the one he eventually got.

First, he had to get through sixteen weeks of basic training, which he
recalled as "sheer hell." In a 1975 recollection he hinted darkly of suicides
and murder among the unlucky grunts on the base. For his part, Rod decided
to suck it up and endure whatever he had to. "Everybody else was bitching
about going into the service," he told interviewer Ben Vaughn late in his life.
"I swore to God I wasn't going to bitch. They could give me the most difficult
KP (kitchen police duty), whatever it was—I did it. There was no way I was
going to bitch. I was going to learn."

Still, he did try to find ways to get outside the Fort Ord gates. He claimed to be a Buddhist after he learned that soldiers could gain Sunday leave if they practiced a faith not observed at the base chapel. (Rod had been baptized as a Mormon when he was eight years old at the insistence of his stepfather.) The army brass eventually caught on, shaved his head, and ordered him to run laps in the summer sun as punishment. If Rod took it stoically, he surely had flashbacks of the brutal treatment he'd received at the Nevada School of Industry five years earlier.

Better times were coming, though. At some point after his induction, someone in charge would have looked at Private McKuen's paperwork and seen "radio announcer" in his employment background. The U. S. military was busily staffing its psychological warfare units during this time, drawing upon professional broadcasters in the civilian world for these posts. The Lonesome Boy of KROW was perfect for the teams of propaganda spinners assigned to help undermine the fighting will of the North Korean forces.

Rod was sent to the Army Information School at Fort Slocum, New York, a campus-like base on a small island on Long Island Sound. Its ivy-covered brick buildings and coed student body offered the closest thing to a college setting McKuen ever found himself in. For eight weeks, Rod's communications skills were honed and shaped into effective tools for spreading pro-American messages. He already knew a thing or two about seducing a radio audience—now he was ready to learn the dark arts of psychological warfare.

While at the school, Rod tested out media manipulation techniques for fun and profit. On behalf of himself and a fellow soldier, he sent off letters to dozens of newspapers across the U. S. bemoaning a lack of mail from hometown folks. He and his cohort gave Fort Ord as their return address, allowing them to claim a different town as home in each letter. The *Reno Gazette-Journal* was among the papers that published the following request from Privates Rod McKuen and Joe Moline: "Wonder if you might print our plea for some mail. Since coming in the army we haven't had any. Maybe some of your readers could write and give us some news from home. Sure hope so." Readers around the country responded to these plaintive appeals with cakes, cookies, and other gifts, as well as sympathetic letters.

After completing the Army Information School course, Rod was sent to Fort Lawton in Washington before being shipped out to Asia. While working on the post's newspaper, he decided to try boosting the career of film actress Mala Powers as an experiment. He claimed credit for getting her chosen as "the girl we'd most like to go down with" by the paratroopers at Fort Benning, among other honors. Servicemen around the country wrote fan letters to Powers's studio, receiving in return photos of the star dressed in fatigues. (Projects like this served as test runs for Rod's later promotional effects on his own behalf.)

Tokyo was McKuen's next destination. He was assigned to duty with the Voice of the United Nations Central Command, an American-dominated propaganda agency tasked with subverting Communist morale. Rod joined a team of psychological warfare scribes in churning out copy that was then translated by native speakers into Korean, Mandarin, Cantonese, and Russian. The scripts were group efforts, sometimes as brief as thirty seconds—not the best showcase for individual talent. Still, Rod found a way to put his own stamp on VUNC's radio programming.

"One of my creations was Moran, a sort of Korean Tokyo Rose who spoke quietly and played sentimental music," he said. "All I did was adapt my old Oakland radio show *Rendezvous with Rod* for a smooth-talking and sexy-voiced Korean girl to speak . . . Every night she opened her show with the tagline 'Hello, my midnight companion . . . it's me, Moran, again. You ought to come south. It's beautiful here. Your family's here. I'm here . . . ' It worked so well that I was named by Communist Korea as an official war criminal.'"

Rod also claimed to have invented the slogan "Make Love, Not War" as a psychological warfare tool around this time. The idea was to beguile enemy soldiers with visions of Venus instead of Mars and sap their will to fight. It was only later, he said, that he began using the phrase onstage in the sixties, when a younger generation adopted it as their own. It seems just barely plausible that "Make Love, Not War" could have slipped into one of Moran's murmured messages, though (as with so many McKuen claims) the truth will probably never be known.

Between his bursts of creativity, Rod felt bored and restricted by military life. He wasn't used to playing by someone else's rules when dreaming up creative schemes: "We were headquartered in Tokyo in what was called the Finance Building. I remember the sergeant came by and I was thinking, sitting there in front of the typewriter, and he slapped me on the head and said, 'Why aren't you creating?' I thought to myself, 'I've got to get out of this . . . I've got to get back to entertaining.'"

Itching to hit the stage, Rod started slipping out of the Finance Building after a day's worth of propaganda writing and heading over to the Ginza Strip, a Tokyo nightclub district with a somewhat seedy reputation. He soon landed a five-month gig singing at Maxim's, a popular Ginza venue that attracted both American and Japanese customers. Along with jazz and folk songs, Rod's set list included rock 'n' roll numbers, still something of a novelty in 1953–54. According to his own description, he came onstage wearing tight pants and stripped to the waist, ready to surrender to the "loud and sensual beat" of the music. Maxim's took out a newspaper ad featuring a picture of Rod "belting a song bare-chested in an ape-like stance." Apparently, this was the wrong kind of message for a PFC to be sending the local population—once McKuen's commanding officer saw the photo, he brought charges against the private that resulted in a summary court-martial, confinement to quarters, and a $50 fine. Rod's days churning out steamy dialogue for Moran were over.

Disciplined but not totally disgraced, Rod was reassigned to the Korean Civil Assistance Command, headquartered in Seoul, an agency charged with improving the image of the United States among the civilian population. KCAC men were not required to wear regulation uniforms and could essentially write their own orders. Rod and fellow private Bruce Sutherland traveled the countryside together accompanied by a driver and translator, stopping at mountain villages and urban centers to tack up posters, show movies, and otherwise spread a positive message about American aid. The ragged, slightly rascally team of McKuen and Sutherland would arrive at officers' clubs and be received as undercover operatives out on a secret fact-finding mission. No doubt Rod savored this kind of freewheeling disregard for typical military protocol.

Overall, Rod's accounts of his shenanigans in Korea sound like fodder for TV military sitcoms like *M*A*S*H* or *The Phil Silvers Show* (a.k.a. *Sergeant Bilko*). He cast himself as the hero of droll escapades involving wrecked jeeps, lovestruck nurses, and bamboozled sergeants. If his stories seem a bit heightened for effect, what does sound credible is his value to the U. S. military as an entertainer and goodwill ambassador. If Rod could draw crowds on the Ginza, he could also make good money at NCO clubs singing rousing American folk ballads like "Shenandoah." The army included him in an entertainment unit that took him from Korea to Hong Kong, Thailand, and back to Japan. Rod's boyish vigor and willingness to tackle just about any musical style would have been an asset to any talent package.

There were less pleasant sides to his year in Korea. Rod encountered severe poverty and witnessed a public execution by firing squad in the city of Daegu. From what he saw, American efforts to help the Korean people by supplying them with consumer products were often counterproductive. Starving people were sent bicycles; children choked to death on gifts of bubble gum. Rod expressed his feelings about what he saw in a series of antiwar/anti-military poems published over twenty years later. (He also claimed to have written and published a novel during this time called *Elephant in the Rice Paddy* that drew upon his experiences in Japan and Korea. Rod said the book was quickly suppressed by the U. S. Army; in any case, no copies or records of its publication appear to have survived.)

There is one more unverifiable story from Rod's army hitch that deserves mention. In a 1976 issue of his *Inside Stanyan* newsletter, he described a long-distance relationship with Helen, a young woman he'd met during his days at KROW. While serving overseas, Rod poured out his heart to her in some fifteen hundred letters—she wrote back at a much more leisurely rate. A crisis point came when Helen told him she was pregnant by another man and contemplating suicide. He wrote back immediately and offered to marry her. Much to his relief, she turned him down. Though he wanted to help her, Rod knew he shouldn't get married "until I was in a situation where I really knew myself." This hunger for self-discovery—wrapped up in a search for his father as well as an authentic sexual identity—would become a dominant theme in his work. Whether there was a Helen or not is less important than the choices Rod pondered in stories like this.

Rod was in the middle of his Korean adventures when his debut poetry book . . . *and autumn came* was published by Pageant Press in August 1954. This slender volume was drawn from the verse he had been writing since high school; some of it had been featured on his KROW show. Rod collected $750 from friends to pay for the initial print run of five hundred. Though humble in length and format, the book served notice that Rod wanted to be taken seriously as a budding literary artist.

It's hard to miss the influence of *This Is My Beloved* on Rod's early writing. As in Walter Benton's famous work, the poems in . . . *and autumn came* are dated like journal entries, presented in chronological order, and grouped into numbered sections. Also like Benton's pieces, they are meant to trace a love affair from its first blossoming through its painful decay and bittersweet aftermath. Rod does inject some postwar alienation and social satire into this formula. His free verse (all lowercase, with occasional italics) veers from cozy, whimsical imagery ("you laugh like a bolt of calico / you smile like strawberries and cream") to plainspoken declarations of despair ("everything is last night / nothing is tomorrow") and quirky self-examinations ("physical love is a funny shape / at least mine is"). There are quick sketches of Bay Area locales

like Sausalito and San Francisco's McAllister Street. And there are lines that
skirt deeper revelations—after describing a one-night stand, Rod admits to
"feeling like a male prostitute."

Whatever its lasting merits, . . . *and autumn came* served as a useful calling
card after Rod was mustered out of the army in May 1955. He headed back to
the Bay Area and plunged into the live entertainment scene with the help of
his KROW comrade Phyllis Diller. She had started performing as a stand-up
comic at the Purple Onion, a hip little club crammed into a cellar on Colum-
bus Avenue in San Francisco's North Beach neighborhood. Diller's demanding gig required four sets a night, six nights a week. She shared the bill with
two musical acts; a spot opened up and Phyllis brought Rod on board. The
pay was probably in the ten-bucks-a-night range—still, the chance to play this
happening venue was too good for him to pass up. (McKuen wasn't the only
emerging poet to play the club—a young calypso singer/dancer named Maya
Angelou first gained renown at the Purple Onion around this time.)

Rod struck some on the North Beach scene as a young man in a hurry
who made up for any artistic shortcomings with ingenuity and chutzpah.
That was the opinion of folk singer Randy Sparks, who had been performing
with Diller before Rod got his gig in the summer of '55: "Rod had a bio and
a press kit with the photos of all the places he'd supposedly been. He had just
gotten out of the army, and the first picture you looked at when you looked at
his promotional book was one of Harry Belafonte with his arm around Rod.
We didn't have Photoshop then, but there were ways to doctor a photo. In my
opinion, that was a doctored photo. And he was trying to get away with it. It
was amazing . . . "

It's fair to say Rod knew how to work a publicity angle. But he also knew
how to please a crowd in an intimate room like the Purple Onion. Sharing the bill with Diller and singer Ketty Frierson (who went on to record
as Ketty Lester), he filled his fifteen-minute slot with folk songs, calypso
tunes, and a smattering of poetry. (Among his showstoppers was the Korean

national anthem performed in calypso rhythm.) Squeezed onto the club's four-by-six-foot stage, Rod found a way to appeal to both local bar cruisers and Midwestern tourists who frequented the venue. Even then, his peculiar mixture of casual cheeriness and brooding melancholy had a way of reaching an audience above and beyond his strengths as a singer. Women especially responded to his gangly good looks and sensitive persona. At twenty-two, he was still the waiflike Lonesome Boy, a romantic outsider who stood out among the sharp-edged satirists and cool Beat bards who came to define the North Beach scene.

The district's array of clubs and cafés attracted a growing stream of out-of-towners eager to sample the bohemian atmosphere and semi-decadent attractions. Among those who checked out the Purple Onion in the summer of '55 was Cobina Wright Sr., a legendary (or at least durable) socialite/columnist with an eye for interesting people. Hailed as "New York's most fabulous hostess," Wright had married into wealth after a middling career in opera and the movies. Her real talent was blending the worlds of high society and show business at her parties. She detected a hint of star quality in Rod's stage act and urged him to give Hollywood a try. He was ready for a change, so he caught a bus south a week later.

Instant stardom didn't await Rod once he got to L. A. "Life as a protégé of Cobina's consisted mainly of singing at parties," Rod recalled. His luck started to change in November, when influential syndicated columnist Mike Connolly reported that Universal-International had "interviewed" him for a film role. Rather than crediting Wright's influence, Rod usually told the story of his big break this way: "I got my first acting job by jumping on the back of a prop truck and getting on the Universal Studios lot. I knew they were casting for a teenage movie called *Rock, Pretty Baby!* [at that point titled *Crazy Love*] and I found out where they were doing it. I sat in the (casting) office all day and the girl said, 'What was your name again?' 'Rod McKuen—it must be there someplace.' 'No, I don't think so . . . but you've been here all day . . .'"

Rod was then screen-tested by talent director Jim Pratt and given a seven-year contract with U-I.

Tracing Rod's activities in 1956 can get complicated, but fragments of information indicate he spent time building up his singing career as well as preparing for his Hollywood screen debut. He'd won an ally in Connolly, a powerful showbiz figure who combined a right-wing, fiercely anti-Communist outlook with a closeted gay lifestyle. Among Connolly's friends was Henry Willson, an agent whose influence helped turn Rock Hudson, Rory Calhoun, and Tab Hunter into stars (he also named them). Connolly was a frequent guest at Willson's A-list pool parties, where handsome young male actors came to be seen, evaluated, and hopefully taken up by an influential older man. Stars were born—or at least created—out of such encounters. According to Hollywood historian Val Holley, "All you had to do was hang out at Henry Willson's pool to meet everyone you had to meet in terms of being passed along the gay publicity circuit."

Of course, more dreams were dashed than fulfilled. "One agent would promise some young guy that he'd make him a star in exchange for sex," said actor/author John Gilmore. "But somehow the big break never came, and the agent would pass him to one of the other agents, who'd sleep with him and then pass him on."

Where did Rod fit into this Hollywood beefcake demimonde? There's no direct evidence putting him poolside at Willson's place. There *is* this item in Connolly's February 21, 1956 column, however: "Rod McKuen broke in his act at the Bar of Music, singing 'Rock Around Rock Hudson,' subtitled 'What Next, Henry?' a Blackboard Jungle-type roundelay & rocked the room." The above suggests that Rod knew enough about Willson's status as Hudson's patron/creator to satirize it even if he wasn't part of the inner circle. It also catches him gearing up for the teenage-rocker exploitation films he was about to appear in at Universal. The Bar of Music connection is likewise significant—the club was an intimate cabaret room on Beverly Boulevard with a

loyal gay clientele and a somewhat shady reputation. Popular female imper-
sonator Arthur Blake performed there regularly.

By April, Rod had begun working on an album for Liberty Records.
Released later that year, his *Songs for a Lazy Afternoon* LP presented him as an
eclectic artist who handled folk tunes, calypso numbers, and adult pop fare
with equal self-assurance. Much of the material is self-composed or written
in collaboration with jazz guitarist Barney Kessel. Rod's vocals are warm and
caressing on the romantic songs, hearty and assertive on the dramatic folk ballads. His ability to interpret a range of styles is impressive, even if the music
here doesn't coalesce into a single style. Overall, the album suggests an artist
not quite fully formed, but eager to please.

In the cover photo for *Songs for a Lazy Afternoon*, Rod sits on a log in an
outdoorsy setting and stares dreamily into the distance; there's a single daisy
in the foreground. He is barefoot and wears a red shirt and blue jeans. His
looks suggest a Nature Boy–like image, as well as a certain dandiness (the red
shirt) and poetic sensitivity (the daisy). According to a story Randy Sparks
heard from his manager Jack Daley, Rod's bare feet helped him land at least
one choice TV gig: "[Rod's manager] Chuck Weedn got a copy of that album
to Ralph Levy, Jack Benny's producer. He had to have him on Jack's show
because Ralph was a foot fetish man. That's all it took."

Mike Connolly contributed liner notes to the album that underscored
Rod's loner persona: "If late some evening you should drive down a Hollywood street, and notice a tall boy, slightly bent over, with his shoulders
pushed forward—walking along whistling or singing to himself, chances are
it might be Rod McKuen . . . " The image of the brooding young man out of
step with the rest of the crowd had grown fashionable by the mid-fifties. The
greatest of all these conflicted antiheroes was James Dean, whose short but
sensational Hollywood career helped redefine Hollywood masculinity and
challenge the dominance of macho stars like John Wayne and Gary Cooper.
Dean was killed in a car crash in September 1955, around the time Rod came

south looking for movie work. The moment was right for twentysomething men with pompadour hairdos, awkward slouches, and simmering, ambiguous sexuality to get screen tests for the next *Rebel Without a Cause.*

Publicists began referring to Rod as a "James Dean look-alike" as early as February '56. In October, the Associated Press carried the following news flash: "Actor-songwriter Rod McKuen has discovered his face is not necessarily his fortune. 'I was standing on a corner a while back,' he said, 'when a girl came up to me. She yelled, "Don't look so much like James Dean," slapped my face and ran off.'" Did the press flacks at Universal hope Rod could be slapped into stardom? Whatever the truth behind this story, it's easy to see how McKuen's slight resemblance to Dean might have been useful as publicity fodder.

Rod's debut as a major studio player was less than overwhelming. *Rock, Pretty Baby!* assembled a group of appealing young male men and cast them as a teenage rock 'n' roll combo looking for a break in some generic mid-American town. John Saxon and Sal Mineo were the featured male stars; Rod took lower billing as Ox Bentley, a gangling, good-natured bass player who acts as a steadying influence among his bandmates. Besides giving sage advice to his pal Saxon ("You knucklehead, you gotta stop acting like dames were never invented!"), Rod gets to sing his self-composed tunes "Happy Is a Boy Named Me" and "Picnic by the Sea" and shamble through various malt shops and band rehearsal rooms. If he was looking for a smoldering James Dean–like role to show off his acting skills, Ox wasn't it.

Rock, Pretty Baby! hit theaters in December 1956 and was reasonably successful. Rod went on a four-month promotional tour for the film that took him back to his old haunts in Oakland. Playing the part of hometown boy made good, he spoke to a class at his alma mater Tech High and attended a screening of the film at T&D Theatre, where he'd served as usher and publicist eight years earlier. While in town, Rod told an *Oakland Tribune* reporter he had turned down the chance for the title role in *The James Dean Story* biopic because "it wouldn't lead to anything but oblivion" if he allowed himself to be typecast. He also let it slip that he had written 450 songs to date and sold twenty thousand copies of his records after his appearance on Jack Benny's *Shower of Stars*, while emphasizing that "acting is what I want to do most of all."

Rod played the studio game as best he could. Part of his full-time role as budding movie star called for him to go on dates with available starlets, whatever his private preferences might be. He was frequently paired with Corky Hale, a jazz pianist/harpist who was also dating Frank Sinatra and Mel Tormé at the time. "We'd go to all the movie premieres together," she recalled. "And there were lots of parties—he was very outgoing at those. He was a sweet, lovely guy." Among the high points of Rod and Corky's time together was a swanky affair thrown by Lance Reventlow, the socialite son of Barbara Hutton, reputedly one of the wealthiest women in the world. A photographer captured the couple dressed up in caveman-style furs, with Corky flashing Rod a sexy look. Though their relationship was strictly platonic, the two of them stayed in touch and eventually formed a musical combo and recorded together.

There's no doubt Rod enjoyed the perks of being a film actor, including hobnobbing with the superrich. But he was too savvy not to realize his movie career wasn't on the fast track. "I don't think they gave him much of a chance at Universal," Hale said. "I thought, 'Gee, Rod, I wish they'd give you some decent roles.'" His next film, 1958's *Summer Love*, was a sequel to *Rock, Pretty Baby!* with many of the same players (plus fresh faces like Molly Bee, Jill St. John, and Shelley Fabares). Rod was back as the easygoing Ox Bentley and given a few numbers to sing. His brief status as a contender for Jimmy Dean's crown seemed far behind him.

If there was one thing Rod had learned to prize, it was control of his own destiny. Essentially on his own since age eleven, he wasn't the kind to trust his career to anyone but himself. There was no Henry Willson figure changing his name, shaping his image, and telling him what to do next. Rod may have developed the habit of stretching and fudging the details of his résumé, but he was painfully aware of whether he was moving ahead or falling behind. And he wasn't afraid to work hard to get what he wanted on his own terms.

Rod needed help in making the most of his opportunities. He found an ally in Chuck Weedn. A shadowy presence in Rod's history who served as his manager and may have been his romantic partner for a year or so, as well, Weedn was hired by HiFi Records as chief A&R man in mid-1958, around the time Rod began recording for the label. Whether Chuck was responsible for Rod coming to HiFi or the other way around is unclear. What does seem evident is that Weedn helped McKuen boost his career in both music and film. Randy Sparks recalls visiting the two of them at an apartment they shared: "There was no place to sit, as every flat space was covered by letters, notes, and envelopes, all written by Rod and his manager to himself. This was, I was told, their daily output of fan mail, all supposedly from hot and bothered girls. [My manager] Jack Daley and I were pressured to sign a few of the messages to achieve 'a better diversity in handwriting.' Studio execs, I heard, couldn't understand how Rod McKuen received more fan mail than Rock Hudson." (Weedn's sister Betty tells a similar story of Chuck enlisting his mother and various other family members to churn out faux fan letters for Rod.)

Despite this guerrilla promotion, Rod was hedging his bets about screen stardom. He continued to write and perform poetry, cultivating a Bay Area bohemian persona distinctive from the teen movie sidekick image that Universal seemed to be locking him into. By the late '50s, the existential angst and erotic frankness associated with Allen Ginsberg and his Beat Generation comrades was no longer a strictly underground taste. *San Francisco Chronicle* columnist Herb Caen dubbed their imitators "beatniks," kicking off a fad that spawned endless exposes and parodies throughout pop culture. Rod was ready to get in on the action with a pair of spoken-word albums that had at least tangential Beat connections.

Released by HiFi in late '58, *Time of Desire* took Rod's Lonesome Boy persona several steps further with its steamy musings about furtive encounters in dim-lit bars and furnished rooms. The poems move between San Francisco, Los Angeles, and Tokyo and often present McKuen as an erotically tormented voyeur watching couples wandering city streets or splashing in the ocean. Rod's vocals retain a certain boyish quality, making his readings sound like Tom Sawyer adrift in a Henry Miller–esque sexual wonderland. The cool jazz combo backing him adds the right coffeehouse touch. As he'd done in his KROW days, Rod plays here with salacious themes and imagery without descending into outright smut. According to the album's liner notes, "*Time of Desire* was not conceived for the purist nor was it written for the pornographic mind—though both will probably have plenty to talk about after hearing it."

January 1959 found Rod back in San Francisco, reading his *Time of Desire* poems with jazz group backup at the Cellar on Green Street. The likes of Kenneth Rexroth, Lawrence Ferlinghetti, and (possibly) Jack Kerouac had given readings there, lending other poets who held forth in its tiny confines a secondhand Beat Generation glow. Rod was positioning himself as a sort of beatnik fellow traveler who mingled with the hipster crowd while remaining true to his loner self. He floated a rumor in the press that he would appear in *The Beat Generation*, a low-budget MGM film. While this didn't pan out, he did release an album in early 1959 that would become a beatnik exploitation cult classic.

Like *Time of Desire, Beatsville* was recorded by Rod in a single session at HiFi's studios with a seasoned crew of session players providing jazzy backup. Some of its poems had been read by him at the Cellar to a presumably beatnik-inflected audience. Sorting out bona fide Beat voices from parodists and poseurs was difficult back then—in Rod's case, he came across more as an observer (or infiltrator) than a member of any movement. This stance gives *Beatsville* a wry yet humane tone that makes its intentions hard to pin down. The sketches of misfit young men and women offered in these poems mostly ring true. If Rod doesn't take characters like "Frieda, who strips at the drop of a benny" or "Raffia the poet, who is not only an angry young man but a dirty old man as well," very seriously, he does seem to identify with their outsider status overall.

Rod suggests that everyone in *Beatsville* is playacting on some level. "I try to be a good beatnik, but it's hard," he admits in "No Pictures, Please." "I got a pad with a torn Picasso on the wall and a dirty red tablecloth . . . And if you come home with me I'll give you a cheese sandwich and wine in a cracked cup . . . Ohhh . . . my white bucks gave me away." Blowing your cover was something he could sympathize with. Rod had been changing costumes and adjusting identities ever since childhood. This may provide the odd note of authenticity that makes *Beatsville* more than a send-up of a passing fad. Among McKuen's vast catalog of releases, the album stands as one of his most notable works.

A few months later came "The Beat Generation," a flat-out comedy song Rod wrote and recorded (under the pseudonym DOR) in partnership with voice-over actor Bob McFadden. The pair enlisted Bill Haley & His Comets to provide some rock oomph to this satiric ode to sex, beards, and laziness. (In 1977, Richard Hell based his punk anthem "Blank Generation" on Rod's song.) "The Beat Generation" was included on *Songs Our Mummy Taught Us*, an album's worth of zany tunes riffing on monsters, beatniks, and other pop culture fixations of the moment. The album's key track was "The Mummy," a goofy novelty tune written by Rod and co-performed with McFadden that cracked the Top 40 in September 1959.

It's hard to pin down anything like a coherent direction to Rod's recording career at this point. After releasing his two spoken-word albums on HiFi, he recorded *Songs Our Mummy Taught Us* for Brunswick Records while apparently under contract with Decca. On the later label, he released two albums as a folk/pop singer, *Anywhere I Wander* and *Alone After Dark*. If that weren't enough, he contributed three spoken-word tracks to *The Yellow Unicorn*, an "adults only" poetry/jazz LP released by Imperial. All this label-hopping could have been a sign of creative vitality or desperation, or both. Rod was building a reputation as a versatile journeyman who would try just about anything—an approach that kept him busy but risked his being labeled a jack-of-all-trades sort of artist.

Meanwhile, Universal continued to offer Rod less-than-stellar roles. He was cast as young pioneer Dirk Breslin in 1958's *Wild Heritage*, a nondescript Western also featuring Maureen O'Sullivan, Troy Donahue, and Will Rogers Jr. Though he finally got his name listed above the title, this film wasn't the sort that would raise Rod's stature in Hollywood. Judging by what happened next, all those fan letters he and Weedn had deluged the studio with hadn't had much of an effect.

"Life wasn't all it was cracked up to be at Universal," he told Ben Vaughn in 2009. "*Wild Heritage* was a B movie—it was made to be shown on the second part of a double bill. Then they sent me a script called *The Haunted House on Hot Rod Hill*. I wanted to get out of my contract so bad—I wanted to go to New York and write songs and sing in supper clubs. So I wrote two words on the script and sent it back to the front office. You can guess what those two words were. They let me out of my contract, but I couldn't act for anybody else. No movies, no TV, no stage, nothin'. But I could sing and write songs and sing, because they didn't have a contract with me on that."

With a heartfelt "fuck you," Rod kissed the movies goodbye and closed another chapter in his already crowded showbiz story. From the U. S. propaganda mills of Tokyo to the dark dives of North Beach and the soundstages of Universal City, he had been on a dizzy ride that left him a veteran singer-songwriter-actor at age twenty-six. Rod had a true gift for impressing strangers, making friends, and talking his way into unlikely situations. He had caught lucky breaks others would kill for since coming home from Korea. Now his status as a fresh young talent was beginning to fade around the edges. Anxious to finally find his niche, Rod left L. A. for New York City to take one more shot at love, fame, and reinvention.

Four

~

Mr. Oliver Twist

IF HE COULDN'T be the next James Dean, maybe Rod McKuen could be the next Johnny Mercer. His stated goal for moving to New York City was to establish himself as a songwriter and cabaret performer. He had already achieved some success as a tunesmith, most notably as co-writer of Tommy Sands's 1958 hit "Sing Boy Sing." After his disappointing stint as a Universal contract player, Rod was ready to concentrate on his real strengths in the home of Tin Pan Alley.

There was unfinished business—as well as new possibilities—he left behind in California. Sometime in early 1959, Rod met the man who would become his life partner. Edward Habib was a trim and handsome twenty-four-year-old with a dazzling, toothy smile. The youngest of fourteen children, he had run away from his Fall River, Massachusetts home at sixteen, joined the U. S. Army, and then relocated to San Francisco and taken a bartending job. Rod was gigging at a local club when he encountered Habib. "The story goes, Edward walked into the club, and Rod saw him and just started ad-libbing a song to include references to him," longtime friend Charlie Hallam recalled. "He did that just from looking at Edward." From there, the two began spending time together at Edward's place on Stanyan

Street, the inspiration for a set of lovelorn poems that would later help make Rod famous.

Rod and Edward were destined to have a loving, tormented, but ultimately enduring relationship that would last over fifty years. First, though, Rod was committed to giving New York a try. His foray there was intended to be temporary; Los Angeles would remain his home base. It turned out a little differently. As he put it in *Finding My Father*, he went to New York for a weekend and stayed for four years.

Those years would be marked by deep friendship, nagging poverty, career detours, and creative breakthroughs. The artistic persona Rod would perfect when he returned to California in 1962 began to take shape here. The Lonesome Boy ambled into his thirties with a better grasp of who he was and how he could present himself to a mass audience. New York showed McKuen some bitterly hard times, but also introduced him to people and opportunities that paid off in ways he couldn't have anticipated.

It is likely that Rod's West Coast contacts provided him with introductions to various influential people in the New York entertainment world. His ability to make friends easily combined with his diverse resume made him a credible candidate for a range of projects. By early 1960, he had landed a gig composing music for *CBS Television Workshop*, a series created by innovative producer/director Albert McCleery. Though he lacked musical training and was only minimally skilled on any instrument, Rod was able to come up with some ambitious pieces for the show, including an elaborate eighteen-minute chorale number celebrating life in Manhattan.

McKuen and McCleery both turned up as guests at a Labor Day party given by actor/producer Hale Matthews at his swanky Upper East Side apartment. The son of a wealthy Pittsburgh industrial executive, Matthews was handsome, well connected, a discerning art collector, and "very gay." His dinner parties were known for their gourmet fare and lively company—café society stars like Bobby Short would mingle with newcomers like Rod as Hale played the piano and belted out Cole Porter tunes. High-society sports met ad-agency Mad Men and showbiz riffraff on easy terms here, with romantic undercurrents rippling through the shop talk and gossip.

Like Cobina Wright, Hale Matthews was a rich patron of the arts who could spot young talent in need of moral support and a good meal. Hale would take Rod out on the town in tandem with Richard "Dickie" Scaife, another young Pittsburgh heir who would go on to become a powerful force in Republican Party politics. There's no evidence that Rod and Dickie grew particularly close. But Matthews did introduce McKuen to someone who would become one of Rod's most treasured friends.

Ellen Ehrlich was working as an administrative secretary for the Crusade for Freedom (a CIA-backed broadcasting campaign meant to encourage patriotism in the U. S.) when she met Rod at Matthews's Labor Day party. "We hit it off, mainly because we both loved the film *East of Eden*," she recalled. "I lived on East 50th Street, and he lived just a few blocks away on East 53rd, so we made a date that he should come over and watch *East of Eden* on TV with me. That was the start of it."

Ellen was drawn to Rod's poetic charm and quick, curious mind; he fell for her sophistication and love for the arts. They quickly became a couple, sharing a platonic love affair that endured for the rest of Rod's time in New York. "We were very much emotionally involved," Ehrlich said. "I didn't have any other men in my life. I wasn't looking for other company." She introduced Rod to her mother, who didn't approve of him: "She said, 'What on earth are you doing with this bleach-blond kid?' But I didn't mind that he dyed his hair.

"Rod was quite poor, so we did simple things together. We walked, we had coffee—it was all very low-cost. We always talked, mainly about his childhood and trying to find his father. He quite often called me and woke me up at two or three in morning and read me a song or a poem . . . I knew he wanted to do extraordinary things, though I don't think he knew quite in what direction he wanted to go . . . "

Hungry for fresh influences, Rod tapped into Ellen's extensive knowledge of European theater and music. Bilingual since childhood, she spoke French fluently and took on projects translating French plays for Broadway directors. "I think he might have heard some records [by French songwriters] at my apartment," she said. "He was interested—he wanted to get to Europe and get into that milieu." They went together to see Jacques Brel perform at Carnegie Hall. Rod was thunderstruck—the Belgian singer-songwriter's skills as a composer and charisma as a stage performer gave McKuen a new mark of excellence to aim for. Rod didn't read or speak French, so Ellen translated Brel's lyrics for him. Later, she would accompany him on trips to France as he sought out Brel and other Francophone songwriters.

As companion, muse, and benefactor, Ehrlich was crucial to Rod's growth as an artist. She inspired his song "Ellen's Eyes" and was mentioned in his poems. Their relationship was intimate and complicated, a meeting of hearts and minds that didn't quite fit a conventional label. Rod became famous for celebrating men and women who share a love beyond typical categories and binary sexual niches. Echoes of his chaste but passionate affair with Ellen can be found between the lines of his sixties-era writings.

Like the lovers in his work, Rod and Ellen seemed to live in a world of their own. It was a special place they shared, but it was not the only such place Rod created in his life. Love was meant to be warm and caring, but not exclusive. And there were secrets even lovers kept to themselves.

Sometime in the fall of 1959, Rod met Ben Shecter, a gifted young artist who went on to become a highly successful author, illustrator, and stage designer. Ben tells the story this way: "I was at a party on Long Island, sitting on the deck, and there were helium balloons all tied up there. Rod came up and took a penknife out of his pocket and grabbed the balloons and said, 'These are all the people in your life.' And he cut the strings and the balloons all left. How's that for the start of something? We talked, we went for a walk, and it took me awhile to make the connection that I'd seen him in this awful movie called *Wild Heritage*. I said, 'That was the worst movie I'd ever seen!' And he totally agreed!"

The "very close, understanding friendship" that began between Rod and Ben that day sounds remarkably similar to what Rod shared with Ellen Ehrlich. He knew them both at approximately the same time. They did not know about each other.

Shecter recalls the three or four years he was close to Rod with great fondness: "He was a sweet, gentle man. We would go to Coney Island, the movies, museums together. I think we nurtured each other in a very positive way." Ben took photos of Rod, came up with album titles for him, and wrote liner notes for his *Beatsville* LP. Through all the good times and intimate hours, each maintained their personal freedom: "There was never a dependency upon each other. We lived apart. There was no great emotional commitment."

Two years younger than Rod, Ben was both drawn to his friend and wary of being overshadowed by him. Like many others, he found McKuen both a strong presence and a vulnerable soul: "I think when people met him, he became an indelible part of their lives. He ingratiated himself. The whole thing [about him] was 'Please love me.' I don't think it was desperation—it was a need, like a need you have for chocolate milk or Oreo cookies . . . Rod was like a stray, in need of a home. I have the feeling I was the friend that he never really had."

Ellen and Ben helped to sustain Rod's spirits as he worked hard to keep his career moving. He needed more than love and sympathy to get by, though. His cash flow was precarious, leading him to eventually declare bankruptcy. On the surface, he seemed to be advancing on many fronts— he released albums and singles, formed his own publishing company (Dov Music), landed TV game-show gigs like *To Tell the Truth* (with Ellen's help), and wrote "specialty material" for Elsa Lanchester, the De Castro Sisters, and other supper club acts. Apparently, none of it was enough to keep him out of desperate straits.

"I did anything to make money," Rod said of this time. "I was a male hustler for men and women. I sold blood—I got about ten bucks a pint, which isn't very much. I passed out in Central Park because I'd sold too much blood." To feed himself, Rod would crash events at the Waldorf Astoria: "They have maybe ten conventions a day there. You'd put on your blue suit, see a table with a bunch of badges on it, put a badge on, and you were a member of the group that was meeting. I ate hors d'oeuvres. Because I got ptomaine poisoning so many times, I learned not to eat the fish in the morning or late afternoon. Not to eat the fish, period."

Between visits to the blood bank and the free food table, Rod searched for a coherent artistic direction. He was able to secure recording contracts—sometimes more than one simultaneously—but couldn't seem to deliver a hit album. McKuen veered from style to style with each recording he released, trying to find the right image and the music to match.

Signed to Decca Records as an artist, he emphasized folk and country material like "Sixteen Tons" and "Lonesome Traveler" on 1959's *Anywhere I Wander*. A year later came *Alone After Dark*, an album that featured more of his original pop balladry along with covers of songs from films and Broadway tunes. 1960 also saw the release of *Written in the Stars (The Zodiac Suite)* on Coral Records, a concept album of instrumental pieces. None of these LPs found a wide audience.

Trying out yet another label, Rod released *Stranger in Town* on Kapp Records in 1961. The album's liner notes tried to put a positive spin on the diffuse state of his career thus far, pointing out that McKuen's credits at age twenty-seven "sound like the summation of someone twice his age." Writer Benson Green claimed that Rod's vocal style "fits the much publicized 'soul movement' popularized by singers like Ray Charles" and displayed the qualities of "the French Vocalists, who shrug their shoulders after a deep involvement with a lyric, then go on to the next song." This sort of R&B-existentialist approach is only fitfully present on the album, which follows the early

McKuen pattern of juxtaposing songs by well-known composers (Rodgers and Hart's "He Was Too Good to Me," adapted, as it often was, with a female pronoun; Johnny Mercer's "When the World Was Young") with a few originals.

At least superficially, *Stranger in Town* seemed to be aiming for the resonant melancholy found on such Sinatra LPs as *Only the Lonely* and *In the Wee Small Hours*. McKuen couldn't quite muster enough world-weary sophistication to be convincing, though. On the other hand, he was getting too old to appeal to the bobby-sox crowd. Teen-oriented rock 'n' roll was dominating the charts in late '61, filling the airwaves with tunes like Dion's "Runaround Sue," Bobby Vee's "Take Good Care of My Baby," and Dick and Dee Dee's "The Mountain's High." Rod's music was out of step with such adolescent-oriented fare. Yet he didn't seem ready to be taken seriously as a grown-up artist. Whatever he was offering, it wasn't quite right for either the malt shop set or the cocktail lounge crowd.

Rod's obsessive work ethic sustained him through this difficult period. He maniacally threw his creations up against the wall of public taste in hopes that something would stick. If he hadn't hit the jackpot with the right album yet, he did show signs of anticipating the seismic shift in pop culture the new decade would bring. The conformist Eisenhower fifties were giving way to the age of the individual seeker, a man or woman not so different from the loners Rod couldn't stop writing about. A loosening of restraints and an opening of options could be felt—the voices of outsiders were beginning to be heard in Middle America.

Maybe Rod's moment was about to arrive at last. He had already achieved a modicum of acceptance among the show business establishment while maintaining a foothold in bohemia. Perhaps he was in a position to bridge the gap between the two with a slight adjustment in approach.

In Search of Eros aimed for that sweet spot between the mainstream and the fringe. Released in December 1961 on Epic, the album matched spoken-word pieces with atmospheric jazz backdrops in the manner of his earlier poetry

LPs. Steamy expressions like "Dig your nails in, it only brings us closer" and "I want kisses that know the whole body geography" add spice to reflections upon unattainable love and fading youth. Rod delivers his verse in a steady confiding murmur, avoiding the more dramatic moments that cropped up on 1958's *Time of Desire.*

The literary skill evinced on *Eros* is less important than what its poems are trying to communicate—in fact, the act of personal communication *itself* may be the album's overriding theme. In massaging (and manipulating) the listener's inner fears and longings, Rod was drawing on some of the same skills he'd used writing psychological warfare scripts for the U. S. Army. Yet it also seems likely the album's content was inspired by his real-life romantic misadventures.

Whatever its merits might have been, *In Search of Eros* didn't easily fit into the radio playlists of the early sixties. AM stations couldn't handle the free-form verse and mildly salacious content of Rod's work; the experimental formats of FM were still years in the future.

If Rod had missed the brass ring once again, he did edge closer to ultimate success. "Though not dwelling much on it at the time, I had in effect created a new medium, one voice speaking—often quite intimately—to the other (each individual listener) over a quiet musical score," he said years later. "The listener was not a voyeur or even a third party; he or she was engaged in the lovemaking . . . I had this medium all to myself. By the time the imitators started coming on board, I would be too far ahead of them to play catch-up."

Given its culturally timely theme, it might be expected that McKuen would follow up *Eros* with a similar album as soon as possible. Instead, he veered off in a sharply different direction that aimed for the teenage dance market rather than connoisseurs of introspective verse.

Sometime in 1960 or 1961, Rod started co-writing with Gladys Shelley, a veteran pop composer known for her personal flamboyance and hit tunes (most notably "How Did He Look?" first recorded by Joan Merrill in 1941 and later covered by Connie Francis, Eydie Gormé, and Mel Tormé). Judging by the pair's output, the goal of their collaboration was commercial success rather than high art. Gladys wrote the words and Rod supplied the music for a series of ditties that both parodied the pop fads of the moment and shamelessly tried to capitalize on them.

"Oliver Twist" was the Shelley/McKuen number that came closest to becoming a bona fide hit. After unsuccessfully peddling the song to Chubby Checker and Joey Dee (who had both scored big with "twist" material), Rod decided to release it himself. Appearing almost simultaneously with *In Search of Eros* on the tiny Spiral label in December 1961, "Oliver Twist" was a bit sillier than its competitors, boasting such snappy lines as "He raises Dickens with them chickens." In some ways, the song was a throwback to McKuen's comedy numbers with Bob McFadden from two years before. Whether it was a sly put-on or a legit pop tune, the song was a far cry from the dreamy carnal musings found on *In Search of Eros.*

Rod needed a new support team for his latest assault on the charts. Through Shelley, he met Ron Gittman, an aspiring young star-maker who became his personal manager. Gittman gave his financially strapped new client a place to live, spruced up his stage wardrobe, and found him bookings at teen dance spots. "Ronnie was very aggressive, very involved with his acts," said fellow client Chuck Herman. "He took them home, made them dinner, dressed them—it was like Woody Allen in *Broadway Danny Rose.*"

Herman was a member of the Keytones, a versatile Long Island rock 'n' roll combo that became Rod's backup group in early 1962. Gittman introduced the band to McKuen when they were both performing at one of Murray the K's record hops in Brooklyn. The Keytones would go on to back him up at a series of grueling transcontinental gigs that would leave Rod vocally damaged but artistically transformed.

Trudy "Trude" Heller's popular Versailles Club at 9th Street and Sixth Avenue in Manhattan booked McKuen and the group for an eight-week engagement. "Trudy was a very nice woman, but very tough," Herman said. "She liked energy all the time. She'd be kicking and really getting into it."

A young singer named Goldie Zelkowitz—later known as Genya Ravan—also played the Versailles Club around this time. She recalled Heller as a ferocious presence who wanted her money's worth from her acts: "She required rockers to rock—no ballads. She'd go crazy with rage whenever we sang a ballad. I'd look down from the stage and see her getting angry, then she'd run over to the light switch and start flicking it on and off, screaming, 'C'mon! C'mon! Let's twist already! Let's twist the night away! C'mon, baby, let's do the fuckin' twist!'"

Rod squeezed all the dance floor sweat out of "Oliver Twist" he could during his stay at Trude's place. Despite his best efforts, the song sputtered out at no. 76 on the national *Billboard* charts. In the end, "Oliver Twist" may have been too great an act of artistic self-contortion for Rod to pull off.

Selling an ex-Hollywood actor/semi-Beat poet as a teen dance sensation was a heavy lift for Connie de Nave, the publicist brought in by Gittman to help market McKuen. "I didn't understand Rod," she said. "I knew he was talented, but he was like a pizza coming out of the oven with thirty-six ingredients on it. When you bite into a pizza, you expect pepperoni or whatever you ordered. You don't expect ham, pineapple, and maybe two other things on it. With Rod, there was always a surprise."

As a hard-charging press agent for teen idols like Frankie Avalon and Fabian, de Nave was used to promoting fresh faces to the media. Putting over a journeyman artist like McKuen was another matter: "Every place, every newspaper I went to, Rod had been there previously. I'd hear, 'Connie, get the hell out of here, there is no way . . .'" The competition in those days was just too fierce: "There were thousands of young (singers) popping up every other day. His age was a major problem. If you were past twenty-two, you were in trouble."

De Nave knew she was working with a sensitive mature poet trying to fit into a young rock 'n' roller's clothes. Yet she didn't fault him for recording something as silly as "Oliver Twist": "You have to understand something—If I'd been doing *Hamlet* for five years and I had the chance to giggle my ass off and get a different crowd and go to different venues, you're damn right I would've done it."

Once again, McKuen showed his tenacity and resilience when "Oliver Twist" failed to reach the Top 40. In late March 1962 he released the LP *Mr. Oliver Twist* on the Jubilee label. Besides the title track, the album boasted such McKuen/Shelley collaborations as "Oliver Twist Meets the Duke of Oil" (a takeoff of Gene Chandler's current hit "Duke of Earl"), "Celebrity Twist," "Seattle Twist," and "Off Her List (Cause I Can't Twist)." The rest of the LP was rounded out with Ray Charles covers and a few folk songs, including "Twist Along," a familiar Civil War–era tune set to a modern beat.

That last track was indicative of the direction McKuen was heading in. While performing at places like the Versailles, he was also taking his band down the street to Village folk houses where the twist, Frug, Jerk, and the like were strictly uncool. As Herman remembered it, "Folk music was just starting to get hot in '62, '63. We'd play the Cafe Wha? and the Bitter End on Monday and Tuesday nights—we were the first to ever play electric instruments in those rooms. Rod did a lot of traditional folk stuff and turned it around, made his own words up or changed things. He took it seriously and did some really good folk stuff . . . "

(Herman recalls a scruffy twenty-one-year-old Bob Dylan playing for spare change outside Cafe Wha? and the Bitter End on nights when Rod and the Keytones were performing at these clubs, though he has no memories of Dylan and McKuen swapping songs or talking poetry.)

Rod's take on the folk sound was different from that of traditional balladeers or the newer wave of acoustic singer-songwriters. It was a vehicle for him to entertain by any means necessary, whether he was messing with a ballad like "500 Miles" or an up-tempo anthem like "If I Had a Hammer."

Purists wouldn't even deign to classify McKuen as a folk artist, of course. He unashamedly borrowed lines and licks from folk music as he did from a host of styles, working toward the synthesis that would win him massive popularity later in the decade.

Shaking off the aroma of espresso, McKuen and the Keytones were booked for an extended stay in the downstairs lounge of the Copacabana on East 60th Street. This legendary nightspot was known for its tropical decor as well as headliners like Dean Martin, Sammy Davis Jr., and Johnny Mathis. The lounge was for second-tier acts like Rod or the Newton Brothers (featuring a youngster named Wayne). Manager Jules Podell was a hard-boiled character who ran a very tight ship, especially when it came to the small-fry talent.

"I had four shows a night, seven nights a week for months," Rod said. "We were kind of a loud rock group. One time, Jules Podell came over and said to me, 'Turn down the noise or I'll break your fuckin' arm.' And we were there one night when he did have a goon who broke somebody's arm."

It wasn't his arm Rod had to worry about, however—he was starting to dangerously overtax his vocal chords by adding too much roughness to his delivery. "Rod was not a trained singer," said Herman. "He very easily could hurt his throat. He would always try to growl and rasp his voice. Those kind of effects do damage to your throat. He really wasn't cut out to be a hard-ass like Hoyt Axton or Barry McGuire as a singer . . . "

Still, Rod kept going, hitting a punishing circuit of small clubs and bowling alleys across the country with and without the Keytones. (According to Ehrlich, he even sang in grocery stores.) Bad food, cheap lodgings, and visits to local radio stations became a wearying grind. By the time he got to Los Angeles in September '62, he had lost twenty pounds and seriously strained his voice. Rather than getting some needed rest, he began a thirteen-week stint with the Keytones at the Peppermint West, reputedly the hottest club in Hollywood.

The engagement got a lot of attention. Newspaper columnist Walter

Winchell flew out to see Rod perform. Rock Hudson, Jayne Mansfield, Mamie Van Doren, and other Hollywood stars of varying luster caught his act. Not content to play for this older crowd, McKuen and the band also gigged at Pandora's Box, a Sunset Strip teen club soon to become infamous as the site of clashes between long-haired kids and the L. A. P. D. McKuen's repertoire of rocked-up folk and dance fare could please both audiences, a feat that increasingly became difficult as the lines between pop music styles (and generations) grew more distinct.

A year of growling out songs, grinding his hips, and jumping on tables had taken its toll on Rod. The damage done to his voice had only gotten worse by the time he finished the Peppermint West gig. McKuen would say years later that his throat was like "hamburger" and that he was told he would never sing again. "He had a little notebook, and he would write you notes because his doctors told him he shouldn't speak," recalled Ehrlich, who flew in from New York to see Rod perform. "For about six weeks, any communication was through these little notes."

After a regimen of therapy, his voice returned with a raspy edge that gave it added character. He freely admitted that his once robust baritone had been reduced to a husky whisper—"It sounds like I gargle with Dutch Cleanser," he said. Judging by the albums he made after sustaining throat damage, though, Rod could muster a reasonably conventional volume and timbre on certain songs. What seems clear is that he had a new set of vocal shadings to use: muted, misty-toned, evocative of low-lit rooms and pillow talk, perfect for the kind of songs and poems he was about to write.

McKuen said that during his period of vocal convalescence, "I decided that if I couldn't write and sing the kind of material I wanted to, I really didn't want to be a performer at all." Signing with Horizon Records, he recorded *New Sounds in Folk Music* with the Keytones in L. A., an album that mixed original, traditional, and cover songs in the manner of his previous LPs. This 1963 release did contain one important new McKuen tune: "Two-Ten,

Six-Eighteen," a poignant song about a blind veteran coming home to a changed world that would be covered by the Kingston Trio, Jimmie Rodgers, and Waylon Jennings.

The Keytones returned to New York after recording with Rod; they never worked together again. (In response to the Beatles craze, the band shaved their collective heads and became the Eggheads for a while.) McKuen resumed life in L. A., a thirty-year-old former entertainment wunderkind still trying to find his niche in an increasingly segmented music market. New York had offered him love and near-starvation, sent him chasing after a quick hit single, and laid the groundwork for real, substantial success. He was ready to move on.

Ellen and Rod parted company on a good note—as close as they'd been, marriage had never been discussed. He called her frequently from California, and they saw each other occasionally in the decades ahead. In 1969, Ehrlich married Emile Mimran, a billionaire French entrepreneur. Emile felt jealous of Rod at first, though he accepted McKuen over time. Summing up her relationship with Rod after a half century, Ellen called him "the most important man outside of my husband in my life."

For Ben Shecter, Rod's departure from New York marked a clear-cut ending: "We drifted apart. In the time we were together, it was an isolated kind of friendship. The strange thing is, he wanted me to go with him [to California]. And it wasn't the kind of life I wanted. I couldn't live in anyone else's shadow—I have my own path."

For years, Rod McKuen had been writing about rootless, love-starved ramblers, the sorts of men who had intense relationships but left them behind with the turning of the seasons or a change of heart. This was more than an affected literary pose on his part. Rod constant return to the theme of the Loner in his songs and poems was no mere pose. His four-year weekend in New York left behind bruised feelings and bittersweet memories. He would look back on the good and bad times he knew there while pressing on to the success that awaited him out West.

Five

~

Till My Ship Comes In

PUTTING HIS YEARS in New York behind him, Rod returned to his two-story house at the corner of North Gardner Street and Fountain Avenue in the West Hollywood flatlands. Waiting for him was his mother, Clarice, living next door in an attached apartment. McKuen quickly fell in with the folk music circle centered around the Troubadour nightclub on Santa Monica Boulevard. Established in 1957, the venue featured an eclectic lineup of singers and guitar-strummers of varying degrees of professionalism and authenticity. The boundaries of what constituted "real" folk music in L. A. weren't as rigidly defined as they were in places like Greenwich Village and Cambridge, Massachusetts. Show-business calculation crept into the hoot nights; sunny California hedonism toned down the bite of protest songs. Rod found it a congenial environment to write and perform in.

Gravel-voiced folk balladeer Barry McGuire was among those who welcomed Rod into the Troubadour scene. Like McKuen, he had spent time playing clubs in both New York City and various California locales while honing his skills as a singer and songwriter. According to Barry, he was on the verge of joining the New Christy Minstrels when he met Rod in 1962; by the following year they were cowriting for McGuire's upcoming solo album.

McGuire found McKuen talented, resourceful, and always working: "Rod said he was the most published writer in the world because he carried a tape recorder around in his pocket. He recorded everything he said, typed it out, and copyrighted it as poetry. Every day he copyrighted another day of his talking." McKuen's quirks were also evident: "I think his closet had every pair of shoes he'd ever owned. They were all sneakers. He said they were like old friends and had his DNA imprinted in them. They had sentimental value—he'd walked a lot of miles in them . . . "

Rod's house became a meeting place for musicians, actors, and other members of the L. A. entertainment community. McGuire recalled Clarice as a warm and welcoming presence: "Rod's mom was a lovely lady. We used to sit on his front porch and write songs, and she'd make lunch for us. She was a sweetheart—he loved her and she loved him. And I could feel her affection for me. She opened her door to me and made me feel like I was part of her family."

Clarice took on the roles of cook and confidant for a rotating cast of actors and musicians. McKuen's list of future celebrities who stopped by for solace and soup is long and varied, including everyone from Clint Eastwood and Sally Kellerman to Roger Miller and John Denver. According to Rod, Montgomery Clift (an old friend from his days at Universal International) arrived one night, got drunk with Clarice, and passed out on the sofa.

Despite this warm family atmosphere, McGuire picked up on the aura of melancholy that seemed to hang about Rod: "He didn't seem morbid or depressed, just a little bit down. I always thought of it as part of his poetic sensitivity . . . He would laugh, but there was always a little bit of sadness running through his words."

The Troubadour gave McKuen a ready stage for his music and verse—yet his years of experience and eclectic influences kept him distinctly apart from the folk crowd. "Rod seemed to have a career already built in," said Art Podell, an L. A. singer-songwriter who cowrote with him. "The Troubadour was the ideal place for him to go, but the people who came to see him weren't necessarily interested in seeing a folk singer. His audience dressed differently, looked different. Normally, we had a lot of college people, a lot of Hollywood people come. Then all of a sudden, the people of the suburbs came out to see Rod . . . He was enormously attractive to women. The women came to weep and moan over his poems."

Tapping emotion and drawing tears, Rod's performances stood out from what the Troubadour typically offered. "The folk music community was a community of bravado," Podell noted. "It was Woody Guthrie, it was Pete Seeger—it was bold and brawny. Rod was subdued and had a vulnerable persona. Everybody else was singing about sailors and cowboys. He was reciting poetry from a much more sensitive place, and his audience responded differently."

McKuen was in the folk scene, but not of it. Once again, he found himself the Loner who didn't quite fit in with the crowd. According to Podell, "He was accepted, but when the show was over and we all went out to Norm's (a popular L. A. coffee shop) at two o'clock in the morning and sat around and traded songs and stuff, he was never there." Part of it stemmed from his background: "Rod was from San Francisco, a very sophisticated community. He seemed like he came out of the tail end of the Beat Generation and just folded himself into the folk music world . . . Folk music happened to be the thing that was going on, so he just wrote a few folk songs."

There was another reason for Rod's outsider status. Though it wasn't openly mentioned, Rod's sexual orientation was known or suspected by many in L. A. folk circles. The mores of the time held true even among the bohemian types who played the Troubadour. There is no evidence that McKuen lost gigs or record deals during this time because he was perceived as gay. Still, if he was not part of the folk in-crowd, it might not have been entirely his own choice.

"I think Rod at that time was a committed gay person and he kind of separated himself from the world of folk singers," Podell said. "At that point in time, I don't think that kind of open disclosure was beneficial to anybody's career. It never came up in conversation—it was an undertone . . . But nobody discussed it."

To use a contemporary term, Rod set off the gaydar of the L. A. folkies. According to Podell, "The folk music world was a masculine world. Rod's world was a feminine world . . . My first contact with him definitely felt like there was something that was not part of the regular world. The first handshake with Rod was a little bit of an insight into who he was."

McKuen could be both disarmingly open and carefully guarded about his inner life. "I never knew he was gay," McGuire said. "It wouldn't have made any difference if he was. He always treated me like a friend and was straight-ahead with me, gave me good advice, good input."

There were dangers in a lack of discretion back then. Those willing to risk exposure could walk six blocks east from the Troubadour on Santa Monica Boulevard to the Four Star Saloon, a dive bar that became a favorite gay cruising spot in the fifties. In his memoir *Under the Rainbow*, actor John Carlyle described the place as both a "sanctum for the haunted" and a "haven for the elite" where notables like Leonard Bernstein and Rod's friend Montgomery Clift could be found amidst the hustlers and barflies.

The Four Star could be one of the shadowy pickup bars described in so many McKuen poems and songs. If Rod did stop by to sample the atmosphere and action, he ran the risk of arrest and public humiliation. According to Carlyle, "the sensible loners darted home—to avoid being enticed by the lurking vice squad, which meant being vilified on the way to the slammer, being fingerprinted, hiring a lawyer, and drumming up the $500 fine."

The Troubadour and the Four Star were less than a mile apart, but represented very different worlds. Rod navigated the boundaries between them, just as he'd done with the various scenes and circles he had been part of since childhood. His unattached status was reflected in the tolerant, nonconfrontational quality of his work. Rod observed, yearned, commiserated—but always managed to slip away from entrapment. It helped him avoid being easily labeled and allowed him to speak to almost anyone as one individual to another.

Whatever contradictions there were in Rod's life, they didn't interfere with his ability to produce commercially viable work. He showed an increasing skill at combining old-school songwriting conventions with lyrics that addressed the tenor of the times. "Ally, Ally Oxen Free" became a no. 61 single in 1963 for the Kingston Trio—its wistful melody tempered its serious message about pollution and war. "The World I Used to Know" was a commitment-free love ballad somewhat akin to Buffy Sainte-Marie's "Until It's Time for You to Go." Minor-key yet mildly upbeat, it earned Jimmie Rodgers a no. 51 hit in 1964 and was also recorded by Eddy Arnold, Glen Campbell, and Johnny Mathis, among others.

Both "Ally, Ally Oxen Free" and "The World I Used to Know" convey a nostalgic pang that softens their topical content. These and similar songs McKuen was writing leaned toward a sweeter strain in folk balladry that appealed to older or less overtly hip listeners than, say, the protest broadsides of Bob Dylan and Phil Ochs. The songs also showed hints of the French chanson influences that Rod was increasingly drawing upon in his work. Even as he attempted to appeal to the folk music crowd, he was positioning himself to become a chansonnier, the American equivalent of his hero Jacques Brel.

By the time he moved back to Los Angeles, Rod had visited France twice in search of business contacts, cultural enrichment, and (apparently) an erotic adventure or two. At a time when few American songwriters were heading to Europe to collaborate with artists there, Rod was establishing ties with the French music industry that would transform his career. Ehrlich accompanied him on at least one of these trips: "We were together in Paris. Rod would sit at a café and he would ask me to translate something for him, like a song he'd heard on the radio. I did a lot of stuff like that for him—I was really an extra hand. He would have loved to have spoken French, but he didn't."

Back in the States circa 1963, Rod worked up an unauthorized English adaptation of Brel's "Le Moribond." In the original lyrics, a dying man says farewell to those he loved and hated with unsparing honesty ("Goodbye, Antoine, I did not like you very much . . . And it's killing me to die today knowing that you are still alive . . . "). Retitled "Seasons in the Sun," Rod's lyric is more sentimental and forgiving in tone, though still tinged with a certain French fatalism. McKuen submitted it to the Kingston Trio, who included it on their 1963 LP *Time to Think*. A year later, Rod released his own version.

Ehrlich sent Rod's recording of "Seasons in the Sun" to a friend at the French Film Office in New York. From there it found its way to Brel, who thought well enough of it to investigate Rod's own material. Brel especially liked "The Lovers" (a melodramatic McKuen ballad with unmistakable chansonnier overtones), so he translated it and recorded it as "Les Amants de Coeur" ("The Lovers of the Heart") sometime in 1963–64.

Rod discovered what had happened when he visited his French publisher Philippe Boutet in the summer of '64. "I asked him if he had any new songs I might adapt for America," Rod recalled. "He said yes, that he did have one that was fairly new. It had been written by Jacques Brel for the singer Jean Sablon. He then proceeded to play for me a very rough dub of the song. As I listened, I couldn't help feeling I'd heard the song somewhere before, and it was only toward the end of the piece that I realized it was my own song, 'The Lovers.'"

From there, it seemed only natural that the two songwriters should try working together. Boutet put in a call to Brel in Brussels, who suggested that McKuen stay on in Paris until Brel could make it to town for a dentist's appointment. Despite Rod's limited knowledge of French, they began a writing partnership that continued sporadically for a decade. Brel gave his American collaborator plenty of license in adapting his words—sometimes

Rod would adhere closely to the original text, at others change the lyric story lines completely. (Among the most striking examples of the latter was "The Far West," in which Rod moved the setting of Brel's song "La Plat Plays" from Belgium to the Nevada backcountry McKuen had known as a boy.)

Over the years, some Brel purists have wondered why the revered Belgian artist chose to work with the supposedly middlebrow likes of Rod. According to his biographer Alan Clayson, "Brel didn't appear to mind McKuen taking liberties with his lyrics, mainly because, as far as he was concerned, being enormous in Belgium, France, and their colonies was enormous enough." Mort Shuman—another translator of the Belgian's songs—agreed that Brel "was not interested in appealing to the English-speaking world." Still, it seems likely that Brel was pleased when Rod's lyric adaptions helped turn songs like "Ne Me Quitte Pas"—retitled "If You Go Away"—into huge international hits. Over the past half century, "If You Go Away" has been recorded by Frank Sinatra, Dusty Springfield, Barbra Streisand, Ray Charles, Nina Simone, Cyndi Lauper, and many other notable artists. It remains McKuen's greatest claim to fame as a songwriter.

For his part, Rod considered Brel the most brilliant performer he had ever encountered: "When I first saw Jacques Brel, I wept. I think I wept as much because I thought, *I'll never be this good an entertainer* . . . He moved me so much, [despite my] not even understanding what he was saying." By 1965, Rod had fully embraced his friend Jacques as a role model and presented himself to audiences as a full-fledged American chansonnier.

Aligning himself with French singer-songwriters was more than just another attempt at reinvention on Rod's part, though. There were real affinities between his work and the chanson tradition. Like McKuen, chansonniers presented themselves as outsiders who were both romantically passionate and subtly subversive of middle-class sexual mores. They loved personal freedom, celebrated comradeship among men, and were skeptical of lasting relationships with the fickle female species. They sang of loss, longing, and regret in

less-than-perfect voices—critics compared the vocals of beloved chansonnier
Charles Aznavour to that of a bleating goat. (If this is the case, Rod's damaged
vocal chords were a definite plus in putting his material over.)

More than anything, it was the emotional openness of Brel and his kind
that Rod related to. "We don't have the chansonniers in America, the people
who write songs about what's happening every day and then go onstage and live
them," he told NBC News' Edwin Newman. "It's as though there is something
inside the American male, I suppose, that makes him afraid to cry or afraid
to get emotionally involved in his songs, and maybe the reason my things are
successful is because some people live the things I do vicariously . . . "

As a chansonnier, Rod could escape being trapped in the niches where the
American music industry tended to pigeonhole artists. He could avoid falling into the chasm that had opened up between the pop styles embraced by
audiences slightly older than he was and the folk-rock sounds that teens and
twentysomethings had made their own. With a little European polish, his
sentimental tendencies could seem mature and sophisticated. McKuen had
played at being a beatnik and didn't even try to be taken for a hippie. But he
wore the clothes of a Parisian-style singing poet with convincing ease.

On the verge of real success at last, Rod found an ally in a fellow artist who
had already entered the big time. Though their close association was relatively
brief, Glenn Yarbrough proved crucial in helping McKuen find a mass audience for his songs and poetry.

Blessed with a lyric tenor of almost unearthly purity, the burly, baby-faced
Yarbrough was an ideal interpreter of McKuen's ballads. Formerly with the
Limeliters, Glenn had been active in the folk world for over a decade by the
time he began recording Rod's compositions on the 1963 album *Time to Move
On.* In certain ways, the two men were similar—both were born in the early
1930s, had served in the military during the Korean War, and felt equally at
home performing in coffeehouses and supper clubs. Yarbrough's penchant for
suits, ties, and neatly trimmed hair placed him on the more conservative side

of folk. If his looks were clean-cut and sober, his voice was full-bodied and deeply emotional, able to extract every bit of romantic longing out of a lyric.

Yarbrough went on to release a dozen more albums featuring Rod's songs; five of them were devoted entirely to McKuen material. Glenn helped Rod earn a modicum of financial security and set McKuen on the path toward reigniting his own recording career. He also played an unexpected role in launching Rod as a poet and entrepreneur.

When the two met, Glenn had established himself as a solo artist, while Rod was just beginning his career upswing. "I had just become successful on my own," Yarbrough said. "I'd recorded one or two of Rod's songs—'Isle in The Water' and 'The Lovers' among them. I've forgotten now how I got them, but I'm pretty sure I didn't know him at the time.

"One day he came walking down my driveway in the Hollywood Hills, dropping sheet music and all sorts of stuff. He didn't drive, so he'd taken a cab up there. He wanted me to hear his material. I prefer to have songs sent to me, but I couldn't just turn him away. He sang some songs for me, and I offered him a three-year contract to work with him exclusively. We set up a publishing company together, and he lived in a cottage on my property."

Rod moved into Glenn's guest house sometime in 1962. Offering a panoramic view of Laurel Canyon, the little cottage became a McKuen song factory that supplied Yarbrough with a steady stream of tunes. It also enabled Rod to invite Edward Habib to move in with him. "Rod finally talked Edward into coming down to L. A. when he rented Glenn's place," McKuen's friend Charlie Hallam recalled. "Edward was saying, 'What am I going to do there? How am I going to work?' Rod said, 'I'll find work for you.'" Soon, Habib would become McKuen's collaborator in business as well as his romantic partner.

"Rod was really, really ambitious," said Yarbrough's second wife, Annie Graves. "He was a writing machine—his mind must've been constantly working. He had to share it, whatever it was. He'd just go to Glenn and say, 'Here's a new one.' And Glenn loved his work."

As with so many of his relationships, McKuen was close (in this case literally) to Yarbrough—yet the two of them remained apart. "Rod and Glenn were not social friends," Yarbrough's assistant Paula Bailey said. "Rod stayed pretty much with Eddie on the other side of the driveway. Even though Glenn lived on the same property and they lived in a little place, you'd almost think they would've been over to the big house a lot of the time. They weren't."

If Rod and Glenn kept a respectful distance personally, they drew closer artistically as the sixties wore on. In 1966, Glenn released *The Lonely Things: The Love Songs of Rod McKuen* on RCA. The album would prove to be a turning point for both men. Arranged with elegant restraint by Mort Garson, the LP contained some of the best songs and poems Rod had written over the past several years.

The regret and longing that ran through the album was in tune with Yarbrough's life at the time: "I was going through a bitter divorce, and was kind of down and out—well, down, but not out. The songs on *The Lonely Things* were so depressing. I didn't think anybody would want to hear them. It turned out to be the biggest album I'd ever made."

Lincoln Mayorga's sparsely evocative piano is at the center of *The Lonely Things*, dressed up by intermittently lush strings arranged by Garson. Yarbrough is in peak balladeer form, showing off his shivery vibrato to full advantage as he interprets quietly angst-ridden ballads (the title track), bittersweet salutes to lost love ("Channing Way, 2"), rueful breakup numbers ("People Change"), and happy/sad toasts to the musician's life ("A Kind of Loving"). Rod's penchant for unabashed sentimentality is balanced by Glenn's mixture of suavity and earnestness, making this one of the best showcases of McKuen's work ever released.

"The Women" stands out in this set for its misogynistic overtones. Rod retained the edge of Brel's lyric, which portrays women as scheming, faithless enemies of men. "Glenn was recording it at a session, and three generations of females in his life sat in stony silence during the playback," Rod said. "A

Rod McKuen on film set, late 1950s. (Jim Pierson)

A late-1950s McKuen publicity photo. Note Rod's James Dean--esque look.
(Jim Pierson)

Released in 1956, Rod's
debut album, *Songs for a
Lazy Afternoon*, presented
him as a sensitive artist with
Nature Boy overtones.

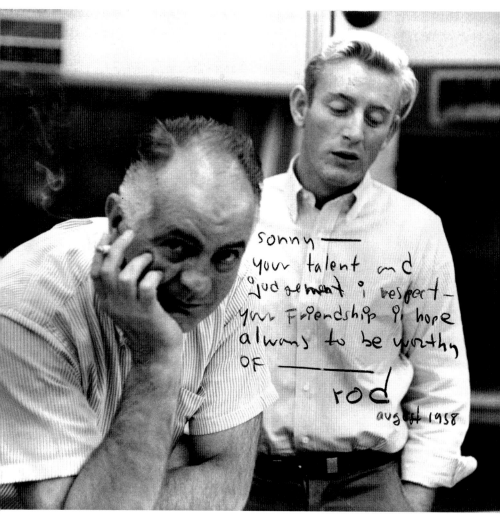

Rod in the recording studio with arranger Sonny Burke, 1958. Sonny worked for Decca Records during Rod's brief time as an artist there. (Jim Pierson)

Rod in caveman costume with friend Corky Hale at a Hollywood costume party, 1959. (Jim Pierson)

Rod's 1959 *Beatsville* LP was both a satiric and sympathetic look at the poets and poseurs he encountered as part of the Bay Area's bohemian community. (Jim Pierson)

Rod saw himself in the chansonnier tradition of Belgian singer-composer Jacques Brel. "If You Go Away" and "Seasons in the Sun" were among their collaborations.

Rod during his 1960s stint as an RCA recording artist. (Jim Pierson)

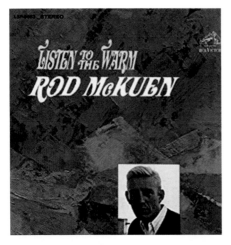

Listen to the Warm (1967) accompanied Rod's poetry book of the same title. Its look was inspired by the abstract cover art of Stan Getz's Brazilian-themed LPs of the 1960s. (Jim Pierson)

Rod with presidential candidate Robert F. Kennedy, 1968. McKuen campaigned for both Democrats and Republicans over the years. (Jim Pierson)

Rod with Frank Sinatra during sessions for *A Man Alone* (1969), an album devoted to
Sinatra's interpretations of McKuen songs and poems. (Jim Pierson)

Rod's special fondness for cats was captured in
"A Cat Named Sloopy" and other writings.
(Jim Pierson)

Rod with beloved companion Mr. Kelly. (Jim Pierson)

daughter who was just being quiet, a former wife who glared at a current girl-friend, and Glenn's mother, who said to me, 'Are we really like that?' To which I replied, 'Yes, and more.'"

Nestled among the songs were moody free-verse vignettes like "Night Song" and "Brownstone." According to the album's liner notes, these and other McKuen poems were taken from the book *Stanyan Street & Other Sorrows*. Those interested were invited to write to a post office box in Hollywood for copies. Requests began to pour in for the book—the only problem was, no such book had been published.

To be accurate, Rod did have an assortment of poems he'd written and performed that were ready for publication. He hadn't put out a book of verse in over a decade; his earlier attempts had reached a tiny readership. When he saw the demand was there, he took a few weeks out to write more poems, gather an assortment of older pieces, and cobble together a small volume. Stanyan Music—a company McKuen and Yarbrough had launched to handle Rod's songs—published the book in the latter half of 1966.

The life of *Stanyan Street & Other Sorrows* could have ended with a burst of mail-order sales. Sensing bigger opportunities, McKuen decided to aggressively market the book in stores. Then and now, selling poetry books wasn't the best bet for making money—it's an even shakier proposition than trying to write hit songs. Attempting to do so without the help of an established publisher was even more difficult. Rod had recently signed with RCA Records as an artist. It would have made more sense for him to concentrate on reviving his recording career than to spend time pushing his little volume of verse. Still, he took on the challenge with gusto.

Rod enlisted Edward for his grassroots marketing campaign. "I would go driving up and down the state of California with a car loaded with Rod's books," Habib said. "I'd go through the telephone book and get addresses of bookstores. I'd go to the stores and say, 'Can you handle five books? If they don't sell by next week I'll come and pick them up.' Things were beginning to break for Rod, and I'd go back to the bookstores and they'd not only order more books, they'd double the order. Before you know it, they'd be ordering fifty or sixty copies at a time. And before we knew it, we went through sixty-five thousand copies."

A little dealmaking helped spur sales, Rod recalled: "Ed would go up and down the (West) Coast, and he'd say, 'If you want to buy one copy, we'll give you seventy percent off. If you want to buy five copies, we'll give you sixty percent off. If you want to buy ten copies, we'll give you forty percent off.' I knew nothing about this."

Edward also made sure Rod plugged *Stanyan Street* at his concerts: "I'd pick up the book, read a poem, hold up the book so everyone could see it, and say, 'By the way, my brother has asked me to tell you that this is available in the lobby.' Which is one of the reasons I never learned any of my poems by heart."

Today, live performers attempt to keep their careers afloat by selling a variety of merchandise at shows. Back in 1966, it was definitely uncommon for an entertainer like McKuen to self-publish a book of poetry and promote it from the stage. At best, it would have been seen as a small, thoughtful gesture for the fans, or an act of vanity. But Rod took it seriously and so did his audience. Going beyond his core following, he reached out to a vast potential readership, one that few thought even existed.

Stanyan Street & Other Sorrows was an unlikely candidate to make publishing history. Its eighty-four pages contained poems dating back to 1954, as well as a handful of lyrics to lesser-known McKuen songs. The book jacket—featuring modish Jezebel font lettering and a drawing of a San Francisco–style Victorian house—added to its whimsical vibe. At first glance, the volume seemed as lightweight and innocuous as a Christmas stocking stuffer.

This smallness of scale was key to its success. McKuen's poems—direct, confiding, wistful but free of cynicism or jadedness—purposefully avoided grand themes. The emphasis on fleeting moments involving specific people (usually the author) went against the pop culture mood of the moment. The protests, riots, and public flaunting of convention that were becoming fodder for music, novels, and movies were far away from the intimate longings found in *Stanyan Street*. A year earlier, Rod's friend Barry McGuire topped the charts with "Eve of Destruction," a declaration of outrage at the world's incurable ills. Rod scored his career breakthrough by heading in a very different direction.

Anyone who had followed McKuen's work over the past decade would have recognized the style and subject matter of *Stanyan Street*. Afternoon encounters and one-night stands are captured in imagery both carnal ("I knew the hills and gullies of your being / the curves / the turns . . . ") and quirky ("I'd lie down in your shadows' shadow / and live on sounds your stomach makes"). The poems mourn the demolition of neighborhood landmarks as well as the passing of friends. Self-acceptance and compassion for others (except motorists who run over animals) are the dominant notes here. A survivor's stubborn pride tempers the bittersweet tone in lines like "My only forced submission has been the rape of time . . . "

Stanyan Street's contents could be taken as autobiography, folk wisdom, tips for self-healing—but was it really *poetry*? McKuen didn't bother to get the approval of any school, movement, or authority figure before offering his book to the world. Once again, he was the outsider, the man without pedigree or credentials, finding his own path around the gatekeepers.

1966 saw the publication of books by such critically recognized poets as John Ashbery, Ted Berrigan, LeRoi Jones (later known as Amiri Baraka), Anne Sexton, and Robert Creeley. The readership for their verse was highly literate, often fervent—and limited. Sales of poetry books were (at best) in the low thousands. Poets usually didn't get reviewed in mainstream publications or make appearances on television. Most of the truly famous poets of the past fifty years—iconic figures like T. S. Eliot, Robert Frost, and Carl Sandburg—had already died or would by the end of the decade.

The Beat poets came closest to achieving a mass audience. Allen Ginsberg in particular was widely read and an acknowledged influence on a younger generation of poets and songwriters. McKuen had at least a passing association with the Beats—he had traveled in the same Bay Area circles and saluted/satirized the movement on albums like *Beatsville*. But Rod didn't set himself up as a voice for a self-identified subculture, as some of the Beat writers did. He was a loner even among the rebels and dropouts.

Whether he was producing genuine poetry, journal jottings, or mere doggerel, McKuen was connecting with a wider public than an Ashbery or a Berrigan or even a Ginsberg could reach. *Stanyan Street & Other Sorrows* would go through multiple editions and sell thousands of copies within the first year of its publication. The book reinforced an upturn in Rod's fortunes as a songwriter and recording artist. After so many false starts, near misses, and small victories, he'd finally gotten a clear shot at unequivocal success.

With *Stanyan Street*, McKuen began to find a readership among people who didn't typically make a place for poetry in their lives. He would be called an imposter, a faux poet, a crassly commercial panderer for doing so. This line of criticism hearkened back to the label of illegitimacy Rod had been trying to overcome ever since his birth to an unwed mother in a charity hospital. Over the next decade, he would legitimize himself as an artist in the eyes of millions around the world.

A year or so before *Stanyan Street* was published, Paula Bailey had encountered McKuen in the driveway behind Glenn Yarbrough's house: "Rod came out and said to me, 'I'm so frustrated . . . will I ever become famous?' He knew he was talented. He was really putting out a lot of stuff. It was not long after that that things began happening for him . . . "

Rod was about to reach heights of fame no one could have anticipated. The eternal Stranger in Town was about to arrive in spectacular fashion.

Six

~

Sloopy and the Summer of Love

THE YEAR 1967 would be remembered for a number of cultural milestones—*Sgt. Pepper's Lonely Hearts Club Band, The Graduate,* the musical *Hair,* the Summer of Love. America was going through convulsions that year, manifested in the terrible (riots in Detroit and Washington, D. C.), the unsettling (Timothy Leary's call to "Turn on, tune in, drop out"), and the absurd (the banana-peel smoking pseudo fad). People were called upon to take sides in the generation gap, the war in Vietnam, the battle between the hippies and the straights. Everything seemed polarized, unmoored, headed for meltdown.

Rod McKuen stood for something different. As the year began, he was riding a rising wave of popularity that transcended musical and literary categories as it attracted an unlikely mix of older and younger fans. Both as a musician and poet, he was finally reaping the rewards of his long years as a journeyman entertainer and self-published writer. In a time of loud, fierce expression, his music and verse spoke to America's gentler instincts. There were millions waiting to embrace what he had to offer.

For a decade, Rod had seemingly spread himself too thin as an artist, dabbling in music, movies, and the printed word while trying to grab onto whatever craze seemed useful at the time. Now he was able to unify his performing, songwriting, and poetry into a cohesive whole. Landing a new deal with RCA Records, he had released five albums of original songs on the label by the end of 1967. The LPs—most of them benefitting from Neely Plumb's tasteful, focused production—presented McKuen as a mature, worldly observer of the human condition. Rather than feeling like a departure from what he did as a performer, his poetry tapped the same veins of experience and emotion found in his songs. Books, records, concerts, and TV appearances all served to reinforce each other. Rod was building a personal brand in ways few if any entertainers had ever done before.

He did so by reaching an audience over thirty that didn't relate to the protest ballads and rock anthems of the moment—but he won converts among the younger, hipper crowd, as well. It would be a mistake to regard him as a spokesman for an emerging "silent majority" of conservative Americans. Beneath its often placid surface, his work reflected the deep cultural changes that had taken place since World War II.

Rod had always been the misfit, the odd man out of any scene he was part of. Too mainstream to be classed as underground yet too quirky to be a conventional showbiz act, he never convincingly placed himself in a company of peers. By 1967, though, the whole country seemed to be full of misfits, not all of whom declared themselves with long hair and eccentric dress. These men and women became Rod's special constituency.

In a few years, critics would call Rod the voice of Middle America. But it was not the Middle America celebrated in TV programs like *Father Knows Best* and *The Donna Reed Show* that he represented. McKuen did not win a vast audience celebrating well-ordered and smugly content nuclear families. His expressions of loneliness and yearning resonated with the unobtrusively alienated, the quietly disaffected. Unlike the protesters and hippies defying the Establishment, they didn't broadcast their inability to fully take part in the good life. Rod gave voice to what they couldn't or wouldn't say.

Commentators had been noticing the growing dissatisfaction among "normal" Americans for a good ten years. "Togetherness"—a term coined in 1954 by *McCall's Magazine* for what happy families experienced—had become an unattainable goal for many. Best-selling books like Betty Friedan's *The Feminine Mystique* (1963) probed into "the problem that has no name" that beset housewives who supposedly should have been content with their lot. Women in particular were said to be repressing their feelings and squelching their dreams.

Superficially at least, the public arena was more open than ever before. *Playboy, Sex and the Single Girl*, the topless swimsuit, and the birth-control pill were all part of the American mainstream, indicators that the old Puritan morality had been breached for good. Freedom for the body and spirit became mixed up with drug-induced mind expansion and political rebellion, a heady brew that gave 1967 its special glow. But on a more ordinary level, sex was spoken of as a simple way to overcome loneliness, a language that transcended words. Popular San Francisco topless dancer Carol Doda was quoted describing her act as a way to "communicate with people."

The idea of loneliness as a sort of free-floating national crisis was a familiar talking point by the middle of the sixties. *The Lonely Crowd*—the title of an influential 1950 sociological study—had become a national catchphrase. "All the lonely people / Where do they all come from?" asked the Beatles in 1966's "Eleanor Rigby." It was a question McKuen had been asking in his songs and poems for nearly twenty years.

McKuen's obsession with loneliness—as well as the need for loners to be alone—was in sync with the prevailing mood of 1967. Still, he declined to join the Flower Power bandwagon of acid-dipped utopianism. He was too old, possibly too jaded, and surely too authentic a loner to issue a manifesto like John Phillips's "San Francisco (Be Sure to Wear Flowers in Your Hair)," a no. 4 single that July. Rod's work spoke of individual connections forged by strangers of no definite age, gender, or degree of hipness. *Stanyan Street*'s verse radiated freedom and a certain benign paganism without adopting the us-against-them slogans so prevalent in the Summer of Love.

The casual, scribbled-note quality of Rod's poetry was a different sort of challenge to Establishment orthodoxy than the coded drug references and insinuating surrealism of Bob Dylan or John Lennon. Likewise, McKuen offered empathy and insight without the formality of highbrow literary standards. He worked within the context of pop culture, the vast arena of expression occupied by TV shows, comic books, Top 40 radio, romance magazines, science-fiction novels, and other diversions beneath the consideration of serious critics. Derided as middlebrow trash, such mass-produced entertainment was becoming more and more meaningful to American consumers.

It is significant that McKuen's mass-culture breakthrough in 1966–67 coincided with that of Charles Schulz, whose *Peanuts* comic strip offered a poignant sort of whimsy not unlike that found in Rod's work. Both men were fond of sentimental catchphrases like "I'm strong, but I like roses" (McKuen) or "Happiness is a warm puppy" (Schulz). Robert L. Short's 1965 best seller *The Gospel According to Peanuts* found biblical truths in the doings of Linus, Snoopy, and Charlie Brown. McKuen likewise appealed to the spiritual yearnings of his readers and listeners with a simply stated message of love, inclusion, and acceptance. (McKuen and Schulz became friends around this time and went on to collaborate on the 1969 animated film *A Boy Named Charlie Brown*.)

The creators of *Stanyan Street* and *Peanuts* shared one more thing in common: a feel for merchandising that made their work iconic and ubiquitous. Charlie Brown and his friends were everywhere in the mid-sixties, including on the radio (thanks to the Royal Guardsmen's "Snoopy vs. the Red Baron," a no. 2 hit in December 1966). In much the same fashion, McKuen moved quickly to capitalize on his career breakthrough with a steady stream of books, records, and live shows that elevated him from cult-figure status into genuine celebrityhood.

Rod was more than ready for his big moment. Though he had built up a core of true believers over the years, it was easy for others in the music world to typecast him as a second-tier artist who would never reach a large audience, at least in the States. All of this changed at the start of '67. McKuen had been dealt a new hand, and he played it with a blend of bohemian nonchalance and keen business savvy. From now on, there would be no more half-assed fad-chasing schemes and lame low-budget deals. Rod was done with being undervalued and shortchanged.

Rod instructed his agent, Helen Brann, to find him a deal with a major publisher. His work—and his amazing success as an independent author—attracted the attention of Random House poetry editor Nan Talese. "I checked his figures with our West Coast reps, and they told me he was a phenomenon," she said. "He was coming to New York and we met; I offered him a $750 advance, which he accepted."

Talese recognized that McKuen wasn't a typical poet arriving with literary cachet but limited sales potential. She arranged for him to speak to company reps at an upcoming sales conference: "I introduced him, and then he addressed the group, and he told them about selling books out of the trunk of his car. He said it was difficult, and the reps loved it. They gave him a standing ovation."

McKuen kept up his casual persona during negotiations with Random House. As Rod recalled, "Bob Bernstein, who was head of the company then, took me to lunch and said, 'What would it cost me to have you give us *Stanyan Street*?' I said, 'I'm not interested—we published it, and it's my baby.' My brother [Edward Habib] kicked me under the table. Bob said, 'What do you want?' I said, 'There's nothing I want.' My brother said, 'Oh, yes, you do—you want a new Mercedes.' I said, 'I do?' So the book was sold for a new Mercedes." (According to Talese, Bernstein acquired the rights to *Stanyan Street* for $10,000.)

Around the same time Rod was securing his book deal, Warner Bros. Records released *The Sea*, his collaborative project with arranger/composer Anita Kerr. At first listen, the album seemed like just another McKuen poetry release, this time dressed up with orchestral backdrops and environmental sound effects. Overall, though, *The Sea* was more focused in its conception and execution—as well as in its marketing—than Rod's earlier spoken-word recordings had been.

Officially, *The Sea* wasn't a McKuen release at all; the album was credited to the San Sebastian Strings, a studio ensemble under the direction of Kerr. The name sounded exotic yet vague, comparable to the 101 Strings, the Mystic Moods Orchestra, and other instrumental units gaining attention around that time. The latter group anticipated *The Sea*'s blend of symphonic melodies and aquatic sound effects with its 1966 LP *One Stormy Night*. "Mood music" was becoming a genre, appealing to hi-fi aficionados and FM radio listeners with its gauzy, evocative soundscapes. Kerr and McKuen took this template and added poetry that was both intimate and impersonal, creating a dreamy, almost hypnotic ambience.

Kerr's musical skills were crucial to the project. A veteran arranger with wide experience in Nashville and L. A., she had first worked with Rod on his 1966 LP *Through European Windows*. In December of that year, McKuen approached her about collaborating on a sea-themed project that had been simmering in his mind for some time. He said, "I gave her some ideas about the music, but when I heard it for the first time, it was such a revelation that I tore up all my ideas and started all over again." (Actually, a number of *The Sea*'s poems had already been published in *Stanyan Street* or had appeared on earlier McKuen albums.)

Because he was still signed to RCA, McKuen couldn't read his work on *The Sea*. An anonymous actor was chosen for the narrator's role instead. "The name doesn't matter," Rod wrote in his liner notes. "It is more important that it is someone you might like to know, or someone you might like to have say to you the things that are being said here." The mysterious voice belonged to actor/singer Jesse Pearson, best known for his starring role in the 1963 film *Bye Bye Birdie*. A few years older than McKuen, Pearson brought a tender sort of gravitas to his performance, reciting Rod's words with a rich purr that suggested sexual languor spread over endless sunny days.

The ebb and flow of the tides frames the album's tracks, setting an even rhythmic pace sustained by the words and music. The narrator seems adrift on currents of reverie, reaching out to a lover one moment, sliding back into fears and doubts the next. Suggestively tactile imagery ("You've been at the beach so long you even taste like the sun") blend in with philosophical reflections ("You have to make the good times yourself . . . take the little times and make them into big times . . . ") Kerr's billowing strings enhance *The Sea*'s tranquil mood, though slinky jazz riffs and bursts of Latin brass add some welcome vigor to the foggy atmosphere.

The album was a significant departure for McKuen on a number of levels. By sharing artistic control with Kerr and stepping away from the vocal mic, he depersonalized the project without losing the confiding quality of his poems. Rod's name was on the album, but its contents didn't have to be taken as an act of self-expression on his part. With *The Sea*, he moved away from the singer-songwriter-poet mode toward the more ambiguous role of lifestyle product creator. The McKuen brand—applied to products ranging from calendars and greeting cards to jackets and luggage over the next decade—began to take shape here.

The Sea proved to be an unexpected hit, earning gold certification and remaining on the *Billboard* album charts for 143 weeks. Though classified as an easy listening release, the album managed to sound hip enough to distinguish it from the lounge crooners, big-band retreads, and instrumental cover-tune collections that defined the genre. People found more than just music here—the album's cumulative effect was soothing, steadying, even healing. In a year when Americans felt overloaded and under siege, *The Sea* offered a refuge from the madness of 1967.

A number of *The Sea*'s poems were included in *Listen to the Warm*, Rod's first official title for Random House. This volume followed the *Stanyan Street* formula of combining free-form verses with song lyrics. Like McKuen's earlier volume, soft-lit erotica and yearning nostalgia are leavened with cheeky comments about current pop culture. There are a few antiwar poems as well.

Talese recalls that she chose the book's title and suggested its abstract orange and yellow cover art (inspired by similar artwork for a jazz LP by Stan Getz and João Gilberto). Both emphasize the sensual quality of Rod's verse—he delights in recounting both scenes of nature and the everyday minutiae of city life, with special emphasis on food and the naked human body. "Listen to the Warm" suggests the weightless contentment of the womb, a place beyond the cares of adulthood. Juxtaposing bedroom reveries with snapshots of lost toys and the changing seasons, McKuen's poems appealed to primal needs in ways that made their aesthetic value almost beside the point.

With *Listen to the Warm*, Rod increasingly edged across the boundaries of poetry into the realm of self-help literature. More than craft, wit, or originality, he was offering *himself* in the book's 114 pages. The intimate details of his poems risked disapproval and ridicule—the occasional awkward phrase actually strengthened their impact. In turn, he gave the reader permission to feel vulnerable or needy without embarrassment. The therapeutic element in all of this was undeniable.

McKuen's years as a songwriter taught him how important it was to go for the emotional jugular as quickly as possible. His penchant for the sentimental separated him both from the hipper pop artists and the literary establishment of the day. It also helped make him a fortune.

No poem in *Listen to the Warm* tugged at the heartstrings harder than "A Cat Named Sloopy." This signature work—often performed by McKuen in concert and on television—summed up much of what people either loved or hated about him.

Rod's backstory about the poem was typically whimsical and self-effacing. "Really, [Sloopy] is an amalgamation of two cats," he told TV talk-show host Mike Douglas in 1969. "One was called A Marvelous Cat and the other was named Sloopy. Sloopy had one yellow eye and one blue eye and was a Persian or something and was completely deaf . . . I had the cat when I was living in New York and feeling very sorry for myself, and I was very broke and I hated the city and everybody, and the cat was very nice to me."

"Sloopy" lovingly recalls the affection and understanding the pet gave him before Rod's negligence caused her to run away. The poem was a crowd-pleaser, but not for those with finicky literary standards. Dogs and cats were considered fit subject matter for children's books and Disney movies, but not legitimate topics for serious fiction or poetry. For an adult man to claim that his cat was "the only human thing that ever gave back love to me" was to invite ridicule and the wrong kind of pity. Rod offered his confession without a hint of embarrassment.

He was on to something. Whatever the poem's literary merits, "Sloopy" resonated deeply with both lonely singles and animal lovers (and some folks were both, of course). Today, America is a cat-obsessed nation, with an endless deluge of products, services, and videos celebrating the nation's most popular pet. McKuen's willingness to extol the human qualities of his cat was definitely ahead of its time in 1967. With "Sloopy," Rod emerged as a spokesman for the value and dignity of animals, a cause he would devote increasing time to in the following decade.

"Sloopy" is also notable for Rod's description of himself as a "midnight cowboy" (who sought out the company of strangers "to live an hour-long cowboy's life"). McKuen claimed to have invented this evocative phrase, which was then supposedly borrowed by his author friend James Leo Herlihy to be used as the title of the 1965 novel about New York street hustlers. Considering that "A Cat Named Sloopy" appeared in print in 1967, this seems questionable. According to at least one source, Herlihy got the term from Tennessee Williams, who called Marlon Brando a "real midnight cowboy" during a rehearsal for *A Streetcar Named Desire* in 1948.

That McKuen alluded to his adventures in New York's commercial sex

underground while celebrating his devotion to his pet cat shows how willing
he was to skirt the edges of respectable morality in his work. Even at his most
treacly, he only thinly disguised who he was and how he had lived.

The LP version of *Listen to the Warm* was released by RCA three months
after the book appeared. Opening with an orchestrated reading of "A Cat
Named Sloopy," the album interspersed poems from the book with songs that
leaned toward light jazz and bossa nova stylings. Arthur Greenslade's arrange-
ments give the tracks a cinematic quality, making McKuen's vocals feel like
film narration at times. There are no hearty folk sing-alongs or Brel-esque
dramatic recitations here—the mood is wistful, bruise-tender, and nostalgic,
right down to Rod's final cries for Sloopy at the album's close.

The print and audio iterations of *Listen to the Warm* reached a surprisingly
broad-based audience as the Summer of Love settled into a sullen, divisive
autumn. Rod's work could be leafed through over cocktails in a suburban
ranch home or meditated upon by candlelight at a hippie crash pad. The
boundaries between hip and straight were still somewhat fluid in late 1967;
voices that fell between the two extremes could be heard by both sides if
pitched in the right key. Counterculture arbiters like *Rolling Stone* (launched
in November) had not yet laid down firm criteria for judging singer-songwriters. At that point, McKuen was still garnering positive reviews in places
like *Stereo Review* and the *San Francisco Examiner*. The reaction against him
among critics would not fully emerge until a year or so later.

Rod never pretended to be a hippie. His photo on the cover of the *Listen
to the Warm* LP shows him with a conservative haircut that kept his sideburns
short and the bangs out of his eyes. There would be no awkward attempts to
be "with-it," no photo shoots in bell-bottoms or a Nehru jacket. Rod's sweater/
jeans/sneakers ensemble allowed him to skirt the hip dress code without favor-
ing the telltale suit and tie of the older generation. You could easily imagine
him ambling from the lounge to the love-in, blending into both scenes, always
the loner who never quite joins the party.

By the end of '67, McKuen had become a true phenomenon, transcending the labels of songwriter, entertainer, and poet. Some in the media saw a comparison with author-philosopher Kahlil Gibran, whose inspirational 1923 classic *The Prophet* presented eternal truths in simple poetic terms. There were plenty of seekers on both sides of the generation gap who wanted spiritual answers that went beyond religious dogmatism. Even clerics like Father James Kavanaugh—author of the 1967 best seller *A Modern Priest Looks at His Outdated Church*—sought to break away from tired old teachings about sex and marriage. (Kavanaugh later quit the priesthood and became a poet.) McKuen became one more unconventional writer/teacher who seemed to suggest a more authentic and fulfilling way to live. Though he never claimed the term, he was taking on the status of a New Age guru.

Life magazine picked up on this in its February 9, 1968 profile of Rod. Writer Jack Fincher noted that while McKuen's work often "skip[ped] prettily like a flat stone across a sea of poetic clichés," it carried a message of wide appeal: "Don't fear to bare your emotions. *Be* sentimental. Be natural. Don't stay cool, stay warm."

According to Fincher, Rod's growing legion of "fanatically dedicated" believers included a Jesuit seminarian who compared McKuen to Jesus Christ. Fincher also noted that some of these fans emerged from backstage visits with their hero "looking as if they had just been blessed by a pop Pope." The article's lead photo underscores these claims—Rod stands onstage with eyes closed, arms stretched outward, palms open and tilted heavenward, as if calling down blessings from above. A neatly groomed nightclub crowd (mostly young and female) looks up at him in rapture.

Over the next few years, McKuen would acknowledge his status as a spiritual teacher. To Fincher, he stressed his therapeutic role without making great claims about his art: "It just happens I've said something at a time when people need to be talked to . . . I'm not a poet; I'm a stringer of words. My stuff is conversational, one man saying as simply and honestly as he can how he feels about people and about himself. It's a tremendous outlet for people."

Whether he was a sage, a poet, or a mere word-stringer, Rod made history with *Listen to the Warm*. The book sold over one million copies in hardback within a year of its publication, far outselling any previous McKuen volume (as well as such titles as *The Rise and Fall of the Third Reich, Gone with the Wind* and *The Random House Dictionary of the English Language*). Combined with the sales of *Stanyan Street* (which would exceed two million copies), the LP version of *Listen to the Warm, The Sea,* and other recording projects, Rod's commercial achievement was truly staggering.

Rod's ability to keep a level head amidst this outpouring of success was remarkable. He had learned a great deal about remaining steady and self-controlled under trying circumstances. Almost twenty years had gone by since he'd begun his showbiz career as a teenage broadcaster in Oakland. He'd been mishandled by Hollywood, poorly promoted by record companies, forced to sell his blood and his body to survive. Now that his big break had finally come, he was going to make the most of it, even if it meant damaging some friendships along the way.

One of the casualties was Rod's publishing partnership with Glenn Yarbrough. The arrangement between the two had included the guest house behind Yarbrough's house, where Rod and Edward Habib had lived. Now that Rod was on the verge of superstardom, the deal didn't look quite so attractive: "I had a tip that the *Life* magazine story on me was coming out—as far as I knew, I was going to have the cover. [*Note: He didn't get it.*] And I had to gather all the cash to buy Glenn out before the story hit. It was $25,000, which was a lot of money—but I also knew it wasn't a lot of money for those songs. I booked about six months of gigs and used the advances to help pay Glenn."

For his part, Yarbrough was ready to end his connection with McKuen. Though both had benefited from working together, conflicts over money had soured their relationship. "I told Rod just to pay me back for the publishing company and get out of my life," Glenn said.

From now on, Rod would do his best to be fully in control of career, financially as well as creatively. His frenetic pace of writing, recording, performing, promoting, and dealmaking continued to accelerate in 1968. A bout of hepatitis barely slowed him down—fueled by endless cups of coffee and unfulfilled dreams, he seized his cultural moment and wouldn't let go. With hardly a moment to reflect upon how far he'd come, Rod was almost continuously on the road or in the studio, feeding and expanding the market he created, reaching millions and *making* millions, helping the lonely to feel a little more warm.

Seven

~

A Man Alone and Others

IT WAS A rarified roster of cultural heavyweights who gathered on an April 1968 evening at New York's tony 21 Club. Random House founder Bennett Cerf invited an A-plus list of famous names to help celebrate the success of his recently signed author Rod McKuen, a poet many of them had heard about but perhaps only a few had actually read. If they had seen Rod before, it may have been at the Waldorf Astoria when he was scarfing up canapés while wearing a stolen name tag. It hardly mattered now, as Rod brushed his cascading bleached blond hair out of his eyes and flashed his Tom Sawyer smile at the American royalty gathered around him.

Rod had been to swanky Hollywood parties before, but never an affair like this. Walter Cronkite, Ed Sullivan, John Steinbeck, Richard Rodgers, Diana Vreeland—some of the foremost tastemakers of the mid-twentieth century were there to certify his status as an emerging celebrity. What did they see when they looked at this not-young, not-old man with a fourth-grade education who was making Random House a fortune with, of all things, poetry? Did they see a primitive talent, a parvenu, a gate-crasher? Did they respond to his calming charisma, or did they feel uneasy about legitimizing an author lacking highbrow credentials and connections?

For his part, Cerf was enjoying the show, relishing the coup he'd pulled off by signing a rank outsider without the approval of his upper-crust friends. As he surveyed the room and noted Rod's ability to chat up the blue-blooded likes of Gloria Vanderbilt and George Plimpton, he thought about the naysayers too finicky in their literary tastes to accept McKuen. When *Time* sniffed that Rod was "Edgar Guest with lemon juice," Cerf responded, "Nevertheless, he sells five or six thousand copies a week. I'd like to find a few more Rod McKuens!"

The 21 party was one more validation of Rod's emerging status as a media superstar. After more than a decade hovering on the outskirts of artistic success, he was ready to collect his rewards for all of his hard work and sheer endurance. Not that he intended to slack off—there would be no letup in his eighteen-hour workdays or relentless travel schedule. Breaking sales records and earning the adulation of crowds had become almost routine by early '68. Rod had more than proven himself in the marketplace. But this was only the beginning.

At the same time, friends and colleagues were worried about McKuen's health. "I am concerned about you," Nan Talese wrote Rod the same week his *Life* profile hit the stands. "Please try not to over-extend your energy . . . I'm not being a spoil-sport; I just want to warn you what can happen when the balloon goes up so high . . . I'm not asking you to be less ambitious. I am only asking you not to spread yourself too thin."

If Talese had concerns that Rod might be facing burnout, Random House overall seemed happy to promote him as an unstoppable creative force out to conquer every corner of the popular arts. The company's press releases and internal memos touted him as a "phenomenon," a "cult hero," an "international personality." Staff publicist Selma Shapiro reflected Random House's genuine amazement and delight over Rod's success in an October 1968 story pitch to *Newsweek*: "In one year's time, there are now over 900,000 copies in print of his three books of poetry. We find that, frankly, incredible. He has more offers for screen plays, scores, television appearances, specials, and so forth, than he can keep track of. He is charming, kind, and very, very hard-working—and he is also a good businessman." In selling McKuen, Shapiro emphasized his relentless drive and mass acceptance over the aesthetic value of his output.

Not everybody in the media establishment was convinced by such appeals. "Rod McKuen is part of an interesting phenomenon," *Esquire* editor Byron Dobell wrote Talese. "But I could only see quoting from his lyrics (in *Esquire*) to show the banality of the phenomenon. There are two or three touching moments in all these words but his lack of discrimination . . . well, I think he's *terrible* (,) but some said the same of Robert Burns!"

Random House may not have sold Rod McKuen as the new Carl Sandburg—much less Robbie Burns—but its editors and executives knew they had signed a writer with a unique ability to reach a vast readership. By all indications, it was the under-thirty set who were primarily buying his books. As one West Coast sales rep put it, Rod appealed to the same romantic yearnings as Kahlil Gibran's *The Prophet*, only with a fresh, beatnik-inflected touch. Considering his later reputation as the chosen poet of the unhip and ordinary, it's worth noting that Random House took out ads for Rod's first two books in underground newspapers like the *Los Angeles Free Press*, the *Berkeley Barb*, and the *Village Voice*. Marketing to the Now Generation was an inexact science for mainstream publishers like Random House—but the sales figures for *Stanyan Street* and *Listen to the Warm* were undeniable. Whatever McKuen offered, the kids wanted it.

Rod's relationship with his publisher was a congenial one, at least for the first three years. He worked closely with Talese on the content, packaging, and marketing of his books. She lent a sympathetic ear to his problems, encouraged his creative schemes (within reason), and tried to help him manage the impact of his fame. Early on, he showed her his business savvy with detailed letters that hashed out the intricacies of his publishing contract. Rod was particularly keen on making sure his songwriting copyrights were separate from his Random House deal. From the start, Nan knew McKuen was no misty-headed bohemian who considered himself beyond such mundane things as money. He insisted upon a larger advance for each book; his royalties were paid quarterly, an almost unheard-of arrangement in the book publishing world.

In an unusual show of trust for him, Rod listened to Talese's editorial critique of his next poetry collection, *Lonesome Cities*. She suggested he tone down the eroticism of poems like "Morning, Three" ("There are some parts of you that have no highways. Hairy forests cover even well-worn paths"). Mindful of his image as well as his writing, she was concerned about including the poem "For Jack Fincher" "because here I think you are singling yourself out as being well-known, and I believe that one of the ways the reader empathizes with you is because you are not a 'celebrity' but have the emotions and understanding of those who buy your poetry." (The poem was deleted from the book).

Talese also dealt with a steady stream of good, clever, and dubious ideas from Rod. He was writing a children's book, working on a novel, turning *Stanyan Street* into a screenplay. (None of these went very far.) He told Random House he was working on an autobiography titled *Uphill All the Way*, then said he was turning the project over to Ed Habib. More substantial were his plans for Christmas-themed books, calendars, and a line of small, inexpensive gift books to be copublished by his own Stanyan company. Rather than heed Nan's warning about being spread too thin, Rod was pouring his creativity over as much of the marketplace as he could, as quickly as possible.

Stanyan Street and *Listen to the Warm* had earned Rod the freedom to attempt just about anything. He was able to blur the distinctions between his roles as singer, songwriter, poet, and businessman in ways that were unique for the era. The fact that Random House and RCA Records shared the same ownership worked to his benefit. Ultimately, he turned down a high-dollar offer to stay with RCA in favor of signing a new recording deal with Warner Bros.-Seven Arts, the label that had done so well with *The Sea*. (He also managed to buy the rights to his RCA albums, allowing him to rerelease them himself.)

Rod joined the Warner Bros. roster just as it was bolstering its counter-culture cachet with rock acts like Jimi Hendrix, Neil Young, Jethro Tull, the Grateful Dead, and the Mothers of Invention. Rod's music wouldn't be confused with the edgier fare released by these artists. Still, national promotion chief (and soon-to-be president) Joe Smith knew there was a market for McKuen's albums: "It was single women, for the most part—guys had no interest in it. Airline stewardesses, they were a big audience for him. When I'd fly somewhere and had a couple of Rod's records with me, I was a hero on the plane."

As with Random House, Rod's dealings with his new record label were complicated. He was making so much money from books and other sources that he chose to acquire the rights to master recordings from the Warner Bros. catalog in lieu of royalties for his own album sales. That way, he could rerelease classic albums by Ethel Merman, Dinah Shore, and other singers he loved on his own Stanyan label while avoiding paying additional taxes on his already enormous earnings. He had learned a thing or two from a decade's worth of disappointing record deals.

"Rod was a scam guy," Smith said. "I mean, if there was a little edge to be gotten by doing something, he would do it. He was an opportunist. He had been a poor kid, and then all of a sudden he made it, and he was going to grab everything he could out there. He was a whirlwind, doing concerts, making records, scamming here and there. You had to watch him all the time." This could lead to some testy moments: "He would make me crazy . . . he called constantly. I had my people say, 'Joe Smith is in a meeting.' And so the next thing I see, there are three people walking with big placards reading 'Joe Smith is in a meeting' outside my office. Rod would hire people to walk with the signs . . ."

Despite such minor irritations, McKuen and Smith got along well for the most part. (In fact, Rod asked Joe—a former disc jockey—to do the narration honors for the San Sebastian Strings LP *For Lovers.*) Warner Bros. enjoyed success with such releases as Rod's 1969 live album *At Carnegie Hall.* Capturing McKuen performing to a sold-out crowd on the night of his thirty-sixth birthday, the album's set list that includes tunes from his folk days ("Ally, Ally Oxen Free"), dips into his Brel collaborations ("If You Go Away," "Amsterdam"), samples his recent soundtrack compositions ("Champion Charlie Brown"), and sprinkles on some favorite poems ("A Cat Named Sloopy," "Stanyan Street"). Overall, Rod lives up to his billing as an American chansonnier as he fronts a full orchestra without letting the spotlight stray from his voice and material. *At Carnegie Hall* became Rod's highest-charting LP (no. 96 in *Billboard*) and remains in print; if there's a definitive McKuen album, this is probably it.

Selling out Carnegie Hall was just one box for Rod to check off on his feverish career agenda. He took on assignments as a film composer, heading to London to score the art-house flick *Joanna* and the box-office smash *The Prime of Miss Jean Brodie.* For the latter he wrote "Jean," earning himself an Oscar nomination and Golden Globe award. A version recorded by pop singer Oliver became a no. 2 hit in the United States. *A Boy Named Charlie Brown* came next, matching Rod's whimsical songs with Lee Mendelson's animated treatment of Charles Schulz's beloved Peanuts gang. (Mendelson also produced *The Loner*, Rod's first network TV special, broadcast in May 1969.)

One project offered an especially sweet kind of validation. In March 1969, Frank Sinatra recorded *A Man Alone*, an LP devoted entirely to McKuen material. It came about through the efforts of mutual friend Bennett Cerf, who invited Frank over for dinner one night and played him the soundtrack to *Joanna*. Sinatra was favorably impressed and, when he met Rod at the aforementioned 21 Club party a few months later, the two started talking about an album. "I had tried for years to reach Frank; wrote songs with him in mind, but could never get to him," Rod said. "When we finally met, instead of just offering to do just one or two [songs], he promised me an entire album, which he'd never done before for any other composer. It was incredible."

The creative team-up of the Loner and the Chairman of the Board seemed a little strange to some. Yet the pairing had a certain logic, given Sinatra's quest to stay musically relevant and commercially viable. "His career was at a crossroads," daughter Tina Sinatra later wrote of this period. "The Beatles were outselling him in the record stores. The nightclub era—*his* era—stood in eclipse, and he'd yet to plot his next move." The man known as "The Voice" had definitively interpreted songs by Rodgers and Hart, Johnny Mercer, and other classic songwriters of an earlier time. The music of the kids, though, was giving him trouble—he'd recorded contemporary fare like "Both Sides, Now," "Yesterday," and "Mrs. Robinson" with mixed results. Maybe McKuen would be a better fit—Rod was older and more steeped in the Great American Songbook school of composition than the likes of Lennon–McCartney or Paul Simon. True, he was on the sentimental side—but wasn't Frank an incurable romantic underneath his tough-guy veneer?

Rod took the prospect of working with Frank very seriously. He recorded a demo of the entire Sinatra album—a blend of previously recorded tunes, new songs, and spoken-word interludes—with a forty-piece orchestra. "My vocals weren't as good as they could have been because of the time restraint," McKuen said. "FS had called me on a Tuesday and said, 'Be here Friday to play the demo and a couple of friends. I'm making a spaghetti dinner, and you and our album are invited.' 'Here' was his apartment in New York City, and I was in London. Of course, I hadn't completed the album the way I wanted it to be . . . (But) when I caught the TWA red-eye on Thursday I had a finished acetate and a cassette of the demo in my carry-on bag. I had really put my heart and soul into every line that I wrote for this great man, and listening to the cassette with headphones on a 747 while sailing through the night sky was thrilling. There was nothing humble in my attitude, and it never crossed my mind that The Man wouldn't like it."

According to Rod, the album brought tears to Sinatra's eyes when he heard it—"You really nailed me," Frank said. Whatever the Chairman's emotional state might have been, he recorded McKuen's material with his usual brisk efficiency, completing work in three sessions. Engineer Lee Herschberg remembers Rod present for at least some of the recording: "He would be out there in the studio, occasionally, discussing the lyrics with Frank, maybe how to interpret or accentuate them in certain ways. In the end, that was always up to Sinatra."

A Man Alone was released to moderate sales and mixed reviews. "A chief complaint was 'the Sinatra in conversation tracks,'" Rod recalled. "He hadn't attempted anything like this before, and some critics were taken aback. My reason for writing them was simple. FS was an Oscar-winning actor and he had the chops to pull it off, and I was giving him the chance to show that side of his talent on record . . . I consider none of the spoken tracks to be poetry, and they were not meant to be. They are mind-thoughts that link the songs. In hindsight perhaps four spoken-word tracks were two too many, and I probably should have included a couple of songs in their stead."

In some respects, *A Man Alone* is a follow-up to the brooding, regret-drenched Sinatra albums of a decade earlier, recasting the midnight angst of *In the Wee Small Hours* and *Only the Lonely* for a late-'60s audience. Rod assembled a loosely strung narrative of loss, nostalgia, and acceptance that jibed with the moodier aspects of Frank's persona. Still, for all of the singer's masterful timing and phrasing, he couldn't quite put his own stamp on the songwriter's words. When Sinatra complains about petty lies told by newspaper boys and laundrymen ("From Promise to Promise"), he seems to be reflecting McKuen's view of the world rather than his own. Rod casts Frank as a loner straight out of *Stanyan Street*, and Frank manages to pull off the role for the most part. But often there's a sense of interpreting rather than embodying the material.

If there's an unqualified success here, it's Sinatra's rendition of "Love's Been

Good to Me." Glenn Yarbrough and the Kingston Trio had each previously interpreted this song as a wistful folk ballad. Frank drew a poignant dignity from its lyrics that earlier versions had only hinted at, enhanced by the strings and harpsichord of Don Costa's elegant arrangement. He delivers slightly Victorian lines like "We used to go a-courtin' along October Hill" with a saloon singer's easy panache. Conveying tenderness as well as inner strength, "Love's Been Good to Me" was the best track on *A Man Alone*; arguably, it is the best song McKuen ever wrote. Released as a single, it reached no. 8 on both the U. S. adult contemporary and British pop charts (though it sputtered out at no. 75 on the pop charts in the States).

A Man Alone proved to be a commercial disappointment; Sinatra discussed doing another album's worth of McKuen tunes, but nothing came of it. No matter—there were other icons of his youth that Rod wanted to work with. At the top of the list was his old friend Rock Hudson.

The two had first met when they were both under contract to Universal Pictures. At the time, Rod was a fledgling contract player making teenage exploitation movies; Rock was the no. 1 box-office star in the world. Hudson was shooting the action film *Twilight for the Gods* on the studio lot when McKuen met him in 1958. As Rod recalled, Rock was grappling with various personal issues (among them his divorce from Phyllis Gates) and needed some distraction: "I acted as a calming influence . . . Rock was a smart cookie and hated the fact that Universal took advantage of his popularity by rushing him from one film to another . . . We spent a lot of nights knocking a few back and, with or without friends, the nights usually ended up around the piano . . . "

The two became close enough pals that Rock paid the recording costs for Rod's second Liberty album, *Kiss Me Again Stranger*. Oddly, the LP was going to be credited to Roy Fitzgerald (Rock's legal name). This may have been a way for Rod to put out another LP on Liberty under a pseudonym, after he'd signed a deal with HiFi or Decca (his recording contract situation was rather tangled at this point). It may also have also signaled Rock's desire to be recognized as a singer (or at least associated with one). In any case, the Roy Fitzgerald album remained in the can.

It seems clear that Rod was smitten with Rock—but then, so was much of Hollywood and the world at large. As the greatest closeted gay star of his era, Hudson breezed through affairs with countless eager partners under a cloak of protection provided by the movie industry press. He was drawn to the rugged outdoors type, the sort of image Rod cultivated. If Rock had looked deeper, he would have noticed how much he had in common with the younger actor— both men had been abandoned by their biological fathers, suffered abuse from their stepdads, left home early, and served in the military. There was a real connection between them, one that outlasted their initial good times together. By most accounts, though, Rod was the one who carried the torch.

Hudson and McKuen kept in touch and occasionally saw each other after the latter had moved to New York City. By the late sixties, Rod's career was ascending while Rock's beefcake mystique was beginning to fade. Younger, less hunky actors like Dustin Hoffman made Hudson seem like a relic of an earlier era. No longer ranked among the top ten box-office draws, he needed fresh outlets for his talents. That's when Rod stepped up with an appealing offer.

Sometime in early 1969, Rod convinced Rock to make an album with him. According to Hudson biographer Mark Griffin, it wasn't meant to be a vanity project: "Rock was very serious about it. He had always wanted to be Gene Kelly, a song and dance man." Hudson had dabbled in singing before— in 1959, he had warbled a few casual numbers in his film *Pillow Talk*. With his career entering a transitional phase, it seemed like a good time to try his luck with a full-fledged LP. McKuen would supply the songs, the arrangers, and the musicians. Rock covered the $80,000 cost of the March 1970 sessions at Chappell and Philips studios in London.

Photographer David Nutter was on hand to document Rock and Rod in the studio. He recalled the sessions running smoothly—except for one volatile incident: "A young man came 'round, obviously a boyfriend or something, and Rock left the studio. Rod was infatuated with Rock—he became distraught and laid down in front of the sixty-piece orchestra. Rod said to me he was going to kill himself—I thought it was so insane, so over the top, and it was in front of people. I thought, 'How embarrassing,' so I took him over to the pub and I tried to make him laugh. I kept saying, 'You mustn't kill yourself—it's not worth it.' I was trying to make light of it, because it was so silly."

After this outburst blew over, the *Rock, Gently* album was wrapped up successfully and slated for release in July. "Rock was thrilled with the experience, and with the result," Hudson's longtime companion Tom Clark recalled in a 1989 memoir. "He brought the tapes home and we played them over and over, and he smiled appreciatively. Actually, the poor guy simply couldn't sing. He did have a nice voice—full, rich, resonant—[but] he had problems with such niceties as pitch and key and things like that." An honest listening to *Rock, Gently* confirms Clark's assessment—Hudson's renditions of McKuen signature tunes like "Love's Been Good to Me" and "Jean" are pleasant but thin, the sort of performances that would please Rock's devoted fans but not translate into hit records.

Launching Rock Hudson as a recording artist was only part of the game plan, however. Rock and Rod announced they had formed an independent film company, R and R Productions. They told the press that Rod was set to write a screenplay and make his debut as a director on their first movie, with Rock as the star. An adaptation of McKuen's poetry collection *In Someone's Shadow* was mentioned as a possible project. First, though, R and R was set to do a film version of a mostly autobiographical novel called *Chuck: An Experience*.

The story of *Chuck* is bizarre—and revealing—enough to explore in detail, even though it never got very far as a film project. The reasons Rod was drawn to this book and considered it movie material say a good deal about where he was at personally and professionally in 1970. *Chuck* dealt with issues unresolved in Rod's life—and played with fantasies he was only beginning to acknowledge to his vast public.

Published by Doubleday in May 1969, the book tells the tale of Carl, a successful Cleveland writer who discovers he has a twenty-one-year-old illegitimate son named Chuck living in Los Angeles. Carl seeks him out, and together they embark on a series of adventures that include pot smoking, visits to Tijuana brothels, dalliances with Hollywood starlets, and near-busts by the cops. The father feels alienated from his wife and three children back home, and starts spending more and more time with his son, toward whom he feels a curious erotic attraction. Adding a darker element is Chuck's unhealthy attachment to an older woman known as "the Bitch," who is addicted to heroin and wears dentures. In a moment of high drama, Carl grapples with her, steps on her upper plate, and liberates his son from her clutches. Father and son go on to share a house in North Hollywood, where a towel-clad Chuck entertains his dad with private accordion concerts around the swimming pool.

Chuck: An Experience was written under the pseudonym Carl Sterland by Roy Newquist, a veteran Chicago journalist and broadcaster known for his in-depth interviews with Joan Crawford, Elizabeth Taylor, Richard Burton, and other film legends. "Ninety-nine percent of this is truth, in all its awkwardness and pain and discomfort and complication and beauty," the author states at the start of the book. Sterland/Newquist presents his story as both personal confession and sociological reportage—but actually, it comes across as soft-core sexploitation akin to the works of Jacqueline Susann, Harold Robbins, and Penelope Ashe ("author" of the 1969 bestseller *Naked Came the Stranger*). Whatever its literary merits, *Chuck* does reflect the shifting morals and sexual confusion of its era, albeit in lurid, prurient fashion. (And, according to Newquist's son and daughter, it *is* mostly true.)

The 1970 Bantam paperback edition of *Chuck* announced on its cover that the book was "to be made into a major motion picture starring Rock Hudson and directed by Rod McKuen." Why would Rod select this semi-obscure and undeniably tawdry novel for his directorial debut? It seems unlikely he would have missed the undercurrents of incest and misogyny running through its pages. Even if he didn't have any artistic qualms, his keen business sense would have told him that a good chunk of his audience would be offended by its casual drug use, titillating sex scenes, and uncomfortable depictions of father-son relations. Why would he risk his career—as well as Rock's—to bring this story to the screen?

It's possible Rod saw this tale of a middle-aged man's sexual awakening as having potential to be a box-office hit à la *Midnight Cowboy*. What seems even more likely is that he found elements in *Chuck* so meaningful and relevant to his own life that he was willing to gamble on its acceptance by his fans and the public at large. True, he had to confront the sleazy depictions of whorehouse romps and drug debauchery (not to mention the novel's stilted, turgid prose) if he wanted to make something positive out of the book. What he would have responded to was Newquist's desire for an intimate connection with another man, be it as a friend, son, or lover. "What Chuck and I have brought to each other, I refuse to analyze," Newquist wrote, adding later that "love is hell when you can't screw the object of your affections." This sort of tormenting ambiguity runs through much of McKuen's work as well. Beyond its ugly scenes and bad writing, *Chuck* is a book about abandoning fixed roles, crossing boundaries, and surrendering to love—all themes Rod felt were part of his message to the world.

McKuen and Newquist were at least casual friends at the time Chuck was optioned by R and R Productions. Moreover, Rod and Rock screen-tested the real-life Chuck (an aspiring actor) to play himself in the film. Hudson was said to have reservations about this because his proposed costar was taller than he was. Or maybe the whole project had simply grown too weird for Rock's tastes. In any case, the announced June '70 starting date for filming came and went. The *Chuck* movie may have been a fantasy all along—there's no evidence a screenplay was ever written.

The movie's demise was probably connected to the souring of Rod and Rock's partnership overall. Hudson was angry that *Rock, Gently* was to be sold as a mail-order item by Stanyan Records rather than receive major-label marketing via Warner Bros. "If [Rod] had told me from the beginning that that was how he was going to distribute the album, I wouldn't have minded," he told Tom Clark at the time. "But the fact that he was so devious about it is what really ticks me off. I'm just not about to forgive him." As it turned out, *Rock, Gently* sold in small numbers; Rod still had copies on hand to sell by mail in 2005.

R and R Productions fizzled out amidst these hurt feelings. Hudson was still angry when McKuen came knocking at his back door on Christmas Day 1970, interrupting a holiday party in progress. Clark recalls Rod standing in Rock's kitchen, bedraggled and rain-soaked, as he wished his old friend a merry Christmas. Though they would see each other at Hollywood social events after that, the old intimacy between the two had ended. Rod never acknowledged the breakup and spoke warmly of Hudson years after his death: "Rock was a misunderstood, complicated man, but one of the good guys . . . "

Rod was often accused of scheming and scamming his way to the heights of pop cultural fame. Tastemakers in the music and book publishing worlds recognized his rare gift for image-building and intuitive marketing sense. Judging by how he used his fame, though, it's clear Rod was motivated by more than a desire to maintain a predictable revenue stream. Having Frank Sinatra record his songs was a rare honor that exceeded any dollar value. If more questionable ventures like working with Rock Hudson didn't work out so well, they were still risks worth taking for the fun of it. It was all for the best that some of Rod's projects didn't pan out—*Chuck* probably fell into this category.

Anyone who worked with Rod McKuen knew he was both practical and capricious, careful with his plans and prone to chase ideas down rabbit holes. Editors and record execs who worried about his talents being exhausted were selling him short. More likely, Rod would exhaust *them* with his never-ending efforts to take on more projects, win more fans, and legitimize his stature as an artist in any medium he chose. As he approached the peak of his career, there seemed to be no one who could hold him back.

Eight

~

Mush, Money, and Fun with Fondue

WHEN IT CAME to Rod McKuen, critics could debate the quality of his work—but they couldn't argue with his numbers. Sales of his work in print and on record set new standards for what a creative artist could achieve in the era of mass communication. Decades before Howard Stern claimed the title, Rod was on his way to becoming a true King of All Media, reaching millions through radio airplay, movie soundtracks, TV appearances, newspaper interviews, and concert tours. His songs and poems could be praised, ridiculed, embraced, or discarded—but they couldn't be ignored.

Rod's accomplishments as a Random House author were particularly staggering. As of January 1971, he had sold over three million volumes of poetry. As copublisher of various Stanyan Book titles, he racked up an additional 1.25 million in sales. All told, his books accounted for 4 percent of the company's total sales volume for 1970. Judging from letters and memos from this time, Random House was filled with elation bordering on dizziness over the wild ride Rod had taken them on. Within a year or so, he was leading Random House into new publishing ventures that went far beyond his role as the best-selling poet of his—and possibly of all—time.

In late 1969, Rod and his copublisher finalized plans to "carve out a big chunk of the exploding gift book market" with a new line of slender, attractively jacketed volumes. The first dozen Stanyan books in this series included everything from collections of quotes from Henry David Thoreau and W. C. Fields to bite-size sentimental offerings like *I'm Your Friend So I Bought You This Book* and *Be Gentle with Me for I Have Never Loved Anyone As Much As I Love You*. Initial sales were encouraging enough to justify publishing *The Stanyan Book of Cats, God's Greatest Hits, Stop the War*, and *Fun with Fondue*, among other titles. Special racks were created to display the gift books in stores; retailers were required to order at least a few of them if they wanted to stock McKuen's best sellers.

Once Rod brainstormed an idea (or at least a snappy title), his small but hardworking staff would be tasked with coming up with the copy and designing the book. Heading the editorial team was Jane Wilkie, an experienced magazine feature writer capable of cranking out reams of copy under tight deadlines. She worked closely with Random House editorial assistant Susan Schwartz, who recalls Wilkie as "a typical Southern California girl—petite, blonde, well-tanned, very smart and funny." The two of them completed at least two dozen Stanyan gift books together, sometimes under trying circumstances.

Take *Hundreds of Things to Do on a Rainy Day*, for instance. "I'm concerned about this one," Wilkie wrote Talese. "Enclosed are 3 pages of new stuff I'd written. When I showed them to Rod, he said everything must be a one-liner . . . If carried though in this manner the whole book will, in my estimation, become inane and worthless. Not only is something like this difficult to sustain for the reader, but he is suggesting 'things' that are not things to do." She managed to complete the sixty-one-page volume, which offered such time-filling tips as "Learn to whistle through your teeth," "Caulk anything that is leaking" and "List the wives of Henry VIII and the husbands of Elizabeth Taylor." The book went into at least three printings.

If Random House thought projects like this would cheapen Rod's stature as a poet or its standing as a publisher of quality books, there's no evidence of it from surviving letters or memos. The company trusted—or at least went along with—his inspired abilities at brand building. And really, there was no conceptual conflict between the small shared intimacies in his poems and the potpourri of wisdom and trivia that filled his gift books. As both a writer and marketer, Rod had perfected the ability to evoke immediate emotional responses with a minimum of embellishment. The Stanyan books acted like aspirin tablets on bored brains and jangled nerves, relieving stress and perking up the reader's spirits in short, quick bursts. They were slight, but they made you feel better.

More Stanyan merchandise was on its way. The first annual Rod McKuen Calendar & Datebook appeared in 1969, stuffed with obscure holidays, poetic nuggets, Pop Art graphics, and aphorisms on how to live a better life. Rod was ahead of his time in offering merchandise like this. His friend Morgan Ames recalls him showing her an early version of his calendar: "He said, 'You know, I'm going to publish this.' I had never heard of anything like that. I said, 'Oh, Rod, if you could package your fingernail clippings, you'd sell those too!' I laughed at him and he laughed, too. He didn't get offended. His attitude was like: 'Isn't this fun?' I think in many ways he was stunned by his own success and he wanted to ride it for all it was worth."

Projects like this further monetized Rod's popularity—but they were also welcomed by his fans as ways to bond ever more closely with him. Together, artist and audience created a community of surprising loyalty and longevity. Over the years, Rod had built a cult following into a mass phenomenon by fostering a personal relationship with those who listened to him or came to see him perform. "When I did my radio show, I was speaking to one person," he recalled in 2011. "I've done that my whole career. When I'm onstage, whether it's for three thousand or thirty-five thousand people, I always try to relate one to one. I think that's the secret of any success I've had."

The affection and reverence of Rod's faithful only deepened in the early seventies. He reportedly received a thousand love letters a week, along with assorted gifts and marriage proposals. Though his work was snapped up by a surprisingly broad range of consumers, a core demographic could be identified. Writer Marcia Seligson sketched this group portrait of a McKuen concert audience in a 1972 *McCall's* article: "The average age, I would guess, is eighteen; mostly female, entirely white . . . Utterly respectable, clean-shaven, and straight. The head drum majorette at Grand Rapids High, the TWA reservations clerk, the home ec major at North Dakota U. (with her date, the physical education major) . . . normal, nice, naïve, still capable of intense hero worship—and the hero they have chosen to worship boundlessly is Rod McKuen."

Similar descriptions of McKuen fans turn up in numerous articles from this period. When interviewed, his concertgoers tended to give the same reasons for their devotion to Rod. "He knows about love, he makes you feel for love, believe in love," one young man told Seligson. Added a teenage girl: "You *know* he's talking about himself and his own life, and that's why it seems so important, why he's such a real person." For those who embraced his work, Rod had the ability—and the courage—to put shameful or difficult emotions into words. As one of them put it: "He speaks for me, says exactly what I feel most deeply and can't say myself. Nobody else can express my feelings like Rod." More than crafting appealing songs and poems, McKuen served as a voice for the shy, the inhibited, the inarticulate.

McKuen's goal of connecting with people one to one was more than just a slogan. It would be unthinkable for, say, Frank Sinatra or Bob Dylan to field questions and shake hands with admirers after performing. Yet even at the height of his fame, Rod would spend hours talking with fans in post-concert rap sessions that covered everything from his artistic philosophy and moral beliefs to his stands on political issues of the day. Though he continued to resist the "guru" label, he resembled a lay pastor or human-potential teacher at such gatherings. "I don't want anybody to follow me," he told *The New York*

Times Magazine in 1971. "But if I can be of service by what I've learned, I owe people at least an honest answer."

Early in his career, Rod recognized the benefits of building a loyal audience through personal contact. He would send out hundreds (later thousands) of signed postcards to fan-club members while on vacation in Europe. Lasting friendships could grow out of a casual inquiry about his work. This happened with Allen Weitzel, a student at San Jose State University who had been taking English classes with Beat poet Michael McClure in the late 1960s. Weitzel started his decades-long correspondence with Rod with an exchange of notes about a *Stanyan Street* poem; within a year or so, McKuen was phoning him after midnight to talk over his writing and career decisions. "He loved to talk, and I was a good audience for him," Weitzel said. "When we'd be on the phone for two hours, I'd probably command ten minutes of that time . . . I was very pleased about anything he'd say about the poems I sent him. In later years, he'd write and ask about my family. My attitude towards him never changed. I always thought it was nice of him to take the time to contact me."

This kind of story is not uncommon of Rod's career. Until the end of his days, he remained an unusually accessible celebrity who maintained long-distance connections with "ordinary" folks as well as the posh and privileged. Beyond his undeniable need for more attention and revenue, McKuen genuinely seemed to care about his fans, both individually and collectively. In public events and private acts of kindness, he lived up to the compassionate ideals he expressed as an artist. There is ample evidence to refute the frequently raised charge that McKuen was in it only for the money.

Rod earned the love and trust of millions by speaking *to* them and *for* them. By 1971, his status as the most popular poet in the world—in *history,* by some measures—was secure. Not everyone was happy about this, however. McKuen's work became a flash point in a bitter culture war over artistic standards in a consumer-driven society. When Poetry Society of America president Charles Angoff called Rod's poetry "a social plague," he was echoing the judgment of America's literary elite. The Lonesome Boy had become either a healer of souls or a threat to civilization. As Seligson put it in *McCall's*, "There is no other figure on the cultural scene in this country who is so utterly revered by his fans and held in such mocking contempt by his nonfans."

The debate over Rod McKuen and what he stood for kicked off in November 1967, when *Time* dismissed his poetry as little more than "sweet love, lonely rooms, silent rain, quiet snow, and lost cats." Prior to this, he had received mostly positive reviews for his albums and live shows, with an occasional mention of his verse. It was only after Random House published *Listen to the Warm* that his work was received with intense hostility by academics and leading media outlets. Critics were first amused, and then horrified that Rod's verse was making the best-seller lists. The attacks on him (and his readers) grew nasty and often apocalyptic in tone, as if his popularity was a harbinger of imminent cultural collapse.

Professor Karl Shapiro's scathing assessment of McKuen in the November 24, 1968 issue of *Book World* was particularly influential. A former U. S. poet laureate and editor of *Poetry* magazine, Shapiro was known as an erudite, unpredictable critic who upheld traditional literary values while championing such modernists as Henry Miller. To him, Rod's work was the latest example of a disturbing trend that began with the "bored, hysterical and narcissistic drivel" served up by Allen Ginsberg and the Beats. "It is irrelevant to speak of McKuen as a poet," Shapiro wrote. "His poetry is not even trash." Lowbrow entertainment by "crooners" like Rod was acceptable in its place, "but the deliberate obtrusion of the howler or the crooner upon the literary minority can serve no other purpose than to destroy the sensibilities of everyone concerned."

According to Shapiro, McKuen's fans pressured *Book World* to drop the professor as a reviewer after these comments were published. This prompted further rants against a composite cultural corrupter Shapiro dubbed "Dylan McGoon" (an amalgam of Bob Dylan and Rod McKuen). The pervasive influence of McGoonesque writing was part of an erosion of standards that led to student violence on college campuses, he believed. He singled out the book trade for particular scorn: "The greed and cynicism of even the best publishers appalls me; the wild exploitation of primitivism by the Media has rendered us insensible and made us a prey to every disease of esthetic decadence which the lower reaches of the imagination can concoct." (Were you listening, Bennett Cerf?)

Shapiro's argument that McKuen was bringing lower class standards to the elite world of poetry was stated even more bluntly by fellow poet and academic Louis Coxe in a January 1970 *New Republic* review. What began as a critique of Rod's latest poetry volumes veered into an attack on the slack minds and stunted tastes of McKuen's readership. "People who ordinarily read scarcely at all can fall in and out of this poetry with no damage done and nothing taken away," Coxe wrote. "What McKuen guarantees is that a certain California sexual daydreaming can be yours for the asking, even if you do move your lips rapidly as you read." Of course, the writer of such vapid verse was spewing it out cynically: "McKuen is no dope and knows what he is doing, i.e., weeping nostalgically all the way to the bank or the broker's."

Perhaps the most famous takedown of McKuen was Nora Ephron's article "Mush," appearing in *Esquire*'s June 1971 issue (and included in her book *Wallflower at the Orgy*). She linked him with *Love Story* novelist Erich Segal as a peddler of sentimental pabulum, describing their work collectively as "pure treacle, with a message that is perfect escapism in the throes of future shock; the world has not changed, the old values prevail . . . The optimism comes in nice small packages that allow for the slowest reader with the shortest concentration span and smallest vocabulary."

Like Shapiro (whom she quotes in her article), Ephron couldn't hide her disdain for the lowbrows who were drawn to such dross. What's most interesting is her view that McKuen's work expresses an urge to escape into a Pollyanna world of old-fashioned values. (Shapiro thought it represented an attack on tradition and would lead to insurrection, even violence.) Actually, the anonymous sexual encounters and general sense of alienation found in *Stanyan Street* and subsequent books reflect a moral code that was quite different from proprieties of the Good Old Days. Like many critics, Ephron couldn't see the subversive undercurrents amidst the nostalgic treacle.

Most of all, "Mush" found vacuity at the center of Rod's poetic vision. "What is McKuen trying to say?" Ephron asked at the end of the article. Quoting one of his poems, she concludes: "Nothing."

Obviously, innumerable McKuen fans disagreed with this opinion. Some wrote in to their local newspapers to push back against negative articles. In response to an attack on Rod as a "marshmallow poet," Jacksonville, Florida high school student Ann Marie Myers asked "how it can be so wrong to indulge in sentimentality now and then . . . (McKuen) gives us a portion of his mind and invites us to understand and feel it. And he succeeds magnificently." William Anderson of Norfolk, Virginia, pointed out that "in this violent, confusing society, there are surprisingly still a lot of sensitive, simple human beings. Rod McKuen is writing for these people who still seek beauty and understand it and who crave this beauty to overcome the all-too-obvious decay of it." Rather than a sign of cultural decadence, Rod's devotees saw his work as offering relief from the breakdown of modern society.

There were those in the literary world who defended Rod. "McKuen's work was plainspoken, romantic, and of course completely out of the academic loop," recalled award-winning poet/novelist Aram Saroyan. "He wrote sincerely out of his own need, which wasn't the worst reason to pick up a pen . . . I think he drew from a broader pool of resources than more academic poets who had nothing approaching his popular success. He was honest about his emotional limits—he was a poet of the morning after, when the romance is still fresh but not likely to endure. And millions of readers identified with that."

Poet/critic Robert Peters likewise felt that Rod was treated unfairly: "The hypocrisy of poets and critics who praise poets writing worse than McKuen irritates me . . . He has to be the only poet in America who is dismissed out of hand by peers who won't read him. The assumptions (and I confess to having shared it) is that someone so popular must be bad!" To prove his point, Peters put together a quiz to see if readers could pick out lines by McKuen from those written by academy-approved poets like Robert Creeley, W. S. Merwin, Derek Walcott, and Robert Lowell. He found that few who took the test could distinguish Rod's work from that of the others.

The accumulating critical jeers forced Rod to respond. Karl Shapiro particularly got under his skin. At first, Rod shrugged him off with a flippant "Who cares what he thinks?" Then he decided to address his foe directly in his poem "Driving Through Davis," calling Shapiro "a white-haired loser" who was "a sort of poet once until his talent dried and dried for lack of any nourishment." Rod again struck back at Shapiro as a failed poet in a 1972 *Saturday Review* interview: "He accused me of fostering unrest in the country and inducing kids to burn down buildings . . . I suspect a certain amount of sour grapes there. I also suspect that, if students were burning down buildings on Mr. Shapiro's campus, he was among those responsible for it." Such personal attacks were unusual for McKuen—clearly, the White-Haired Loser's words hit a nerve.

At first, Rod was reluctant to make great literary claims for his work. "I never really call it poetry, myself," he told NBC News' Edwin Newman in 1968. "I was always afraid of the word *poetry* because when I was a kid I never liked poetry very much." In the same interview, he edged toward claiming the "poet" label by broadening the definition of the craft: "I speak in simple terms and simple language. To me the definition of poetry is anything that for a minute or whatever little time is necessary transmits some kind of warmth or feeling toward one other human being. And that can be a sentence or a poem or a piece of music or the way somebody looks when they turn a corner, or the way somebody smiles at you that you might never, ever see again." This response was typical of how Rod resisted narrow categories—it reads like one of his poems. And, of course, it was just the sort of amorphous, nontraditional reframing of what poetry was that infuriated the likes of Karl Shapiro and Louis Coxe.

Four years later, Rod dropped his shyness about using the P-word: "I do consider myself a serious poet . . . I take pride in my work, and I think I'm a good poet. And I know I'll be a better one if I have the time. I consider myself honest, and I do believe that honesty helps an artist do his best." He was not ashamed about what he had achieved: "How dare I make a living writing poetry? They want you to be a pale kid who comes out from under a rock every few years and who delivers a sheaf of paper full of maxims . . . It's not a modest thing to say, but what the hell—I like my poetry. I feel I work hard at it and I'm speaking the language, and it's very, very pleasing to me that I'm getting through to people, millions of people."

Rod claimed that he exposed critical bias against him through a devious strategy: "When I started getting bad reviews for my poetry, I decided I'd give the critics what they wanted. I did a book of sonnets with another publisher under a pseudonym. It got great reviews but had lousy sales. So I did another. It got literally rave reviews. Then I did a third. This one really hits the top. 'After the pap of Rod McKuen,' one guy said, "it is refreshing to come across the brilliant poetry of . . . '" (There is no hard information to verify that these books were published or reviewed.)

There's no indication that Rod's bad press had any effect on his sales. The main things critics condemned his writing for—sentimentality, simplicity of expression, a fondness for the ordinary in themes and images—were not issues for his readers. What fans liked about his work—its compassion for the lonely and vulnerable, its celebrations of life's small, tender moments, and all-inclusive sense of the spiritual—were either overlooked by the critics or rejected by them. The great Rod McKuen debate was one more manifestation of the culture wars beginning to divide America in the late 1960s. As with so many battles great and small, the argument over the value of his work pitted populists against elitists. And as with so many other conflicts in a capitalist society, it was settled by the marketplace—at least temporarily. Rod was justified in thinking he'd won the argument.

Rod McKuen had been writing poetry for nearly twenty years before he made significant money from it. He practiced the craft as a sincere amateur without the blessing of the literary in-crowd. Being a poet was one more way to break through the barrier of loneliness between himself and the world, one more aspect of his composite identity as an artist. The output of words and music, poems and advertising slogans, inspirational thought and marketing hustle—they were all part of the same desire to touch, reach, and hold people. Rod didn't conceal his fusion of art, inspiration, and commerce from his followers—they felt a part of it all. Really, building a brand was another name for bringing people together. Each new product was an entry point into the World of Rod.

If the love of his fans sustained him, Rod was still hungry for more. Classical music offered him yet another creative field to invade and conquer. Rod had been releasing instrumental pop albums as far back as 1960 and may have discussed putting out his classically influenced material on RCA's Red Seal label some years later. By the early seventies, he was ready to fully emerge as a composer of symphonies and chamber music. Through Stanyan, he released a series of albums with dignified titles like *Concerto No. 1 for Four Harpsichords and Orchestra* and *Symphony No. 1: "All Men Love Something."* (More whimsically, he also released *Concerto for Balloon & Orchestra and Three Overtures.*) He gained enough credibility with such works to receive commissions to write music for the Edmonton and Louisville symphony orchestras.

Overall, these compositions sound like an amalgam of Aaron Copland–like Western elements, stage musical melodies, and film soundtrack excerpts. "Rod's classical pieces never really made a significant mark, because they were essentially lyric themes fleshed out in something akin to symphonic form," said *New York Times* classical music critic Robert Sherman about his friend's work. "I felt that his concertos and other pieces were basically song melodies stretched out and expanded. They were pleasantly attractive, but I don't remember any being original or otherwise significant."

According to singer and music scholar Michael Feinstein, McKuen commissioned others to turn his musical ideas into fully formed classical pieces: "Stan Freeman—who was a remarkable composer and a fine musician—was hired to ghostwrite for Rod. He told me that Rod said, 'I want to write a concerto for oboe and this and that instrument,' and then he hummed a couple of melodies. Stan extrapolated and created something. Stan was laughing about it, because it was so silly. But it was a job and he did his job."

Whatever his reasons, Rod took pride in being recognized as a classical composer. He insisted he had taught himself the rules of composition and sought musical advice on two occasions from no less than Igor Stravinsky (who cautioned him not to "overlearn"). Rod's classical albums were not an obvious marketing venture on his part—they weren't something his fans were demanding. They reflected his desire for respect and validation outside of the pop culture world, as well as a need to expand his brand.

In a Stanyan press bio, Rod acknowledged that "contemporaries and associates humored him or ignored his classical compositions as peripheral areas of his career." Reactions like that made him more determined than ever to succeed—all his life, he hated to be told he couldn't do something. This seemed as much a motivating principle as the drive to bring in more revenue. Rod was often unusually hardheaded in his business dealings, but he was equally prone to blur the line between serious plans and sheer fantasy. This may account for his habit of announcing half-completed or totally imaginary projects as done deals—the *Chuck* syndrome, you might say. Anyone who partnered with him had to give him room to operate this way.

Random House had given Rod considerable latitude when it agreed to copublish his Stanyan gift books line. Combined with the cross-collateralized deal involving his RCA catalog, it made for a complex and potentially trouble-some relationship between publisher and author. Internal memos in Random House's files reveal tensions over Rod's need to gain financial advantage over deals big and small. Though his relations with Nan Talese remained warm, other editors and executives within the company began to tire of him as a business partner. Rod felt a faltering commitment to his Stanyan projects and began to squabble over money matters. Despite all of this, Random House wanted to keep McKuen on its roster and offered him a $500,000 advance to re-sign in mid-1971. Six months later, he turned it down in favor of an even bigger offer from Simon & Schuster.

The divorce between author and publisher was messy and drawn out. Random House was still contracted with Rod to publish more Stanyan gift book titles, even though its sales force had lost faith in the value of the line. Rod in turn was angry about lowball offers for paperback reprint rights and royalties he felt were wrongly withheld. In February 1973, Rod ended the painful relationship by refusing to turn in further books. "He has won, and in winning, he can have his goddam line," Random House marketing executive Dick Krinsley told Talese. "That's his battle. My winning the war is getting rid of him."

Rod walked away from Random House at the peak of his fame and commercial viability. He was recognized as the best-selling poet in history as well as a platinum-earning songwriter and international concert star. His Stanyan Records label had become the second-largest mail-order record company in the world (right behind the Columbia Record Club). His line of Stanyan gift books had sold over four million copies. He had starred in his own American TV special, hosted a miniseries in Britain, composed hit film soundtracks, and dared to invade the world of classical music. According to his own projections for 1973, he expected to gross $30 million via his various corporations and deals with book publishers and record companies.

It wasn't enough, of course. A week after celebrating his fortieth birthday at a Carnegie Hall concert, Rod paid for a thirty-two-page supplement in *Billboard* to announce a host of new projects for the coming year. Equal parts résumé, business prospectus, and personal manifesto, this document aggressively presents Rod as a "modern Horatio Alger" with a "determination to succeed." In an introductory essay, Stanyan staff writer Jane Wilkie tries to temper her portrait of McKuen the media mogul with softening colors: "No man creates an empire without a streak of steel in his psyche. Yet those who know him say that McKuen's stunning success stemmed not from the tycoon/tyrant syndrome, but rather an effort to erase the self doubts incurred from childhood . . . His day covers myriad projects that are shelved only when he finally goes to sleep. None of this frenetic activity is to make money per se; there still lingers the compulsion to prove himself to himself."

What is described above is not the usual way a company CEO celebrates sales and drums up excitement for new ventures. But then, Rod was something exceedingly rare in the American business world: an artist who was transforming his personality, taste, and life experiences into a seemingly unlimited range of products and services. According to his *Billboard* supplement, the diversification of the McKuen brand would continue with the launching of a nationwide Stanyan record-store chain, as well as a greeting card line. And then there was Rod McKuen Casuals . . .

The ad copy for this new product line was enticing: "Millions are into his books and records and songs and in the coming year, many millions more will be in his pants . . . and jackets, and sweaters and sneakers." McKuen Casuals was intended to be "a full clothing line . . . patterned after the star's distinctive wardrobe style." Rod had hired "his own wholesale clothing personnel to merchandise the entire line as a display special in department stores and clothing chains." Profits from sales of the clothing line were to benefit Animal Concern, a nonprofit Rod established to fund wildlife preservation efforts and scholarships for students of veterinary medicine. (It is unclear if any items beyond a unisex "Muk-About" jacket were manufactured and sold.

"Fly-About" nylon travel bags were also offered through Stanyan's mail-order catalog.)

Most of the plans Rod unveiled in *Billboard* never came to pass. Still, that he'd chosen such a high-profile forum to assert his accomplishments and dreams was significant in and of itself. As he took a victory lap and made a pitch for investors, he felt obliged to say he wasn't interested in "money per se"—a remarkable admission for someone forging a business empire. As he moved forward into the mid-seventies, Rod relied upon the continuing loyalty of his community of fans to follow him through whatever changes he embraced. They would understand what drove him even if the suits and pundits didn't.

Rod himself had undergone a makeover around this time. He grew a beard and let his hair revert to its natural brown, signaling a transition into sagacious middle age. Loose-fitting open-collared shirts began to edge out sweaters in his public wardrobe, though jeans and sneakers remained a constant onstage and off. Freshened up and looking forward, McKuen readied himself for a shifting pop marketplace.

The cultural milieu of the moment offered Rod a range of choices. He could become part of the emerging singer-songwriter boom, continue to cash in on the nostalgia of the older generation, expand his reach as a writer into novels or nonfiction. He might even transition into the role of a human-potential advocate and social-change activist. It all seemed possible.

"The man enjoys creating," Rod's bio in *Billboard* asserted. His greatest creation was still himself—and it was very much a work in progress.

Nine

A Kind of Loving

IN EARLY 1970, Rod McKuen moved into a thirty-room mansion on Angelo Drive in Beverly Hills and promptly filled it with dogs, cats, his treasure trove of collectibles, and a few select people he cared about. Before that, he had been living in a small stucco house on Montcalm Avenue in the Hollywood Hills that provided a spectacular view but didn't allow enough room for the tens of thousands of records, books, and other pieces of personal memorabilia he had accumulated over the years. Rod's new residence was a rambling architectural mishmash that blended Spanish, English Regency, and Italian touches in the mode favored by 1920s-era movie stars. Rod made it his own with personal touches like a state-of-the-art music room, Greco-Roman statuary, and a white-jacketed butler to usher visitors in. "The only reason I have this place is so the animals can have enough space to run around in," he said. The sheer ostentation of the mansion must have appealed to his childhood Hollywood dreams as well.

Except for a brief interlude in New York in the late 1970s, Rod would make the Angelo Drive mansion his primary address for the rest of his life. For much of his forties, he was away on tour, vacationing, or just wandering about the world, both out of professional need and personal desire. Later, as his career wound down, Angelo Drive would become the center of Rod's world, the one place he truly belonged.

"Home" would always be a mythic concept for Rod, an expression of his search for family and his own identity. The death of his mother from lung cancer in April 1971 severed the longest and deepest emotional connection he ever knew. Clarice Hooper's life didn't blossom into happiness after her son became a rich celebrity. Her drinking increased as she grew more isolated and withdrawn; Rod and Ed tried to fix her up with eligible bachelors and find ways to cut down her consumption of wine and vodka. She took an interest in Rod's career and gave him advice on his business dealings. Overall, though, Clarice's world continued to shrink as her son and his partner led their own lives. As Rod recalled in *Finding My Father*, his mother took so little pleasure in life that he and Ed decided to let her drink in peace. She died with many questions about her past still unanswered—as he put it, she always seemed about to say something that she could never quite express.

Rod wrote about his loss in "And to Each Season," a song on his 1972 album *Odyssey*, as well as the title poem of his first book for Simon & Schuster. A work of palpable feeling and graceful nature-based imagery, it placed Clarice's passing within the world's eternal cycles of growth, decay, and renewal. Throughout, there is a mature sense of acceptance tempered with regret. "I've no family now but that of man," he stated plainly as he anticipated joining the march of old men passing from the scene.

"Family" for Rod didn't mean his blood relations. His mother's siblings were vague presences in his life. He was estranged from his half brother Bill, who had grown up to be a troubled soul in and out of scrapes with the law. (Rod had to obtain permission for Bill to be let out of prison and escorted to his mother's funeral by plainclothes guards.) There was no one among the Woolever or Hooper clans that Rod felt close to. For all his success at connecting with a vast and adoring public, he was as rootless as he'd ever been.

Edward Habib was there to help ground him. He filled many roles in

Rod's life, roles that changed and shifted over the years. Edward had been the one who sold his friend's books at his shows and negotiated deals to get them into stores. He was given a salary and credited as road manager, photographer, and liner notes writer on album covers and in concert programs. It's unlikely he did any of these things—still, the part he played was an essential one. "Edward was the fire that motivated Rod," Charlie Hallam recalled. "He was the wind beneath the wings of Rod McKuen."

By the early seventies, the initial passion that had brought Rod and Edward together had cooled into a different sort of bond. "Rod never stopped loving Edward, but it was a platonic relationship for all but the first two years," Hallam said. "Edward was a variety man, and he told Rod he was going to leave, because he didn't want to have that kind of intimate relationship anymore. Rod said, 'No, don't leave, stay. I'll make sure you have work and you get paid.' And he stayed."

Rod chose to speak of Edward as his brother—in fact, he mentions in *Finding My Father* that Clarice almost adopted Habib before her death. (He also recalled that she would scold and even discipline him if he misbehaved.) Rod never acknowledged that his relationship with Edward was or had ever been sexual. "He is my brother, father, best friend and partner in almost every way," he wrote on his website late in life. "He is a cute kid all right, but not my lover or my type. Besides, wouldn't that be incest?"

There were times over the decades when mutual anger and resentment nearly drove them apart. Living in a palatial mansion with a faithful partner was a mixed blessing for a born loner like McKuen. Standing in the shadow of a world-class celebrity, Habib needed to carve out space for himself as well. Eventually, the two of them would settle into different parts of the Angelo Drive house, their private domains. Yet they remained bound together in what was marriage in all but name.

Rod chose his words carefully when discussing his private life. His experiences on the fringes of Henry Willson's Hollywood circle in the late fifties taught him how to evade and deflect the sort of talk that could damage a show-business career. Yet his early involvement with the Mattachine Society and recording projects like *In Search of Eros* showed a willingness to risk or even invite exposure. McKuen's ability to gauge the mood of his times while pushing at the margins of acceptability was one of his great talents. Rod was both personally discreet and strategically provocative. He never came out of the closet in standard fashion—that would only label and limit him. But over time he spoke out for sexual freedom in unequivocal terms.

What remained consistent over the decades was Rod's refusal to be classed as anything but an individual. "I don't consider myself as being of any particular sexual persuasion," Rod told *Saturday Review* in a December 1972 interview. "There are as many sexual attitudes as there are people. I'm turned on by people." He expanded upon this to a writer for *The Advocate* four years later: "I think the straights, gays and bi's all do themselves a tremendous disservice by putting themselves into any kind of category. I don't believe that there are only three kinds of sexuality any more than there are three categories of need of any kind. I think you'll find there are as many different kinds of sexual needs as you will find intellectual needs."

The above comments sound very reminiscent of today's ideas about sexual fluidity and nonbinary gender identity. Rod demanded a freedom for his desires that millions of Americans now claim as their own. In the 1970s, such an assertion challenged sexual orthodoxy and didn't quite jibe with the arguments of the gay liberation movement. It took nerve for McKuen to march in advance of public opinion. For him, sexual fluidity meant love without restrictions and a path to self-discovery, things worth risking fame and wealth for.

It took awhile for Rod to quit going through the same showbiz charades he'd engaged in during his Hollywood days. As his star began to rise, he felt obligated to explain his status as a single man: "It's very difficult for me to get a woman to understand that she has to make second place to my work," he told Edwin Newman in 1968. Three years later, the press reported that he was regularly dating heiress Charlotte Ford. Rumors flew that the couple were about to get hitched. "When I got the Charlotte questions thrown at me, I told the reporters we had never discussed marriage because we were too busy having such a great time together," Rod said after the alleged affair was over. It was good gossip column fodder, at least.

Confirmed bachelor or not, Rod wanted it known he was a father. He spoke often in interviews about his son, Jean-Marc, born on July 14, 1961 from a liaison with a French woman he'd chosen not to marry. "We just couldn't," he told writer Nathaniel Freedland in 1969. "I didn't want my son to wear a burden of guilt because he was illegitimate. Yet to have married and divorced to have given him a surname would have been a dishonest thing to do." Over the years, Rod would elaborate on his relationship with his son, offering that he visited him while on his European tours. By the seventies, Jean-Marc was showing promise as a jazz pianist, attending college, and developing a remarkable resemblance to his dad. Because of kidnapping concerns, Rod said, he never wanted to divulge where his son lived or identify him by his full name.

According to Rod, he became more distant from Jean-Marc and daughter Marie-France (about whom he never spoke in detail) as they grew older. In response to a question about his son posted on his website in 1999, he said, "Since I wasn't there for him when he needed me, I don't even feel right about calling him my son. He has a wonderful mother and (step) father that have raised him to be a young man any parents could be proud of. Though, from afar, I am very proud." In 2005, he added: "My kids have long been out of college and I assume they are making their own way in life & paying their own bills. I'm not completely sure of this since I hear from them only every other millennium. However, with Jean-Marc and Marie-France no news is usually good news."

There is no information that confirms Rod McKuen ever had children. To the author's knowledge, no one else has ever mentioned meeting or communicating with them. At least four of his closest friends either doubt or flat-out deny that Jean-Marc and Marie-France ever existed. After Rod's death, no son or daughter came forward to claim anything from his estate. Yet he spoke about having a child to his attorney on his deathbed. It was vitally important to him that the world thought of him as a parent.

David Nutter recalled an odd incident from 1971: "We were filming outdoors in London and there was this young boy there. Rod told everybody that this was his long-lost son, but it was obviously somebody else's son who happened to be there at the time for the shoot. I thought it was really kind of strange. Rod was a little bit of a fantasizer about stuff like that."

Assuming his children were imaginary, what were Rod's reasons for maintaining this fiction? It may be that he initially wanted to bolster his image as a heterosexual male. Once the story was launched, it was easier to keep talking about his son and daughter over the decades than to stop. But there are probably more deep-seated motivations for Rod developing the tale of his two out-of-wedlock children. His account of Jean-Marc's life mirrors Rod's own experiences; by telling this story, Rod's own father's decision not to marry his mother and help raise his child becomes more explicable. Later in his life, Rod's depiction of his relationship with his children grew more troubled—did this indicate that he was now judging his father's actions more harshly, or was he simply growing tired of the story he'd invented? These questions are among the most difficult ones facing anyone trying to solve the riddle of Rod McKuen.

Ultimately, whether Rod's son and daughter were real or not doesn't matter all that much—at worst, it was a fantasy that harmed no one. What *is* important to recognize is McKuen's need to create a loving family around him while maintaining the distance he needed to function as a creative artist. His ability to build loyal and lasting friendships was a constant for him. All his life, Rod took and gave love wherever he could find it.

Rod had a knack for making friends in the most unlikely places. In July 1972 he headed out to Cheyenne, Wyoming, by himself to catch a big rodeo event. While he was at a bar in town, he met up with a pack of amateur pilots who were flying cross-country in vintage open-cockpit biplanes. "My girl-friend saw him and said, 'I think that's Rod McKuen over there,'" recalled Lee Schaller, a dentist who had flown in from California. "She invited him over and we ended up asking him to come flying with us the next morning. I think he was fascinated with the romance of barnstorming across the country in a biplane." Rod stayed in touch with this group and later joined them (again on his own) at a riverside picnic in St. Louis: "He was just one of the guys that day—everybody got pushed off the dock into the river at some point. He did, too." Rod wasn't so intoxicated by his success that he couldn't enjoy this sort of casual camaraderie.

On the other end of the friendship spectrum, Rod started running with a hip younger crowd in Manhattan. Through his publicist Abby Hirsch, he met Henry Edwards, a novelist and pop culture critic with close ties to New York's underground music and theater scenes. "I thought Rod was engaging and smart and generous, a fabulous guy," the writer recalled. "He and I shared a lot of interests, like theater history and his own history starting in San Fran-cisco. I liked him a lot." Edwards offered McKuen an entryway into some of the city's hippest circles: "I took him out—we would go to rock 'n' roll events at places like Max's Kansas City and people would be astonished to see him there with me. Which I think he got a kick out of."

While the trendy young scenesters who met Rod generally liked him, they turned up their noses at his work and what they thought it stood for. "Every-one I knew had nothing but hilarious contempt for him," Edwards admits. "No one liked his work—he was just a phenomenon for the others, the uncool ones, the Middle Americans." Admitting you saw value in McKuen's senti-mental songs and poems went completely against the irony-drenched spirit of in-crowd New Yorkers circa 1972–73. As Edwards recalled, "Things were going through this transformation from the hippies to artifice and show busi-ness. Overnight, it was this amazing pendulum swing to the theatrical rockers like David Bowie."

Things had changed considerably since Rod made his big breakthrough in 1967. Flower power had wilted and faded; glam rock and "divine decadence" were nearing full bloom. During the Summer of Love, McKuen stood at the shifting nexus point between hip and square, and could appeal to readers of both the *Village Voice* and the *Ladies' Home Journal*—five years later, this was no longer true. The gentle eroticism of *Stanyan Street* and *Listen to the Warm* seemed had become the stuff of ancient history—leather and studs had won out over sweaters and sneakers as the preferred attire on the sexual frontier. If he were as cynical a marketing genius as some made him out to be, Rod might have planted his tongue firmly in cheek and played his lonesome romantic image for camp value. That wasn't his style—he refused to descend into conscious self-parody and betray the earnest devotion of his audience.

The Manhattan bath house and cabaret scenes produced an artist Rod was especially drawn to—Bette Midler. The Divine Miss M was all the rage thanks to her irresistible mix of high-camp kitsch and old-fashioned chutzpah. She was making her L. A. debut at the Troubadour in late December '72, so Rod flew her friend Edwards out for the show in hopes of scoring an introduction. McKuen brought Midler and her band back to his mansion for a post-concert dinner party that he hoped would lead to a professional association. Supplying Bette with songs would have hitched Rod to a rising star who shared his love for nostalgia and emotive balladry. It wasn't to be, said Edwards: "She wouldn't have gone near that. She was extremely success-oriented. What would be the advantage? Rod had played Carnegie Hall when we were around—it was not sold out. The second night there was worse . . . "

Whatever Rod's box-office numbers might have been, he continued to circulate and make connections during his visits to New York. Henry Edwards introduced him to Tom Eyen, a veteran of the city's Off-Off-Broadway scene with such notorious stage hits as *The Dirtiest Show in Town* and *Women*

Behind Bars to his credit. Ambitious, hardworking, and gifted with a flair for the outrageous, Eyen wrote and directed plays that would have shocked many if not most of McKuen's fans. Yet the two clicked and began a relationship that lasted several years. "Tom used to brag about dating Rod McKuen," his longtime producer Alan Eichler recalled. "Rod was much older than Tom and definitely not his physical type. He would have been a little square for him— Tom's crowd was very arty. They were really in two different worlds. But there must have been an attraction there—maybe it was just that Rod was famous."

Rod and Tom had the makings of a true power couple in the theater world. It was to be expected that the two would discuss collaborating on a project. In fact, Rod announced that he and Eyen were working on a musical in tandem with Edwards, set for its Broadway premiere sometime in 1974. How Tom's penchant for lurid, sex-charged subject matter would have meshed with Rod's more whimsical shtick is fun to speculate about. There is no evidence this venture went beyond the talking stages, however. Whatever they had shared definitely cooled off by the end of the seventies. Eyen went on to enjoy huge mainstream success with *Dreamgirls* in 1981 before his death ten years later.

Edward Habib seems to have been temporarily out of the picture around this time. "There were a couple of years when Rod's career was hot and Edward felt he wasn't listening to him anymore," Charlie Hallam recalls. "Edward moved out and rented a house in Hawaii. He built a hot dog stand and had somebody else run it for a while. Eventually he got tired of that and went back to San Francisco with a couple of friends. Finally, they talked him into calling Rod." McKuen was glad to hear from Habib and schemed to win him back again: "When Edward came back to Angelo Drive for a visit, Rod had it all set up—he whisked him to the airport and took him on a first-class flight to Paris. And that of course just wowed Edward, so he got his stuff from San Francisco and moved back to Angelo. He stayed there until the end of Rod's life."

Through all these breakups, hookups, and reunions, Rod continued to oversee his network of enterprises and dream up ways to expand his brand. In August 1973, operations for his Cheval/Stanyan Company moved from cramped quarters on the Sunset Strip into a spacious two-story office building on Santa Monica Boulevard in West Hollywood. Rod stopped by only occasionally, leaving the day-to-day duties to faithful staffers like his longtime secretary Gerry Robinson, copyrights administrator Charlotte Brennan, and art director Hy Fujita. If Cheval/Stanyan had a day-to-day overseer, it was Wade Alexander, who kept tabs on the record label, served as Rod's personal manager on occasion, and generally held things together. Hallam—who worked at the offices as gardener—recalled: "Wade filled a lot of roles and was totally loyal. He was like an Encyclopedia of Rod—if there was a question about a book or a song, Rod would call him up and ask, 'Wade, which album was that on?'

"Rod ran a good machine," Hallam continued. "He was very, very controlling, so there were times when he was out of town and certain things would stop because you couldn't do something without his approval. He did not take orders—he only gave them." Always overflowing with ideas, Rod would constantly send down word of new additions to the product line, like the Rod McKuen Tulip, developed by the National Tulip Council of Holland and marketed through the Stanyan catalog.

Flower bulbs were not the bread and butter of Rod McKuen Enterprises, of course. The core of his business continued to be the poetry books and record albums that he released at a steady clip. Covers of Rod's songs also brought in substantial revenue, sometimes from unexpected sources. The biggest windfall of all came when Terry Jacks's recording of "Seasons in the Sun" appeared in late 1973.

As noted earlier, the song was Rod's first attempt to adapt a Jacques Brel composition for English-language markets. Canadian singer-songwriter Jacks first heard the 1963 Kingston Trio version; it later took on special meaning for him, when a close friend was dying of leukemia. Jacks was friendly with the Beach Boys and tried to work up "Seasons in the Sun" with the group. When it failed to progress beyond the demo stage, he decided to record and release it himself on his own independent label. Bell Records licensed the recording for the U. S., where it reached no. 1 on the *Billboard* charts and eventually became the second-biggest single of 1974. The record also topped the charts in twelve other countries. It reportedly sold over six million copies worldwide.

Love it or otherwise, Jacks's version of "Seasons in the Sun" stands as one of McKuen's best-known covers. It still stirs passionate responses, especially on the negative side. Writing in *Slate* in 2005, critic James Sullivan called the recording "an unsurpassed nadir in pop music," noting that the "hectoring nursery-school simplicity" of Jacks's arrangement offered a weird contrast to its "heavy" lyrics. If McKuen's rewrite of Brel's lyric took some of the original edge off, Jacks sweetened things still further by altering the third verse to celebrate the dying man's loving marriage instead of voicing his threats to haunt his cheating wife from beyond the grave. Rod didn't complain publicly about Jacks's tampering with his work—in fact, he piggybacked on the single's enormous popularity by releasing his own new recording of the song and publishing a *Seasons in the Sun* paperback poetry anthology. Why let all that mass media attention go to waste? (Rod later grew peeved when Jacks claimed he was the writer of "Seasons in the Sun" and was further irritated when a slew of artists covered the Jacks-altered version of the song rather than the Brel/McKuen original.)

Scoring a no. 1 record was yet another validation of Rod's songwriting prowess. Ten years earlier, it might have been triumph enough for a struggling ex-"twist" singer hoping to become an American chansonnier. Now it was just one more milestone in a career that had taken him far beyond the boundaries of show business. For all his denials of guru-hood, countless McKuen fans looked to Rod for moral and spiritual guidance during their own fleeting seasons in the sun. His books of poetry were treated as prayer devotionals by many. Gradually, he acknowledged that he was looked upon as more than a writer and entertainer.

In 1975, Rod distilled his thoughts about love and commitment into a marriage ceremony. For some two decades, he had depicted love affairs as transitory interludes between long bouts of loneliness. As he and his fans drew closer, though, the idea of creating vows to sanctify the union of two people (genders unspecified) seemed appropriate to his role as "America's foremost romantic spokesman." As written, the ceremony had a sort of formal informality about it, befitting "a union with no set of rules but those you set upon yourself." Its content is notable for its frequent invocation of God as a loving and omnipresent Father. In most of his previous work, McKuen downplayed traditional religious themes and imagery. Here, he seems to call upon the Lord because he needs Him to give the ritual weight and validity.

The most substantial lines in "The Rod McKuen Marriage Ceremony" are given to the officiating pastor. "This is a vow for forever," he instructs the couple being joined together. "If forever should end for the two of you, or one of you tomorrow, or next year, stay together only as long as you need each other. Go only when your need for the other ends." The pastor's voice sounds distinctly like Rod's, of course. He binds the two people before him loosely, recognizing that love is not a matter of religious dogma or government authority. Yet there's also an invocation of sanctity born out of human need and divine purpose. Between these two extremes is the sort of freedom Rod insisted upon in his own life.

According to its creator, by the mid-seventies "The Rod McKuen Marriage Ceremony" had been used to unite thousands of couples. Though little remembered today, it stands out for its gender-neutral and spiritually inclusive language, a distinct step away from the norms of its era. It also suggests Rod could have built upon his pastorlike role to become a New Age religious leader. The potential was there—his works offered solace, inspiration, and guidance in ways that transcended mere aesthetic value. His personal interactions with fans resembled a lay minister tending to the needs of his flock. McKuen's inner scars and air of melancholy made him a "wounded healer" capable of easing the sorrows in others that resembled his own. There were the seeds of an entire faith in McKuen sayings like "It's not who you love or how you love but that you love."

Rod anticipated the rise of the inspirational mega-celebrity by at least a decade. In the 1980s and 1990s, Oprah Winfrey used her hugely popular TV program to spread a nonjudgmental spiritual message that recalled Rod's underlying beliefs. Oprah's frequent guest Marianne Williamson—like Rod a former nightclub performer and a talented writer—built a fervent New Age following around her charismatic personality and gift for pithy positive affirmations that was likewise suggestive of McKuen's own "cult." It's not a stretch to imagine Rod heading down the same path Winfrey and Williamson took and achieving a similar degree of cultural influence.

From People's Poet to America's Pastor of Love—Rod could have made the leap and brought millions along with him. He didn't lack for a worldwide community of true believers or the media savvy to sell himself as a spiritual authority. Rod hadn't lost his charm, his communications skills, or his genuine empathy for others. It was his own sense of self-worth that was beginning to fail him.

In September 1976, *The Advocate* published an unusually revealing interview with Rod conducted by Newt Deiter, a psychologist and gay activist. Early in their conversation, Rod said he'd gone through an emotional crisis several years earlier: "I had suddenly begun to lose weight—about 20 pounds in two weeks—and it was climaxed by my coming off stage in Connecticut and collapsing . . . It turns out that what I was really doing was killing myself . . . My friend asked me, 'Do you want to live?' I said, 'I don't know; I hadn't really thought much about it, but I am not all that thrilled about life, and no one's ever come back to tell us about what's on the other side, if indeed, there is another side . . .'"

One admission led to another: "It turns out that my problem is that in some 40-odd years of living, I had never had a person to talk to—not one single, solitary person I could be frank with . . . I definitely feel an aloneness, one obviously shared with millions of people everywhere. It's not a question of being lonely, it's a question of feeling alone and wondering why I did it all—if I wasn't doing it for somebody, 'cause I wasn't doing it for me. It's rough when you say to somebody, 'Here it is; all I've got belongs to you,' and they reply, 'it isn't enough.'"

Rod was the world's most famous self-proclaimed loner. For the past quarter century, he had dissected, lamented, and celebrated the condition of being apart from the crowd as a radio host, songwriter, and poet. But he had never before talked about being alone with quite this note of hopelessness and despair. Rod had always spoken of a few select people in his life who loved and understood him. Here, he acknowledged a chasm between himself and the rest of the human species that no amount of fame, money, sex, or artistic fulfilment had ever overcome. He was beloved by millions, rewarded as few writers and no poets had ever been, and yet it all seemed meaningless.

To step away from the brink, Rod had to confront his past. He had spent decades trying to delay reckoning with the psychic wounds sustained in his childhood. The first and deepest of these was the disappearance of his father. It was time for Rod to find out who he really was.

Ten

Mac and Anita

F ROM CHILDHOOD ONWARD, Rod wondered about the man who had romanced, seduced, and abandoned his mother. Close friends like Ellen Ehrlich remember how often he talked about the mysterious Mr. McKuen, who vanished before his birth. In his poem "Alamo Junction," he wrote about reading obituaries in the towns he passed through, hoping he would find "a man who spells his name the same as me." Rod grew up imagining his father was a fighter pilot or a movie star. At age forty-two, the fantasies had faded but the desire to meet him had not: "If he's a skid row bum, that's fine with me. I just want to say hello, to tell him everything turned out OK, to thank him. He gave me life and it's been a good life—I'm grateful."

Rod might have gone on fruitlessly looking up variations of the name "McKuen" in telephone directories if he hadn't received a call from Dick Carlson in November 1975. A successful L. A. broadcast journalist, Carlson had been adopted as a child and later found it difficult to learn the names of his birth parents. He was pitching an idea for a TV documentary about similar searches by adopted children when he heard through a mutual friend that Rod had been trying to find his father for years. Carlson invited him to become involved in the project as both narrator and subject. More than that, he hired a private investigator to conduct a methodical search for "Mack McKuen."

Michael Hamel-Green was an ex–British Army intelligence officer who had moved to San Francisco and opened a detective agency. He took on the McKuen case and began chasing down leads from Rod's mother's past. The initial discoveries were encouraging enough to get Rod to start paying the agency out of his own pocket. The expenses for tracking down stray clues and tenuous tips across the American West came to tens of thousands of dollars. Rod grumbled about the cost, but the results proved to be worth it.

Carlson's documentary, *Home Again*, was broadcast on NBC in January 1976 and met with a positive response. Around that time, Rod decided to use Hamel-Green's research about his case as the basis for the book he ultimately titled *Finding My Father*. According to Carlson, "Michael's reports were voluminous and precise and well written. Rod told me that he walked up and down a hallway in his house reading from the reports, and had what he said transcribed by two secretaries. That's how he wrote a large part of the book. Looking at it, I see where he goes into great detail about things that didn't amount to anything: 'We tracked down Edie Gilbert and he didn't remember those people . . . ' This came directly out of the reports."

Finding My Father's lengthy digressions about false leads and dead ends seem to confirm Carlson's account. But there's more in its pages than just recapitulations of Hamel-Green's fieldwork. The book reflects both Rod's strengths and weaknesses as a writer—it is by turns revealing and evasive, minutely detailed and deliberately vague, bathed in rosy-toned nostalgia and salted with sordid incidents. Poems break up the narrative frequently, reinforcing the sense that this is a subjective account, rather than a work based upon solid proof. At one point, Rod invokes the 1950 Japanese film *Rashomon* to underscore his point that "a hundred half-truths will not make a single fact." *Finding My Father* resembles Kurosawa's masterpiece in its conflicting accounts, multiple points of view, and implied belief that a single truth is beyond our grasp.

Based on Hamel-Green's reports and his own intuition, Rod is led to believe that a onetime sawmill owner and salesman named Rodney Marion McKune (note spelling), known to associates as "Mack," is his father. There would be no tearful reunion between parent and child—McKune had died in 1963 and was buried in a Santa Monica cemetery. In a coda to the story, Rod visits McKune's elderly sister in rural Utah and convinces her he is her long-lost nephew. This connection to a previously unknown family is enough to bring a sense of completion to his search. Rod added that he still longed for a connection with "the Father of us all," a God-like source of all life.

Finding My Father was published in August 1976 and did well in both hardback and paperback editions. And true to form for its author, it drew uneven reviews. *Writing in the Los Angeles Times*, John Charnay called the book "a poignant personal account of [McKuen's] lifelong search for the father he never knew . . . moving and meaningful." An unsigned *Kirkus* review praised the book for its candor while criticizing its rambling style and Rod's willingness to use "his private life for the source of his commercial persona." More damning was Charles Flowers in the Rochester, New York *Democrat and Chronicle*: "[McKuen] pads, repeats and wanders about in the service of another goal, the disingenuous celebration of himself as sensitive human being and skillful poet . . . Nothing [could be] more appalling than his cherubic smiles as he puts the knife to relative or colleague, always without 'meaning' to." Whether he was writing poetry or personal confession, Rod's motives would always be suspect for some critics.

It was impossible for confirmed McKuen haters to approach *Finding My Father* without bias. Admittedly, the book has its flaws. Rod's honesty seems strategic at times—he glosses over significant experiences (like his stint as a lumber-camp hustler) and conflates factual reportage with wish fulfilment. The stories of his childhood are difficult if not impossible to corroborate—

those writing about him (including this author) have had to assay each incident carefully for its factual content. In any case, Rod may not have expected the reader to treat every word as gospel. "I have a very poor memory myself for time and individual circumstances," he says near the end of the book.

Finding My Father is more than an uneasy amalgam of detective story and memoir, though. Rod uses the book to explore the meaning of family during a time of social upheaval. By delving into his own troubled past, he hoped to show that any kind of loving union—no matter how brief or casual—was valid and beautiful. If his web of kinship was tangled, tormented, and at times imaginary, there was no disgrace in that—his newly formed bond with Rodney McKune's sister was more real and vital to him than whatever he shared with various Hoopers and Woolevers. The contradictory fragments of information discovered by Hamel-Green are less important than Rod's insights into the worth of every human being and the right of everyone to find love.

In the end, the theme of overcoming shame is as central to the book as the quest for the elusive Mack McKune. Rod had been a target of shaming of one sort or another all his life. He had felt the absence of his true father long before his Aunt Ruth called him a bastard to his face. His reform-school stint and checkered work history marked him as irregular if not a flat-out deviant. While he never said so publicly, he must have feared disapproval and worse from homophobic mainstream America when he joined the Mattachine Society as a young adult. Once he became successful as an entertainer and author, highbrow critics tried to shame him for what he wrote and how he marketed himself. Rod didn't have the advantage of married birth parents—and he also lacked the artistic bona fides that came with academic and critical approval. In both cases, McKuen insisted on being judged as his own man, on his own merits. If others couldn't or wouldn't legitimize him, he would legitimize himself.

Rather than stew over old injustices done to him, Rod moved beyond his own story to advocate on behalf of others who were "born or adopted under anything but ordinary circumstances." In early 1976, he contacted California State Senator William Campbell, who was working on legislation to make it easier for adult adoptees to gain access to their birth records. McKuen met with Campbell in Sacramento, worked with him to craft a bill, and lobbied state legislators to help get it passed. According to the senator's aide Jerry Heleva, the bill was not an easy sell: "I was very surprised by the virulence of the opponents of adoptee rights. Many adoptive parents viewed this legislation as a betrayal. Rod had warned us that there would be a great deal of emotion about this." (It's worth noting that McKuen's own mother had been unwilling to tell him much if anything about his father.) Campbell's bill eventually passed both houses of the California legislature, but was vetoed by Governor Jerry Brown. (As of 2018, adoptees still need "good and compelling cause" to gain access to their birth records in California.)

Rod continued the fight in a series of newspaper articles the following year. By that time, he had gained some important allies. Among them was then-President Gerald Ford, who been adopted as a child by his mother's second husband and only learned about his biological father at age seventeen. Ford took an interest in McKuen's crusade and met with him after the publication of *Finding My Father.* Rod warmed up to the affable POTUS: "I found Ford to be a most unusual man. A man, who like many men and women in this country have used what was seemingly adverse backgrounds to make themselves a better life . . . We had some good times." Though a self-described lifelong Democrat, Rod campaigned for Ford in 1976 and wrote a heartfelt tribute to him for the *New York Times* when the president left office.

Besides Ford, Rod did some campaigning for Senator John Tunney and other California Democrats in the 1976 election cycle. (Eight years earlier, he had actively supported Robert F. Kennedy for president.) He was encouraged to run for office himself during this time, he said. The idea of McKuen as a political candidate wasn't so far-fetched, considering America's post-Watergate mood. Voters were looking for fresh faces with messages that transcended the usual partisan divides. They were willing to take chances on outsiders running on platforms of love, civility, and brotherhood (Jimmy Carter) and New Age free spirits who talked about big philosophical issues in pop cultural terms (Jerry Brown). In this context, Rod might have connected with the electorate, particularly in Southern California.

For ten years, Rod had built up a massive following that could have been turned into a political base. He was a populist in the most literal sense of the word, reflecting the mainstream tastes and values of millions who felt condescended to by America's elites. Yet Rod never stood for blind reaction against new ideas and unconventional lifestyles. He had publicly opposed the Vietnam War, scored a European hit with an antiwar anthem ("Soldiers Who Want to Be Heroes"), and mocked President Nixon onstage. On several occasions, he claimed he had been included on Nixon's notorious "enemies list" for his outspokenness. He remained a believer in the American political system, however. "Because a few people in high places were caught robbing and raping the country doesn't necessarily mean all politicians are corrupt," he said. "I must say I prefer politicians who are trained politicians. I don't want lawyers running my country. I don't want ad-agency men running it." If Rod's opinions seemed all over the place, they probably were in sync with a good share of the American electorate.

It was probably all for the best that Rod never became a candidate. "I think that to be a good politician you have to compromise, and I don't like to compromise," he noted. If there was one defining quality to Rod's life, it was his insistence on following his own instincts rather than deferring to experts or toeing a party line. He reserved the right to come and go as he pleased, whether in business deals, romantic liaisons, or political causes. As he put it in one of his songs, "I only own myself, but all of me is mine."

Rod hated either-or choices. He demanded the right to do as he wished and be whoever he wanted to be. And just as he opposed the distinction between "legitimate" and "illegitimate" children, he refused to recognize the polarities of "heterosexual" and "homosexual." Still, he knew there were times when you had to take sides. The battle to protect gay rights in Miami was one of those times.

This pivotal conflict erupted in January 1977 when the Dade County Commission passed an ordinance prohibiting discrimination based on "affectional or sexual preference." Seizing leadership of the opposition to this measure was singer Anita Bryant, then in the public eye as the spokesperson for the Florida Citrus Commission. A former Miss America runner-up and all-around icon of wholesomeness, Bryant was constantly reminding TV viewers that "a day without orange juice is like a day without sunshine." Her views on homosexuality were far from sunny, however—she maintained that "homosexuals cannot biologically reproduce children; therefore, they must recruit our children." The idea of gays as schoolteachers particularly infuriated her. She founded Save Our Children to galvanize conservative Dade County voters into repealing the ordinance at the ballot box that June.

A month before the vote, Rod appeared at a Miami press conference called by the Dade County Coalition for Human Rights. He tore into Bryant and what she stood for, calling her "a kind of Ginny Orangeseed spreading bigotry throughout the land." Rather than defending a particular lifestyle, he spoke in broader terms of individual freedom: "I would ask those who may listen to Anita Bryant, 'When are people going to stop taking it upon themselves to be policemen?' I am not interested in Ms. Bryant's personal life, and I am convinced that there are more constructive things for her to do than to infringe on the privacy of individual American citizens." Bryant would be better off trying to improve Florida schools and combating drug abuse, he added.

Save Our Children's response to McKuen was swift—and personal. Spokesman Mike Thompson called Rod's comments "an attack of Judaism and Christianity" by an "out-of-town carpetbagger." Furthermore, "What Mr. McKuen and his fellow perverts do in privacy is their business, [but] what their fellow homosexuals would do in our children's classrooms is our business." Rod had rarely (if ever) been attacked publicly in this way before. In his response, Rod offered Thompson a challenge: "If he can prove I'm a homosexual, I'd be delighted to donate $100,000 to his campaign . . . I've been attracted to men and I've been attracted to women. I have a sixteen-year-old son. You put a label on me."

This was an advanced position for 1977, one that went against the binary beliefs of right-wing evangelicals and even some gay activists. Rod refused to see the fight as one for gay rights per se: "That wasn't why I went after Anita Bryant. By the way, I don't like the word *homosexual*. Those words—*homosexual, heterosexual*, or *bisexual*—were coined within our lifetime to, I suppose help psychiatrists put people in slots . . . I find what people do in bed very boring, unless I'm one of them." Bryant's campaign against ratification of the Equal Rights Amendment was the real reason he spoke out against her, he added.

Despite Rod's bobbing and weaving on this point, it seemed clear he had come to Florida to help uphold an ordinance specifically protecting Dade County's gay residents. He performed at a series of benefit concerts, gave press interviews, and took out full-page ads in *Variety* in support of the cause. Most notably, he wrote and performed a satiric anti-Bryant ditty, "Don't Drink the Orange Juice." Set to a jaunty calypso beat, the tune called for a boycott of the Sunshine State's most famous crop until its citizens took a stand against homophobia. (At one concert in Miami, the song provoked some of Rod's more conservative fans to leave in protest. He responded by tossing oranges at them as they headed for the door.)

Rod was among a legion of writers, intellectuals, and entertainers who denounced Bryant in America and abroad. In the end, such efforts weren't enough to keep the ordinance from going down to defeat by a two-to-one margin at the polls. Still, the campaign marked the emergence of gay activism as a political force in America. Rod continued to voice his support for similar antidiscrimination laws around the country. As for Anita Bryant, her career never recovered from the Miami battle. The Florida Citrus Council declined to renew her contract in 1980; Rod said "Don't Drink the Orange Juice" was responsible. The tune certainly wasn't good advertising for the Sunshine State.

"Don't Drink the Orange Juice" was included on *Slide . . . Easy In*, released on Stanyan's sister label Discus in mid-1977. Packed with funky dance grooves and sweeping Barry White–style orchestrations, the album was intended as a satire of the disco craze. (Much as "Oliver Twist" was meant to be taken as a joke.) The LP veered from boogie-infused Broadway material to instrumental tracks spiked with heavy breathing, barking dogs, and other sound effects. "Amor"—a disco-chanson fusion sung by Rod in French and English—became a surprise hit in France and other European markets.

Slide . . . Easy In's notoriety, though, comes primarily from its salacious gatefold album cover. The hairy, well-muscled arm of gay porn star Bruno is seen grabbing a fistful of something gooey out of a can labeled "Disco," a reference to the practice of using Crisco shortening as a sexual lubricant. (The pun may also be a nod toward the Crisco Disco, a popular Manhattan discotheque of the era.) Other gay culture in-jokes turn up in the album notes, including a thank-you to the FFA (the acronym for the Future Farmers of America—but the Fist Fuckers of America, as well). It was all meant in good, if not entirely clean, fun.

Was Rod turning away from the soft and sentimental image that had made him millions? At first blush, his use of hard-core gay sexual imagery undermined his appeal to the straight Middle Americans who had formed the bedrock of his audience. Though he didn't put his name on the album cover, Rod didn't hide his involvement in *Slide . . . Easy In*—it was advertised in his catalogs next to his more conventional works. Maybe he thought his true believers would laugh off the album (or at least tolerate it) while a new, more adventuresome consumer would pick it up as a novelty. Or maybe he just wanted to mess with people's minds—after all, Rod was the guy who had released a synthesizer noise album titled *Music to Freak Your Friends and*

Break Your Lease (under the nom de plume "Heins Hoffman-Richter") a few
years earlier.

Prank or not, Rod's "Crisco Disco album" was only the latest iteration
of themes that went back to the beginning of his career. For all his status as
an arch-romantic, he never shied away from celebrating sexual pleasure for
its own sake. His recordings and poems had been testing the boundaries of
acceptable commercial eroticism ever since the late fifties. He had a gift for
gauging what his audience would and would not accept. This was not simply a business calculation—Rod's belief in the free expression of desire in all
its forms was genuine and consistent over his lifetime. He showed courage
when he stood up for gay rights. But he also sensed that attitudes were changing among those mainstream Americans who been his faithful customers for
a decade. All those drum majorettes, phys-ed students, and TWA reservation clerks were not the same people they were ten years ago—many of them
had relaxed their inhibitions and embraced freer lifestyles. Gently, Rod had
nudged them toward a wider conception of what love could be.

In 1967, *Stanyan Street & Other Sorrows* had been a bellwether of changing mores in America. Ten years on, its message of self-acceptance and sinless
love had become commonplace—at its worst, it translated into the selfish
excesses of the Me Decade. For all the human potential movements, swingers'
clubs, fringe cults, activist uprisings, and more that characterized the 1970s,
loneliness was a worse plague than ever. How a born loner found a place in
an uncaring world remained Rod's most obsessive theme. He'd addressed it
with varying degrees of seriousness over the course of his career. And while
he searched for his father and did battle with the forces of bigotry in Florida,
he dealt with his chronic sense of alienation from the crowd in a song cycle
intended for a full-scale musical.

The Black Eagle was described by Rod at various times as an opera or
a "gothic musical" with "overtones of violence, sex, and death." He began
working on it in 1975 or '76 and tested out a number of its songs on tour.

Though never staged, *The Black Eagle* was recorded in London with a symphony orchestra and a full cast, and released as a double-disc LP in 1978. The album's shadowy cover photo of a grim-faced McKuen signaled that this would be a different sort of offering from what his fans had come to expect.

Musically, *The Black Eagle* draws heavily upon familiar Broadway melodic motifs, with operatic chants and arias added for moody gravitas. The songs relate a fable about a nameless Spanish village under the thumb of a repressive Elite in cahoots with the Church. A dreamer named Miguel longs to be free of this place—after various fantastic episodes, he is transformed into a giant eagle who leaves his grieving loved ones behind to discover his higher destiny. Naturally, this role is performed by Rod himself.

It appears Rod spent a good deal of time and money on *The Black Eagle* before putting it aside as an unfinished work. Though only his most hard-core followers heard it in its LP form, the project is significant for its portrayal of a repressed loner who can only find escape from an uncomprehending world by losing his humanity. This was not the stuff of hit stage musicals. Rod was working out his own intractable personal issues on his own dime and didn't care how it might reflect upon his public persona as "America's foremost romantic spokesman."

There continued to be a tension between McKuen's sense of separation from the crowd and his desire to speak for the voiceless millions. He may have been thinking of his youthful days as a solitary wanderer when he embarked upon an investigation of American working life in 1974. For a year or so, Rod took a series of blue-collar jobs in various cities under assumed names. He worked as a garbageman, a waiter, a taxi driver, and a Central Park hot dog vendor, among other gigs. He was invariably recognized ("My voice is the giveaway," he said), but not before he had a chance to talk with ordinary folks about their workaday concerns. Rod said he intended to turn his experiences into his first prose book in time for the 1976 bicentennial. It's easy to imagine McKuen combining his feel for America's lonesome cities with street-level reportage à la Studs Terkel. Nothing along these lines ever appeared, however.

Rod did have a book about America in him, though it took the form of poetic reflections rather than prose reportage. *The Power Bright & Shining: Images of My Country* evoked Walt Whitman in its chantlike recitations of national glory and its affection for the common man. There are salutes to the flag, paeans to Olympic athletes, tributes to big cities and the Great Outdoors. McKuen sounds at various points like an irritated libertarian ("Bureaucracy is busy with its building blocks, making mazes thick as Mondays"), a militant nationalist ("Stop apologizing for America"), a foe of welfare chiselers ("Why work when those who do pay handsomely for me to play?"), and an antiwar crusader ("Don't say you kill in my name or in the name of kind mankind"). Impatience with misguided politicians and a faith in the basic decency of the American people run through the book. Once again, Rod caught the Zeitgeist of his era—the rightward tilt of his book reflects the prevailing mood of his country at the close of the seventies.

The Power Bright & Shining was published in 1980, the year Ronald Reagan won the presidency on a platform of social and economic conservatism. The conditions that allowed McKuen to become a megastar had changed—the times seemed meaner, the American people more mistrustful and segmented. While Rod insisted sales of his books were still strong, it was evident that his latest works couldn't match the phenomenal numbers racked up by *Stanyan Street* or *Listen to the Warm*. Retrenching, he closed the Stanyan offices and let longtime employees like art director Hy Fujita move on. His recording deal with Warner Bros. had ended in the mid-seventies. ("I think it was a natural parting of the ways," label chief Joe Smith recalled. "We'd played that card for a long time and there was a limited market.") With *The Power Bright & Shining*, his contract with Simon & Schuster concluded as well.

Rod remained part of the cultural conversation. Even when treating him with their usual condescension, the press still acknowledged the millions of books and records he'd sold and considered him worth talking to. Reporters still visited his Beverly Hills mansion, where Rod greeted them in his trademark jeans and sweater before showing off his mementos, his gold records, his closet full of tennis shoes. With a new decade dawning, he emphasized his role as a voice for unity and compassion. "After we've come out of this 'me society,' I feel it's important to come into a 'we society,'" he told the *Los Angeles Times*. "It's a very brittle world we live in."

By any measure, Rod McKuen had a remarkable run in the 1970s. He maintained a physically punishing workload while he carved out time to delve into the mysteries of his own existence. As his star power inevitably diminished as the decade wore on, he sought to channel his money and fame into causes he believed in. Rod juggled his roles as artist, entrepreneur, activist, and seeker with manic intensity, even as he knew the inevitable crash would come.

"I'll probably burn myself out by the time I'm 50," Rod told *Newsweek* in 1968. His prediction proved amazingly accurate. But there was more ahead for him than just ashes.

Eleven

~

How Deep is Down?

A T THE PEAK of his fame, Rod McKuen ascended to new heights—literally. He took a ride in a hot-air balloon in early 1975 and was immediately hooked. Sailing above the world at thirteen thousand feet brought him a
rare sense of serenity and freedom. "It just dilated his eyes," says balloon pilot
Ray Gallagher of his first flight with Rod. "He said, 'I speak for a living, but I
am speechless.' He absolutely loved it."

A month later, McKuen invited Gallagher to bring himself and his balloon
over to South Africa, where Rod was in the middle of a concert tour. Enlisting
a cameraman, the poet and the pilot embarked on an aerial safari to Chobe
National Park in nearby Botswana, southern Africa's largest game preserve.
Flying above stampeding herds of wildlife was exhilarating—and dangerous.
"We were only twenty-five feet above the elephants at one point," Gallagher
says. "They were just trumpeting and raising hell. I warned Rod, 'We can't follow the elephants across the Zambezi River—Zambia is right there. Last time
some tourists went over there, they were killed.' I was the pilot in command,
but Rod and the cameraman wouldn't have it. Luckily, I saw a sandbar island
halfway across the river, so I came careening down onto it and we waited for
a tourist boat to come by and pick us up. About thirty minutes later I could

hear the guy driving the boat screaming at us—he told us we were in trouble and that we were putting a lot of people in danger." The cameraman got some great footage and Rod got the thrill of a lifetime.

Rod continued to go ballooning off and on for years afterward. He put photos of hot-air balloons on his book and albums covers and in his annual calendars. He even talked about making a film about the sport (though, like so many other announced projects, it—ironically, in this case—never got off the ground). Ballooning was the perfect escape for a loner who loved to observe the world from a remove. It also served as a metaphor for a spectacular career that had soared up into the sky and was now slowly, steadily coming down to earth.

There were high points as he descended to a more moderate level of stardom. 1978 found Rod flying back and forth between New York and Moscow as part of the American-Soviet production team for *The Unknown War*, a twenty-part documentary series built around little-seen film footage of World War II's Eastern Front. Working closely with Soviet composers and filmmakers, Rod crafted (with assistance from his longtime arranger Skip Redwine) a score laden with heroic marches, stirring romantic themes, and contemplative mood pieces. Sessions with the U. S. S. R. Bolshoi Symphony Orchestra and the Soviet Army Choir added to the soundtrack's richness.

Rod recalled long, stressful but satisfying days working in Moscow on the project: "I had a terrific time, enhanced by Edward sending me footlockers containing fruit bars, Franco-American canned spaghetti and macaroni, Jiffy Pop, and other assorted nonperishables. The people in Russia were wonderful, the food miserable. I mean, how much borscht, potato soup, and caviar can one man eat?" Rod considered his contributions to *The Unknown War* to be among his best work. Unfortunately, a spike in Cold War tensions caused by the Soviet invasion of Afghanistan and the boycott of the 1980 Moscow Olympics kept most episodes from being aired on American television. (The series returned to TV via A&E and the History Channel years later.)

Rod on the beach: "Have you met my friend, the sea?" (Jim Pierson)

The success of *The Sea* (1967) led Rod and composer Anita Kerr to record a series of similarly themed albums. *The Sea*, *The Earth*, and *The Sky* were released as a box set in 1968.

In the mid-1970s Rod kept company with Off-Off-Broadway playwright Tom Eyen (right), known for such notorious productions as *Women Behind Bars*. An announced collaboration on a Broadway show never materialized. (Alan Eichler)

Rod's beard gave him a new look for the 1970s. (Jim Pierson)

Rod with Terry Jacks, circa 1974. McKuen's enthusiasm for Jacks's hit version of "Seasons in the Sun" waned over time. (Jim Pierson)

"When I'm onstage, whether it's for three thousand or thirty-five thousand people, I always try to relate one to one. I think that's the secret of any success I've had." (Jim Pierson)

Released in 1977, *Slide . . . Easy In* boasted a suggestive cover featuring a muscular arm digging into a can of Crisco (labeled "Disco"). The album gave Rod a European hit with "Amor." (Jim Pierson)

Rod made a habit of meeting with fans after shows for autographs and conversation. Some of them became lifelong friends. (Jim Pierson)

Rod received oceans of fan mail over the course of his career. Admirers sent gifts, poems, love notes, and personal confessions. He corresponded with many of his admirers, sometimes for decades. (Jim Pierson)

Edward Habib portrait by Don Bachardy, 2003.
Rod and Edward's troubled relationship lasted
over half a century. (Don Bachardy)

Rod and Edward at their Beverly Hills home in the 1970s. (Jim Pierson)

Rod with old friend and
occasional recording partner
Petula Clark at the Grammy
Museum, Los Angeles,
November 2013.
(Jim Pierson)

Rod continued to perform into his last years: "There was nothing sad or old about
him. He commanded the room." (Jim Pierson)

By the end of the decade, Rod was back in the L. A. social whirl, still enjoying the perks of fame as he mixed with old showbiz friends and the latest crop of rising talent. Michael Feinstein was among the latter when he met Rod at the home of Joe Carberry, a physician known for his well-attended "boy parties." He recalls how McKuen maintained a certain reserve in a room full of temptation: "I was playing the piano at Joe's party, and Rod came over and we tossed tunes back and forth. It was sort of understood that the older gentlemen were there for a reason and the younger ones were there for a reason. And yet I never saw Rod let loose or really party with anybody. There were guys drinking and getting into hot tubs, things going on in other rooms, but Rod seemed to be buttoned-down and carried his deportment well. There was a sense of still having to be a little protective about himself."

Rod was happy to get back to his home base on Angelo Drive. Edward was living there again as well, trying to clean up after too much craziness in Manhattan. "Edward had been partying his brains out," their friend Charlie Hallam said. "[Rod's manager] Wade Alexander brought [Ed] a book on Elvis Presley, talking about all the pills that he took and how he died. Edward was an avid reader of biographies—he read it, and it just shook him up, and he decided, 'I'm outta here.' He dropped everything and flew back to Angelo Drive."

It was a time for taking stock and getting back to basics. After closing down the Cheval/Stanyan offices, Rod had moved his mail-order business to a room at his mansion. According to Hallam, day-to-day business had been neglected while McKuen had been away: "When Rod and Edward came back from New York, they found that the employee left in charge hadn't done anything. The room was a mess, there were six months of old checks lying around—it was total disorder. So they brought me in, and I helped out two or three days a week. There were a lot of repeat customers, [but] it wasn't a big business at that point. Then it slowed down more, and I would come in one day a week to get the orders out."

If Rod's media empire was contracting, his public persona was still upbeat and forward-looking. Signing a new publishing deal with Harper & Row, he aimed for the inspirational book market with *An Outstretched Hand* (1980), a collection of spiritually themed poems and prose pieces, including the Rod McKuen Marriage Ceremony. Counting himself among America's "God-loving and God-fearing people," he states that, while not born again in his faith, he felt comfortable offering "the fundamental rules for being a practicing Christian." Was Rod straining to present his open-ended spiritual beliefs in more orthodox terms here? Perhaps his intention was to provide an alternative to the harshly judgmental Christianity Anita Bryant and her ilk represented. Certainly there was a demand for books that offered hope and healing in nonsectarian terms at the dawn of the eighties. Authors like pop psychologist Leo Buscaglia were reaching millions with a love-centered message not so different from what McKuen had been preaching since the sixties.

An Outstretched Hand might have been a missed opportunity to expand upon Rod's loyal but limited core audience. As he approached fifty, he was less inclined to chase after the fads and fashions of the moment—there were no punk-rock parody records to match his earlier send-ups of beatniks, hippies, twist dancers, and disco fanatics. The media began to treat him as a quaint if persistent holdover from another era, still worthy of notice but no longer hot news. Stories about Rod in the early eighties looked back on his near-incredible sales figures (twenty million hardback books sold was the latest number bandied about) while touting his upcoming projects (often unrealized, like a collaboration with composer Jules Styne on a *Phantom of the Opera* musical). He turned up as a judge at the 1982 Miss America pageant and appeared on regional TV shows. McKuen retained his celebrity status, but he had to work to stay relevant.

Though his star had dimmed, Rod was one of the few celebrity poets on the planet. *Writer's Digest* acknowledged this when they published a lengthy interview with him in February 1984. Distilled from three years' worth of questions submitted by mail, it stands as McKuen's most extensive statement about writing that ever saw print. He offered broad philosophical maxims ("Poetry is not luxury; it is a necessity. The poetry in our lives separates sanity from savagery"), details about his creative habits ("I only stop in mid-thought if I have to. Even a day's work should have a beginning, a middle and an end"), and advice to aspiring poets ("For God's sake, stay away from Robert Service and Kahlil Gibran. Everyone's imitating them. The same goes for Rod McKuen").

The *Writer's Digest* issue featuring McKuen set a sales record for the magazine. Rod was so pleased with how it turned out that he offered interviewer Rose Adkins a job as his secretary/editorial assistant. He was persuasive enough that she quit her position at the magazine, left New York, and began working at his home office that summer. She lasted about a year in his employ.

Before she moved out to L. A., one of Rod's previous secretaries called Adkins and asked her, "Are you sure you know what you're getting into?" By his own admission, Rod could be a temperamental and demanding boss. For the most part, though, Adkins recalls the working environment at Angelo Drive as a pleasant one: "I had a great big office on the first floor with an outstanding view of the hills out one of the windows. Each morning, Edward would bring me a fresh rose in a glass and ask if I wanted coffee. Sometimes he would jump up on the file cabinet and we'd talk for a long time. He and Rod would always ask me if I wanted to eat lunch, but I never did—I was an employee and felt I shouldn't."

Adkins learned Rod's routines and noted his writerly habits: "He was upstairs in his room writing every morning by 8 a.m. on the days I was there. He would tell me to hold his calls, because when he got in the throes of even beginning a poem, he knew he didn't want to stop work on it until he finished with that first draft . . . He wrote longhand all the time. I'll be honest—he had terrible handwriting. I think he did that because he was lazy or because he didn't want anyone to be able to read what he wrote until it was finished.

That's how extreme he would be about protecting what he was writing until it was completed."

Rod's work ethic kept him going most days of the week. At times, though, signs of the clinical depression that sidelined him that decade were evident: "He could get melancholy—at those times, he didn't want anyone around him. He'd call and say, 'I'm going to be working by myself today, and you can go home early or work in the supply room.'" Occasionally, his mood could turn volatile. When Adkins refused to work weekends addressing Christmas cards, Rod lost his temper: "I had told him I wasn't coming in, but he still got real mad at me. When I came in to work on Monday, he said, 'You think you can just show up after quitting?' I told him I hadn't quit, but he was still upset. It was really nasty that Christmas." The experience was unpleasant enough to make Adkins take another job about a week later.

Despite that episode, Adkins remembers McKuen as a kind, compassionate man who felt unworthy in some hard-to-define way. He expressed regret for his behavior that Christmas and kept in touch with her for years afterward. Reflecting on her memories of him, she came to believe that "there was a joy in him that he could never let out. I think he felt that if he was too joyful, people would not like him. He had been hurt so deeply that he didn't trust that people really cared. I cared about him, and I never wanted to hurt him, because I could read the hurt in his poetry."

She was not alone in responding to Rod's vulnerability, of course. He had achieved enormous success by making personal revelations (often less than flattering) part of the larger cultural conversation going on around him. With this in mind, his decision to go public about the sexual abuse he'd suffered as a child can be seen as more than just an act of confession. Rod was purging inner demons, reaching out to his fellow victims, and keeping himself viable as a public figure—all at once.

As he told it, the National Committee for the Prevention of Child Abuse asked him to be their 1982 spokesman after its leaders read about his brutal childhood in *Finding My Father*. Once he took the role, he acknowledged he'd been sexually as well as physically abused by members of the Hooper family. It brought back horrific memories that went to the core of his own sense of self. "All my life I have felt that somehow I did something, that I was asking to be touched, to be victimized, that I must have done something to bring it on," he wrote in *People* magazine. "I am sure that is why I was so confused about my sexual identity . . . Also, I've always had an inferiority complex, and that childhood incident was one of the things that intensified it, for sure. I think that's one of the reasons I've always worked and never taken vacations. I'm always trying to be as good as everybody else."

Speaking in public about his trauma wasn't easy for him. He told Adkins he experienced a panic attack before taking the stage at the National Committee for the Prevention of Child Abuse's annual conference: "He said, 'I don't know what happened to me . . . it never happened before. I got up there and froze. I couldn't even talk.'" He continued to struggle with his memories as he spoke at meetings around the country. "Halfway through the tour, I had to stop," he told the *Philadelphia Inquirer*. "Each time, it would come back in such vivid detail . . . I couldn't sleep . . . I just had to go home."

An overflow of emotional baggage had always accompanied Rod wherever he went. Skillfully unpacking it in public had become his specialty—but the task was becoming harder as time wore on. Part of it stemmed from sheer physical exhaustion. For at least twenty years, McKuen had maintained a punishing work schedule that allowed for little rest or self-reflection. His dimming of energy and decline in sales happened about the same time—it's hard to know which caused which. Rod's career as a recording artist petered out with the release of *Global* in 1981. Though he could still pen a smile-inducing love song, a darker note crept into his music around this time. "Tough at the bottom, tougher at the top / Rough gettin' started, rougher tryin' to stop," he sang ruefully on 1980's *Turntable* LP. Sustaining fame was much less fun than pursuing it.

Harper & Row continued to publish Rod's books into the mid-eighties. His latest poems often felt like postcard messages or travel journal entries, with nostalgia for people and places now gone a recurring theme. Now he seemed to be even more an observer than a participant. *Suspension Bridge* (1984) took him back to San Francisco, where the sight of young men tossing a football around offered "a secret sexercize for those who only watch and want." The search for Eros celebrated in his earlier work had mellowed into a wistful voyeurism. More engaged was "Is There Life After Tower Records?" a story-poem capturing the shopping bustle and casual flirtations at a famous L. A. record store, included in 1986's *Intervals*.

Such flashes of vigor suggested that Rod wanted to stay active and involved. He told *Writer's Digest* there was still a long list of projects he hoped to tackle. But he added that "there are times when I wake up in the morning and the tension in my head and back is so great, I feel like packing it all in. It's as if a great weight were pulling me down and under. Those times don't come often, but when they do, they are real and they are hell."

There were reasons for these bouts of sadness. The AIDS epidemic had struck America with devastating force by the mid-eighties, making McKuen's advocacy for uninhibited love seem grimly out of date. Stanyan photographer Wayne Massey was among the many young men in Rod's circle who succumbed to the disease. The death of old friend Rock Hudson in October 1985 must have also touched McKuen deeply. Rod was a survivor on a field of carnage. The erotic freedom he had championed in the 1960s and seventies had given way to a climate of fear and shame, the very things he had pushed back against in his heyday.

By the middle of the decade, Rod began to suffer depression severe enough to affect his ability to work and interact with people. Looking back in 2011, he linked it with the exhaustive touring schedule he had maintained for over a decade: "I felt that the road kills in a way, so I went into clinical depression . . . I sat around for years making life difficult for my brother, making it difficult for everybody else. I never left the yard for two years. I didn't answer the phone for three years. I wrote, but I never showed it to anyone."

While he may have exaggerated the exact details here, it seems clear that what he experienced was long, bleak, and debilitating. Victims of major depression were still in the shadows in the 1980s—books like William Styron's 1990 memoir *Darkness Visible* hadn't begun to help dispel the stigma of the disease. For a proud workaholic like Rod, the loss of productivity must have further wounded his sense of self. What had been vital now became painful. The man who glutted the market with all things McKuen in the seventies didn't publish another book of poetry for fifteen years.

Fewer friends visited the Angelo Drive mansion during these years. Those who did found Rod leading a subdued though not wholly unpleasant life. "He seemed to enjoy being out from under the pressure," Hallam said. "He gardened a lot. He'd plant tomatoes—every year it would be a ritual for him to try a different kind. He'd give me a bag of tomatoes to take home when I'd visit. They were delicious." New ventures and business schemes had lost their appeal for McKuen: "He didn't have a secretary. There were people who approached him [with projects], but he wouldn't respond."

As he withdrew from the world, money increasingly became a concern. Rod had been reluctant to admit that his royalties had been on the decline since the late seventies. He and Edward had gotten used to an extravagant lifestyle and found it hard to cut back. "I do know that they lived high," said Robyn Whitney, a recording studio owner who became close friends with the two of them. "Edward talked a lot about the incredible amount of people who came to the house, the big parties they gave, how often they went to Paris. Rod came from nothing, so he loved being able to have that huge, rambling house and fill it up with Warhols and Picassos."

Rod's inability to improve his deteriorating finances had a bad effect on his relationship with Edward. "Fighting between them was almost constant," Hallam recalled. "It was all about money . . . Rod wasn't doing anything and couldn't pay the bills. There was no more star element, no more parties at the house. Edward liked standing in the shadows, being behind the star. When the limelight started to die, he became more and more unhappy."

No matter how bad things got, Rod wanted to remain in control of the cash flow. "Rod always deposited money in the master account and then Edward would pay the bills. He never knew how much was coming in, because Rod would always pick up the mail," Hallam said. "I worked at the house doing mail-order—I'd watch Rod go out to the street where the mailbox was, sometimes in his underwear. He never wanted Edward to see the checks coming in."

Resentments and grievances continued to pile up between Rod and Edward. Friends disagreed about who was the worst offender. In Robyn Whitney's view, Edward was "an extremely shy, quiet, self-effacing person who could get stomped on. As much as we loved Rod, we saw him be really tough on Ed, insult him in public, belittle him. I said to Edward once, 'You're a 1950s housewife. Somebody else controls the money, but you make everything pretty and give the parties.' And he laughed."

Nearly everyone who knew Rod and Edward saw them as partners for life. Whether this was healthy was another matter. According to Hallam, "They were codependent all the way. Edward was the other side of Rod McKuen— Rod might know a thousand people and call up whoever he wanted, but really it was him and Edward in that world. And Edward didn't have any identity except with Rod. He lived in Rod's shadow—it was his misery, but he couldn't get out of it. The bond between the two of them was so tight, I always believed that their souls had been entangled with each other for many lifetimes."

The world of Rod McKuen seemed to be growing smaller and more isolated as the nineties approached. But if his personal circle had contracted, there were pockets of admirers scattered around the world who still drew strength and inspiration from his work. The McKuen cult had gone underground, but like most true faiths, it survived even when the rest of humanity turned away. There was still a hard core of believers who continued to read his books, listen to his albums, and keep his words close to their hearts. Rod continued to exchange letters and Christmas cards with loyal fans. Many of them passed their love for McKuen and his work on to their children.

Mainstream pop culture sseemed to be leaving Rod behind. In certain hipper circles, though, there was a revival of interest in his work and mystique. Some of the attraction was ironic—what could be more outré (and therefore cool) than embracing an artist tagged as the King of Kitsch? Rediscovery of Rod was part of a growing fascination with beatniks, 1960s bachelor-pad music, and retro aesthetics in general. LPs like *Listen to the Warm* and *The Sea* sounded like artifacts from a distant, more innocent era and could be appreciated more easily by hipsters than, say, a Barry Manilow album. Rod's songs and poems were part of the collective memory of Generation X, and his influence would show itself in some surprising places.

Kurt Cobain recalled a childhood memory of being brought to tears by Terry Jacks's version of "Seasons in the Sun." By some accounts, it was the first record Cobain ever bought. As the front man for Nirvana, he worked up a shambolic cover of the song that surfaced on the band's 2004 box set *With the Lights Out*. Interviews with Cobain indicate he had something of a love-hate relationship with "Seasons in the Sun" and McKuen's oeuvre in general. He may have been drawn to the undercurrents of pain, loneliness, and alienation running through Rod's work. This odd affinity between the grunge rocker and the poet was detected by *Boston Globe* critic Steve Morse, who wrote that Nirvana's songs featured "moronic ramblings by singer-lyricist Cobain, who had an idiotic tendency to sound like the Rod McKuen of hard rock." (According to Rod, he had been in touch with Kurt shortly before the latter man's suicide in April 1994. They had even discussed writing a song together.)

It took a while for Rod to reemerge into the pop culture milieu of the 1990s. He slowly recovered from depression, thanks to the help of friends, Prozac, and (as he told it) his own willpower: "Overcoming it was the hardest battle I ever fought . . . But one day I woke up and I said, 'What in the hell do you have to be depressed about? Nothing.' It was difficult for me to go back out again. But I was determined that I was not going to let depression get me. And it never has since. I have too much to be thankful for. And I have too little time left to be depressed."

Those who knew Rod suggest he suffered relapses of depression toward the end of his life. That he could be productive again after losing years to the disease's worst effects speaks to his deeply ingrained work ethic and will to survive. Surrendering to illness was akin to admitting shame and losing legitimacy—it could not be tolerated. Rod acknowledged that he was sensitive, vulnerable, and prone to heartache. But he always portrayed himself as a self-made and self-repaired man. No one rescued him from disaster or redeemed him from sins of any kind. His account of beating clinical depression is consistent with how he told the grand narrative of his life overall. In the end, the Loner is his own healer and savior.

Sometime in 1990, Rod began working on recording projects at Private Island Audio, an L. A.-area studio owned by Michael J. McDonald (not to be confused with the famous Doobie Brother) and Robyn Whitney. The couple grew close to him over the next few years, as Rod wrestled with doubts about his career. "When he'd get blue, he'd make some comment like, 'Ah, nobody remembers me. They all think I'm dead,'" Whitney said. "I said, 'Oh, that's so not true.' He didn't have a computer at the time, so I went home and got on the internet and searched for the name 'Rod McKuen.' I ended up printing out seven hundred pages of references to his records and books and all these conversations about him. I took the whole pile to his house and said, 'You haven't disappeared. People remember you—this is what I found on the internet, and I haven't found it all.' He went, 'Really . . . ?' It was a joy to point out to him how loved he still was."

Whitney and McDonald didn't see Rod for another six months. When he returned, he came equipped with a laptop. He had taken computer classes and was ready to join the Internet Age.

Radio, TV, movies, records, books—from the start of his career to the apex of his appeal, Rod McKuen had used every form of media available to build an audience. Now the World Wide Web offered him a chance to reclaim a share of what he'd had—and maybe even recruit new fans. *Stanyan Street & Other Sorrows* was thirty years in the past. Could his whispered intimacies even be heard in the culturally cacophonous 1990s? Onstage, Rod had always tried to relate one-to-one with every fan, no matter how big the crowd. Out in the vastness of cyberspace, he now tried to reconnect with the remnants of his enormous following. At sixty-plus, the Lonesome Boy was seeking a private rendezvous with loyal friends and curious strangers once again.

Twelve

~

The Last of the Wine

R OD MCKUEN'S ROAD to recovery as an artist started at the portals of cyberspace. He needed the love and encouragement of his scattered, depleted, but still extant fan base. There were uncounted men and women across the globe who wanted to reconnect with him—if they could only find him. By the mid-nineties, Rod was becoming computer literate and considering ways the internet could aid in his career revival. He couldn't do it alone, though. Fortunately, there were friends on the other side of the world ready to step in and help.

Ken Blackie was a McKuen true believer living in Johannesburg, South Africa. Like so many others of his kind, he had noticed that Rod had seemingly vanished and wondered what had become of the star. Seizing the initiative, Blackie found contact information for his hero via a fan message board and offered to create a website on Rod's behalf. It took a series of letters, faxes, and phone calls to get an initially dubious Rod to give his consent. With help from tech-savvy friends, Blackie launched mckuen.com on April 29, 1998 (Rod's sixty-fifth birthday).

In keeping with McKuen's fondness for hot-air ballooning, the site was dubbed "A Safe Place to Land." Daily pages titled "Flight Plans" provided the sort of ongoing artist-audience interaction that Stanyan's print newsletters had never quite achieved. Rod can be counted as an early blogger—his diarylike musings and extended posts on the site were both true to his natural writing style and very much in keeping with new internet idioms. Interspersed with Rod's comments were personal testimonials about how his work had changed people's lives for the better.

"Rod has 'donated' his love of life to us all. It would be difficult to imagine what a world would be like without him," offered a female devotee in a December 1999 "Flight Plan" post. A man who had admired McKuen's work since the sixties wrote that with Rod "I always felt I had a friend I could count on to help me over the bad times in my life, and to help make the good times even better." Another woman put her feelings in religious terms: "Somewhere along the way, I paraphrased the Twenty Third Psalm to say 'My Rod and his staff comfort me' . . . Rod is everyman, or rather the ideal that we aspire to . . . My life is richer and more meaningful for having him a part of it. And the journey is so much easier knowing that Rod walks alongside at every step."

Fan sites are meant for effusions like this, of course. Even so, Rod's fans offered messages of exceptionally passionate gratitude. He was literally central to some of their lives. "It is simple enough to say that I owe my life to Rod McKuen," wrote an American fan of thirty years standing. "I was fifteen, alone, scared, and knew that there was no one in the world who could possibly understand me or what I was feeling. Curled up on a bed, waiting for the pills to take effect, I saw Rod's face on an album cover across the room. And then his words poured out from the speakers. As I watched that face, and listened to those words, I suddenly no longer felt alone. And I knew that there was at least ONE other person in the world who knew what I was feeling. And so he gave me the will to live."

According to Blackie, "A Safe Place to Land" attracted between twenty thousand and thirty thousand visits per week at its peak. If this level of traffic didn't necessarily translate into big CD or book sales, it did buoy Rod's spirits and give him hope for a comeback. It was obvious he meant a great deal to a significant number of people on at least four continents. He would come to rely on the site to maintain contact with sympathetic souls even when he sometimes retreated from the world, remaining behind the iron gates on Angelo Drive.

Rod's work had mostly disappeared from retail stores. He lacked the support of a major record label or publishing house, but he did have valuable copyrights to offer. In the mid-nineties, he signed a million-dollar worldwide deal with Delta Entertainment to release recordings from his archives via their budget LaserLight label. This put McKuen compilations and various soundtrack albums he controlled in Walmarts, drugstores, truck stops, and other retail outlets across the country. On the other end of the hipness spectrum, Rod's cult favorite *Beatsville* was rereleased by the small P22 label in 1998. Liner-notes writer Kim Cooper reframed the album as "one of the great lost artifacts of late fifties popular culture, an insider's portrait of a Bohemian community delivered with all the wit, affection, and stylistic confidence it deserved."

1998 also saw Rod back on the charts (at least indirectly) with Madonna's "Drowned World/Substitute for Love," a brooding mood piece that sampled the Rod McKuen–Anita Kerr composition "Why I Follow the Tigers." The track (for which Rod and Anita received cowriting credit) became a hit in Europe, Australia, and other markets, proving there was still gold to be mined from Rod's back catalog.

Life was beginning to brighten up again. As he reactivated his career, other passions stirred. Except for occasional cruising encounters, McKuen had been all but celibate since the 1970s. This changed at the end of the nineties, when he had an affair with a young musician from the Midwest. Charlie Hallam was there the night Danny (not his real name) first visited the mansion: "We were in Rod's little bar room when he told us someone he had met was coming by. Edward was there—he was a bit upset. This young fellow came in, and we all had a drink, and I thought, 'Me and Edward should get out of here.' Edward was being nice—as we were leaving, he said, 'Well, the company was fine . . . ' It was a little awkward."

For the next four to five years, Rod and Danny enjoyed a bantering, flirtatious relationship that was affectionate but often on shaky ground. McKuen tried not to feel overly possessive of his much younger friend when Danny spent time with other men—in some ways, Rod was reliving the commitment issues he himself had faced with casual lovers in his twenties. Danny maintained his connection with Rod as collaborator and employee even as the affair cooled down. Robyn Whitney remembers the musician as "a great guy, real sweet and a really good songwriter. Rod bonded with him over that and I thought, 'Oh, great, he's got somebody to write music with.' I think he wanted to mentor him. And then [Danny] kind of backed away for whatever reason, and the next time I mentioned his name to Rod, he sloughed it off. I think his mood would change and he would get disappointed with people." This seems to have been McKuen's last fling outside of his partnership with Edward.

It had been nearly twenty years since Rod had concertized across the planet. His return to the stage was a gradual process. A series of benefit shows supporting AIDS-related charities in the late nineties gave Rod a chance to reintroduce himself to a select and music-savvy audience. Organizer David Galligan recalls McKuen as an enthusiastic and well-received part of these events. His rendition of Kurt Weill's "September Song" was especially memorable: "Maybe it was because of Rod's age—for whatever reason, it was beautifully wrought and left the audience weeping. It's the best I've ever heard that song sung." The poignant nostalgia of "September Song" could be taken as a comment on McKuen's own career as he sought to reclaim his place in popular culture.

By 2001, Rod was booking small gigs in Southern California, Chicago, and other locales. Reviews of his shows were gentler than in the past—he was now treated as a nostalgia act from the seventies, rather than a threat to the cultural standards of Western civilization. In 2003, Rod parleyed his new infatuation with computers into a sponsorship by Hewlett-Packard for a multicity "Prime of Your Life" tour. He kicked things off with an "Old Fashioned Hollywood Party" attended by close friends like Phyllis Diller, as well as Mickey Rooney, Dom DeLuise, Stella Stevens, astronaut Buzz Aldrin, and other notables. From there, he launched the tour with a return to Carnegie Hall for a seventieth birthday concert on April 30. In 1969, Rod had recorded one of his most popular albums there in front of a sold-out crowd. Attendance was more modest this time around, but warm feelings were still rekindled by McKuen and his eight-piece orchestra.

In interviews, Rod joked that the Prime of Your Life Tour was aimed at "seasoned citizens" of a certain age like himself. At every town along the way, the men and (mostly) women who had mused, swooned, and surrendered to McKuen's songs and poems in their youth sat misty-eyed as he performed, and then waited in line for an autograph, a few words, or a touch of his hand after the show. Rod sat at tables to offer brief but meaningful personal time to fans who brought along old autographed copies of his books for a second signature, presented him with trinkets and sweaters, or just sought to testify to their undying devotion over the decades. McKuen received it all with patience and generosity. "He would stop for hours after his shows and talk with people and take pictures with them," Robyn Whitney said. "I saw him go on with one women for twenty minutes about her cat. There was no one he could say no to."

Basking in the love of his fans helped Rod shake off his spells of melancholy. He was in the mood to accept unlikely offers and try new things. In August 2003, he flew to Maui to appear in the world premiere of *Soulmates*, a rock opera with Christian overtones created by local songwriter Patricia Wilson. The production operated on a shoestring budget, which didn't seem to faze Rod—he reveled in his role as the priest who sings a homily on life's joys and sorrows. Decked out in white clerical robes, spreading his arms in benediction, he embodied the part of a loving spiritual elder perfectly.

Director David Galligan hired aspiring L. A. writer/filmmaker Ben McMillan to serve as Rod's personal assistant during *Soulmates*' brief run. "My job was to drive him around and look after him," McMillan recalls. "We became really good friends—he was seventy, but he had the energy of a much younger man. His wit was just crisp and he was really funny. The first time I hung out with him, I wanted to see if I could go drink for drink with him. Just trying to keep pace with him got me hammered . . . oh, God! He was so much fun."

McMillan had known nothing about Rod McKuen before meeting him. Seeing him onstage in Maui was a revelation: "He was magnetic. Rod had a meticulous kind of presence and control—he just stood there and owned the stage like I've never seen before. There was nothing sad or old about him. He commanded the room." The two of them hit it off well enough that Rod asked Ben to run his mail-order operation for him when they got back to L. A. McMillan agreed to come in every two weeks or so to look after the business. He stayed on for twelve years.

As he went through the mail and sent off orders, McMillan got a sense of Rod's core constituency: "There were genuinely appreciative people from everywhere, along with some crazy ones. There were plenty of thank-you letters, things like, 'My husband just died and Rod McKuen is what we listened to when we first made out.' There would be incoming packages with little cat trinkets, random T-shirts, and long handwritten scribbled letters from people who felt like they were talking to him. Maybe some were too crazy to respond to, but Rod responded to almost everybody with a nice letter and autographs for everyone who requested one."

There was a demand for new product, one Rod struggled to fill. Two new poetry collections—*A Safe Place to Land* and *Rusting in the Rain*—were published by Stanyan in 2001 and 2004, respectively. On the recording front, old friend Petula Clark agreed to sing an album's worth of McKuen songs. Veteran producer Jim Pierson was brought in to oversee the project, released as *Solitude & Sunshine* by Stanyan in 2007. "These were not easy sessions for me," Clark recalled. "Apart from one track, I was singing to tracks that were originally done for Rod. That was not the ideal way to record, but we were both enjoying each other's company. It was wonderful spending time with him again."

"Doing that album with Petula was definitely a new lease on life for Rod," Pierson added. "She had mixed feelings about it, but there were some nice things on there. I do know she didn't like riding with Rod after the recording sessions. He would always veer off the road a little bit, even when he hadn't been drinking. It was like riding with Mr. Magoo."

More ambitious was a sprawling retrospective of Rod's RCA period slated for release by Bear Family Records, a collector-oriented label based in Germany. Pierson had pitched the idea for what evolved into a seven-disc, 195-track box set with an accompanying hardback book. Once McKuen agreed to the project, it began to spiral out of control: "It was like pulling teeth to get Rod to rein it in. We wanted the box set to only be from his RCA sessions, but he started coming up with tracks that may or may not have been from that period. Chronologically, it didn't always gel. Rod was into overkill—he wanted to stuff the ballot box." Released in 2007, *If You Go Away: The RCA Years 1965–1970* probably satiated even the most obsessive McKuen cultist. Gems and throwaway tunes were jumbled together; any linear sense of career progression got lost amidst the sheer mass of material. In this respect, the box set accurately reflects Rod's stubbornly subjective telling of his life and career. Plans for a similar box set from his Warner Bros. years never materialized.

Rod's lifelong devotion to work was thwarted by the lingering effects of depression and related issues. "For the years I knew Rod, it took twenty years to get done what should've taken two," Pierson said. "He didn't take care of himself—sometimes he wouldn't sleep for days. He'd be motivated and then you couldn't get ahold of him for weeks. It was a struggle to get things done."

The passing of friends and colleagues weighed upon McKuen's spirit. Jacques Brel, Rock Hudson, Frank Sinatra, Elizabeth Taylor—so many people he had admired and loved were gone. Phyllis Diller was among the close companions from the showbiz wars who remained available to help relive the old times. But there was no denying that the world Rod used to know was rapidly slipping into history. Rod became increasingly insular and homebound as time wore on.

The Angelo Drive mansion was both a refuge and a prison for Rod and Edward. "That house was kind of like a big tomb," Pierson said. "There had been so much activity, so many great parties there back in the seventies. But over the years, the house got trashed up and rooms got closed off. It reminded me of Gloria Swanson's mansion in *Sunset Boulevard*."

Visitors who came through the tall wooden doors at the front entrance didn't see anything amiss at first. If they turned to left, they would find a kitchen and adjoining breakfast nook kept immaculately clean. From there, though, the tidiness slid into chaos, with countless boxes of unopened CDs and LPs piled up in the main corridor, living room, and dining room. If you wished to avoid tripping over the toppling heaps of records and books, you could take the stairs down into the musty basement. One of the lower-level rooms contained thousands of vinyl records and master tapes packed onto ten-foot-high shelves lining the four walls. The other room housed a once-modern, now-outmoded recording studio Rod had installed in the 1970s.

A grand staircase led up to a second floor that was mostly inaccessible to guests. Rod had used his apartment-size bedroom as his primary work-space amidst the same kind of clutter that dominated the downstairs rooms. Edward's quarters were clean, orderly, and impeccably furnished with designer chairs and costly rugs, the domain of a fastidious man who didn't enjoy being surrounded by room after room of dusty memorabilia and unsold merchandise. The contrast between his room and the rest of the mansion spoke volumes about how the two housemates related to one another.

If the mansion grew too oppressive, Rod and Edward could entertain guests in the well-maintained gardens or invite them over for a dip in the pool. An orchid-filled greenhouse and Greco-Roman statuary added to the elegance of the grounds. On the mansion's left side was a raised area known as Boot Hill. Here Rod buried the many dogs and cats he shared his life with over the years, each animal given its own special plaque. ("We were going to bury Mom there, but decided against it," he would tell friends.)

Tom Truhe and his partner were frequent visitors to the McKuen manse during this time. A Palm Springs oral surgeon who met Rod at an AIDS benefit, Truhe recalls his host's small acts of generosity: "The funniest thing about Rod was, you learned not to say 'I like that' when you were walking around his house, because he would give it to you. He collected martini glasses—the most beautiful ones you'd ever seen—and he'd say, 'It's yours.' Edward would then say, 'Please take it!' It would help get rid of the stuff in the house."

Nearly everyone who knew Rod and Edward agreed that the house was much too big for the two men. At night the rambling expanse of the place felt creepy and vulnerable. There were no working alarms or motion-detector lights; Rod and Edward each kept a gun in their bedrooms in case of intruders. "They asked me many times if I'd stay there by myself and watch the cats, and I told them, 'Not a chance,'" Charlie Hallam said. "There were too many doors, too many windows, too many places for people to get in."

For all its gloom and increasing shabbiness, the mansion was Rod's most cherished possession. Edward felt otherwise. According to Hallam, he wanted to force Rod to sell it in 2005 or '06: "I told Edward, 'If you make Rod sell this house and get out of it, he won't survive. If you take it away from him, he'll lose his mind.' It was a necessity to his life." Rod took comfort in holing up among the artifacts he'd gathered over a lifetime, while Edward found pleasure in getting out of the house for his daily runs up and down Angelo Drive. What they loved and how they lived increasingly diverged.

The fortune McKuen had amassed in the 1960s and seventies was severely reduced by the 2000s. He and Edward continued to maintain expensive habits like dining out at Spago and other pricey restaurants around L. A. Rod had become a compulsive online shopper, ordering tens of thousands of dollars' worth of merchandise every month. Cash flow was a serious problem, so Rod started selling off his valuable Apple computer stock, equipment from his recording studio, and several old-model Mercedes. He took out a million-dollar loan that required monthly payments of $14,000—an obligation Edward became aware of only after Rod's death.

Through it all, Edward remained at the center of Rod's life. There were good times together, including visits with Ellen Ehrlich and her husband when the wealthy couple were staying at their second home in Santa Barbara. Friends grew to expect public bickering between the two men, followed by days or weeks of mutual silence and the inevitable reconciliation. The fights were usually over petty things—a perceived insult, a canceled dinner date, a squabble about a costly purchase. It was a pattern of behavior Rod and Edward had maintained for decades. Still, an uneasy stability was not the same as happiness.

A hunger for love and human connection continued to plague Rod. Writing a letter to poet A. D. Winans on a sleepless night in May 2007, he grieved over the loss of his beloved cat Kubby, "the closest thing I had left to a family." His relations with Edward were as complicated and difficult as ever: "We are too close. Life was never easy with him and I'm sure his appraisal of me would be the same. Still I love him and would do anything for him, but our life together seems increasingly a series of threats and demands and negotiations of silences from me. I am too old to quarrel and find it as waste of time, so the silences between us grows longer."

Lovers, brothers, comrades, codependents—no one will probably ever know for certain what Rod McKuen and Edward Habib meant to each other as they approached the ends of their lives. In Rod's case, the best guess is that he still loved his partner, despite their long-standing and often bitter differences. In 2010, he began performing "Happy Anniversary," a collaboration with Jacques Brel finished many years after the latter's death. Its lyrics describe a couple "still causing one another pain / And using silence to complain" who nevertheless choose to remain together. In the end, Rod sings, they'd be lost without one another. Ruefully bittersweet, "Happy Anniversary" may be the closest thing to a public statement about his life with Edward that Rod ever made.

A year or so earlier, Rod and Edward had told friends they were getting married. California had recently legalized gay marriage, and many longtime couples like themselves were heading to the altar. "Rod said that he'd proposed," Robyn Whitney recalled. "I do special events planning, so I offered to do his wedding. He said, 'No, no, we're just going to the courthouse.' I said, 'Rod, you've waited, what, fifty-five years to do this? You need to make this a big deal, and your house needs to see a big party again.' And Edward said, 'Yeah, we need to have a big party!'"

Tying the knot made practical sense. The Angelo Drive house was in Rod's name; passing it on to Edward would have been easier and less costly, tax-wise, if they were legally married. In the end, though, Rod chose not to go through with it. The sad irony of it all wasn't lost on Whitney: "Rod had created his own wedding ceremony—and then he never used it for himself."

Perhaps Rod was still unwilling to publicly acknowledge his relationship with Edward. Or maybe marriage was a symbol of finality that he wished to avoid. Closing doors and summing things up was difficult for Rod. He rarely talked about mortality and what he might leave behind. For a man who was so proud of shattering sales records and invading every art form he could, he was curiously unconcerned about how he would be remembered.

He did take a couple of steps toward preserving his legacy. One involved setting up a foundation that would fund a combination artists' retreat and archive for his enormous record and book collections. Toward that end, he purchased a stretch of boulder-strewn land in the San Bernardino Mountains northeast of L. A. Though Rod would visit the property from time to time, nothing was ever built up there and the land became a financial burden.

Fans had been waiting for Rod to publish his memoirs for decades. *Finding My Father* had been a veiled and fragmented account of his early years, raising as many questions as it answered. Rod was clearly ambivalent about putting his life on record—he discussed doing so with at least one prospective biographer in the early 1970s, then backed off with the excuse that he needed to wait until a forthcoming critical book about him was published. (This never appeared.) In 2012, McKuen got in touch with his literary agent, Helen Brann, and told her that he was finally writing his autobiography. "With your own story, the right organization of your experiences, the photos, and if you are ready to tell your true story (are you?), you can write a bestseller," she told him. Sketchy evidence indicates that Rod wrote a chapter or two but didn't complete the honest narrative Brann was hoping for.

Those closest to Rod noticed him retreating more and more as he approached eighty. Though his refusal to return calls or answer messages could be maddening, old friends remained fiercely loyal to him. After knowing McKuen for decades, Jim Pierson, Robyn Whitney, and Mike McDonald became something of an extended family and support group for Rod and Edward. Ben McMillan continue to assist with Rod's mail-order business even when his own screenwriting career took off; he would bring his wife and their cats along for visits to the mansion. Rod was still a loner, but in his declining years, he was not alone.

Occasionally, new faces would turn up at his door. Among them were singer Aaron Freeman and Freeman's producer Ben Vaughn, who were invited over for visit after the two recorded an album of all-McKuen material together. *Marvelous Clouds* (2012) was the freshest, most sympathetic take on

Rod's songwriting to appear in decades—its versions of tunes like "As I Love My Own," "Jean," and "The Lovers" were insightful, energetic, and irony-free. In interviews, Freeman (then taking a break from his popular alt-rock duo Ween) said that going through recovery from substance abuse gave him an appreciation for Rod's gentle, life-affirming lyrics. For his part, Rod was delighted with *Marvelous Clouds* and the positive attention it was bringing to his work.

Vaughn returned for several more visits after his first meeting with Rod. "He had this comforting charisma about him—I felt really great in his presence," he recalled. "The minute you were in his sphere, you felt something positive. He was very generous with his time for such a private guy. I came away understanding his fanatical fan base." A vivid impression of the man lingered in his mind: "He looked like a sailor to me, like a thinner Ernest Hemingway with a white beard. He told me that he wasn't recognized on the street anymore, but that people recognized his voice. I was struck by how humble he was for a guy who had been as famous as he had been."

Once an international phenomenon, now an idol of other days living in seclusion, Rod had achieved a measure of peace about the arc of his career. He told Vaughn that a lot of people assumed he was already under the sod—"I get a lot of mail addressed to the estate of Rod McKuen," he said. The live appearances dwindled away; new posts on "A Safe Place to Land" became less frequent, and then stopped in April 2011. In his mansion crammed with memories, Rod looked back upon his own past, much as he had studied the illicit loves of others as a struggling poet. If he came across as humble to visitors like Vaughn, he surely felt the stubborn pride of a self-made man.

"Rod was struck by all that he'd seen and done over the years—I think that's why he couldn't get rid of anything that people had given to him or that he'd collected," Whitney said. "A couple of times he said to me, 'I've had the most astounding life. I've been everywhere and known everybody, and it's just amazing.' He was grateful."

Amazement and gratitude aren't bad notes to exit the stage on. Even Rod couldn't really explain how a taxi dancer's love child ended up in a Beverly Hills mansion with a star on Hollywood Boulevard. Regret was built into the journey from the very beginning—still, it was his life to live as he chose. "If I knew another route I would not use it," he once wrote. "Believe that, for the only lies I tell are to myself."

Coda

~

I'll Say Goodbye

ROD MCKUEN was often accused of sugarcoating the world for mass consumption. But actually, most of the happy times he described in his songs and poems were fleeting. There were pretty butterflies and marvelous clouds floating through the skies of the passing moment, but no promised joy waiting at the end of the rainbow.

In the last years of his life, McKuen became increasingly feeble and bedridden. Injuries sustained falling off a ladder and down a staircase further weakened him. A handyman (Chris) and a maid (Olga) helped him and Edward maintain the house and grounds. But this small household staff could do only so much to keep Rod safe and comfortable as his body failed him.

Edward was worried. He and Rod had grown old together. With decades of near-breakups behind them, they had lived out an indissoluble marriage in all but name. Despite his own health problems—at least one stroke and increasing deafness—Edward was in better shape to look after Rod than vice versa. He knew there was only so much he could do—his partner was independent, ornery, and unwilling to see a doctor. With Rod, the last thing to go would be his sense of control.

The inevitable happened one night in early January 2015. Rod had contracted pneumonia and had been in bed for a week. Against his wishes, Edward and Chris decided to call for medical help. Rod screamed and pleaded to be left in his own bed as he was carried down the stairs and taken to the hospital. After several days' treatment, he was transferred to a rehabilitation center. Edward visited him there once and sometimes twice a day. It was becoming harder for Rod to talk or swallow. As Edward leaned close to hear his old friend's faint voice, he must have known how serious the illness was. But Rod had been through so much in his life that it was hard to imagine him gone. Edward told friends later that he expected McKuen to pull through.

At around 3 a.m. on January 29, Edward was told by phone that Rod had stopped breathing. He met Chris at the rehab facility, only to be told that the patient had been transferred to Cedars-Sinai Medical Center. When the two of them arrived there, Rod had already passed. Edward was in shock as he spent a few moments alone with the man who had shaped his life for fifty years. He could not believe Rod was dead.

Jim Pierson was asked to give a statement to the press. Media outlets around the world reported that Rod had died of respiratory arrest. (The death certificate gave cardiopulmonary arrest as the primary cause.) Obituaries appearing the following day in the *New York Times*, the *Los Angeles Times*, the *Washington Post*, and other papers echoed the raves and jeers of forty years earlier—the massive sales and hostile critical reception for the "King of Kitsch" were cited, along with Rod's convoluted résumé and snatches of his poems. Rod was remembered as a benign mass-appeal artist and charming eccentric with links to the counterculture of the sixties and New Age movement of the seventies. Much of the information in the obits came from Rod's own writings and was repeated without fact-checking; in any case, it all seemed to come from a long time ago.

Rod was buried near his mother in Westwood Memorial Park. The memorial service was kept small, with only Edward and a few others attending.

The aftermath of his death was chaotic and acrimonious. Edward inherited the mansion and the rights to Rod's intellectual property. No provision was made for preserving McKuen's papers or recordings. Friends had tried to get Rod to draw up detailed plans for what would become of his enormous personal archives, to no avail. "Ada Sands [Rod's attorney] was after him for years to get his affairs in order," Pierson recalled. "Even though he had the ego, he didn't put forth effort to get things like that done. It was pathetic and tragic."

Overwhelmed and unprepared for life on his own, Edward withdrew from old friends and hired Charlie Hallam (a licensed real estate agent) to put the Angelo Drive house on the market. Everything else that could not be easily sold, he wanted thrown away as quickly as possible. Some of Rod's more valuable artifacts—art pieces, a few notebooks and manuscripts—were auctioned off to collectors and speculators. The rest went into the garbage.

There's some dispute over why Edward acted as he did. Robyn Whitney thought of him as a sheltered, frightened widower unable to cope with his loss—"He just wanted to be done with it all, as if it would help his grief go away." According to Hallam, the motives for Habib's actions were much more complicated: "Edward wanted to destroy all things Rod McKuen. He had wanted to be done with Rod's business decades ago, and he feared that, if something happened with it, he would get sucked back in and be working again. So he threw everything away, seven [dumpster] bins' worth."

Hallam says he had to talk Edward into saving Rod's huge tape library of master recordings from the trash: "We had ninety-four file drawers and a bunch of other boxes full of all the records of all the deals Rod had made going back to the seventies—Edward wanted to throw all those things into the bin along with the master tapes. He finally said, 'OK, you're gonna take the tapes, but you're going to have to pay to store them.'" Months of negotiations with potential buyers failed to produce a deal. At this writing, the tapes remain in storage, their fate uncertain.

The mansion at 1155 Angelo Drive was sold in October 2015 for $12.9 million. Edward Habib bought a three-bedroom ranch house in the Hollywood Hills and seemed ready to close the door on his long life with Rod. But it wasn't that simple, said Hallam: "I said to him, 'Edward, now you have your own house, just like you've been wanting for the past twenty-five years. If you had the opportunity to go back to Angelo with Rod or be here living your own life for one, what would you do?' He didn't hesitate. He said, 'I'd go back to Angelo with Rod.'"

Edward Habib died on May 12, 2018. He had been suffering from heart disease and the effects of old age. He was buried next to Rod. With his passing, the closest living link to Rod McKuen was gone.

It's tempting to think Rod somehow wanted his legacy to vanish with him after he died. He took few practical steps to ensure his work would be preserved. In so many poems and songs, he had portrayed himself as a wanderer taking comfort where he could and leaving no trace after moving on. Then again, he had always counted on good fortune and a few beautiful strangers to come through in the end. Maybe he knew his legacy would survive if it truly deserved to. As it is, McKuen's memory is held close by a diminished but enduring circle of believers who still find inspiration and healing in his work. In building a brand, Rod created a community that has outlived him.

Whatever the fate of his archives or the status of his copyrights, Rod McKuen's influence still lingers in subtle but discernable ways. At the peak of his popularity, he helped to soften and break down borders between generations, artistic genres, moralities, identities. As songwriter, poet, performer, and human-rights advocate, he insisted that love was a language that needed to be spoken plainly, directly, and without reservation. In these times, when the hunger for human connection has grown only more desperate, McKuen's message has a relevance that transcends concerns of hipness, fashion, and aesthetic taste. From the first time he took to the radio airwaves as a teenage Lonesome Boy to his last days as a kindly elder offering "A Safe Place to Land," Rod never apologized for aiming straight for the heart. He knew it was the warmest place to be.

ACKNOWLEDGMENTS

Tμis book had its genesis in 1986, when Jim Morton agreed to include my essay on Rod McKuen in his small press magazine *Pop Void*. At the time, Rod's name was still a punch line among the hipper precinct of pop culture devotees. Jim's willingness to let me treat my subject seriously encouraged me to think about McKuen's place in history further. Thanks for getting the warmth under way, Jim!

Over the years, Seattle artist Jim Blanchard has burned and sent me CDs of choice McKuen recordings, enabling me to deepen my familiarity with Rod's enormous catalog. He has been an ongoing research source I've very much appreciated.

Television and record producer Jim Pierson became an early ally once this biography got under way in earnest. He has turned into a trusted and exceptionally generous friend. Jim drew upon his huge archive of McKuen TV appearances to supply me with clips from all phases of Rod's career. He was especially helpful in sharing interviews conducted with Rod, Edward Habib, Wade Alexander, Phyllis Diller, and others for his still unfinished McKuen documentary. I've also benefited immensely from Jim's memories of working with Rod over a twenty-year period. I owe you an excellent vegan meal for all of this, Jim. Several, actually.

Music historian/producer Andy Zax has also lent crucial assistance far beyond the bounds of normal generosity. His involvement in McKuen's recording legacy began with a presentation on Rod at Seattle's annual EMP Pop Conference in 2015. He has been unstinting in providing me with insight into Rod's life and work, as well as sharing ultra-rare materials I never thought I'd have access to. Thanks to Andy, I was able to hear recordings of Rod as a teenage radio host and San Francisco club performer. I am hopeful that ongoing efforts to preserve what remains of McKuen's personal archives are successful. I look forward to more marathon conversations with Mr. Zax, whose efforts on my behalf I can never adequately repay.

Early in my research, Robyn Whitney and her husband, Michael J. McDonald, shared intimate stories about Rod, whom they worked with as a studio client for many years. They considered Rod and his partner Edward to be dear friends and gave me a full sense of them as individual people. We spent hours on the phone and at their studio exploring the complexities and paradoxes of Rod and what he meant to those who loved him.

Editor Yuval Taylor provided enthusiastic encouragement once I started writing. He introduced me to writer/archivist Robert Nedelkoff, who helped me sharpen my thoughts about Rod and put me on the trail of some important sources. I'm especially grateful to Robert for connecting me with Columbia University Libraries' Tara L. Key, who used her expertise to dig deeply and discerningly into the Random House archives housed there. The files she uncovered offered a detailed glimpse into Rod's relationship with his first book publisher. (Tara is a founding member of the veteran indie-rock band Antietam, who are worth checking out if you are unfamiliar with them.)

As the book progressed, I was able to interview many people who knew Rod or had insights into the places and scenes he had been part of. I was often amazed at their willingness to share knowledge, stories, and memories so freely. They include Rose Adkins, Morgan Ames, Gordon Anderson, Don Bachardy, Paula Bailey, the late Kaye Ballard, Sharon Barr, Tosh Berman, Helene Blue,

Jonathyne Briggs, Denny Bruce, Holly Yarbrough Burnett, Dr. Joe Carberry, Dick Carlson, Carleton Carpenter, Steve Causey, Jack Cecchini, Petula Clark, Alan Clayton, Kim Cooper, Dickie Davis, Connie de Nave, Laine Donaldson, Ireyne Duncan, Lou Duro, Henry Edwards, Alan Eichler, Dolan Ellis, Clear Englebert, Jack Estes, Todd Everett, Michael Feinstein, Gillian Frank, Sgt. Herb Friedman, Hy Fujita, Ray Gallagher, David Galligan, Bob Gentry, Phyllis Gittman, Annie Yarbrough Graves, the late Gordon Greb, Rebecca Greer, Mark Griffin, Corky Hale, Charles Hallam, Howard Heitmeyer, Jerry Heleva, Judy Henske, Chuck Herman, Lee Hershberg, Abby Hirsch, Val Holley, the late Tab Hunter, Richard Kegler, Paul Knobloch, Johnny Lieske, Jerry Lonn, Murray Lorber, Jim MacKrell, Lincoln Mayorga, Barry McGuire, Ben McMillan, Lee Mendelson, Gene Merlino, Jorge Mester, Ellen Ehrlich Mimran, Karen Newquist, Karl Newquist, David Nutter, Cindy Oliveira, Gigi Perreau, Bookman Peters, Felice Picano, Charles and Pamela Plymell, Art Podell, Sue Rainey, Genya Raven, Steven Reiter, Pat Rocco, Ada Sands, Tommy Sands, Aram Saroyan, Dr. Lee Schaller, Al Schmitt, Bob Shane, Susan Shapiro, Ben Shecter, Robert Sherman, the late Frank Sinatra Jr., Joe Smith, Michael Snyder, Randy Sparks, Judith Tane, Peter Trachtenberg, Donn Trenner, Terry Trotter, Tom Truhe, Tim Turner, Bert Van Breda, Steven Vando, Ben Vaughn, Arjan Vlakveld, Robert Ward, Bob Weedn, Allen F. Weitzel, Carol White, and A. D. Winans.

Thanks to Scott Brown of Eureka Books in Eureka, California, for sharing rare scripts from Rod's early-1950s radio program with me.

Chris Freeman and Dione Oliver at USC's ONE Archives in Los Angeles lent vital assistance in providing documents from Rod's time with the Mattachine Society.

I am indebted to Professor Michael Bronski of Harvard University for helping me place Rod's life and career in the context of LBGTQ history. He enriched this book by sharing his scholarship with me over many months of conversations and email exchanges

Ken Blackie was very helpful in answering questions about the history of "A Safe Place to Land," the Rod McKuen fan website that he continues to archive. This site is an invaluable chronicle of Rod's thoughts from 1998 to 2011, as well as a source for revealing testimonies from McKuenites from around the world.

Special thanks go to Jill Bonney, Jack Goodwin, Eric Yaeger, and Robyn Zadrozny, key members of the ever-faithful Rod Squad, the veteran band of fans who remain true to McKuen and his memory.

Long and sometimes geeky conversations with esteemed friends Sam Allen, Craig Bickhardt, Ted Burke, Joe Davis, Doug Stewart, and Jan Tonnesen tested my McKuen IQ and forced me to defend my opinions about his oeuvre. Regular get-togethers with writing comrades Joann Wilson and Clint Wilhelm at Biddle's Escape coffeehouse in Wilkinsburg, Pennsylvania helped keep me on track. And I cannot forget those long and rollicking drives up and down California with Scott Lawrence Whitman while listening to a tape of *Rod McKuen Takes a San Francisco Hippie Trip* (a bowdlerized version of his *Beatsville* LP). Roll on, Kranko!

Working with David Dunton of the Harvey Klinger Agency was an honor and pleasure throughout the process of making this book a reality. We were in harmony about the direction of the project from our first meeting at his office onward—he knew there was a fascinating story to tell from the start. David remained faithful to the book and made sure it found a good home.

John Cerullo, Bernadette Malavarca, Carol Flannery Cerullo and Clare Cerullo of Backbeat Books have shown patience and understanding as I've brought this book to completion. I'm impressed and gratified that they took on a biography of Rod McKuen purely on the merits of his story. Having a skilled and insightful editorial department on my side has been a true blessing.

My wife, Janet Ingram, has put up with Rod McKuen as a phantom houseguest for quite some time now. I think she finds him interesting and amusing—in any case, she has been completely behind me and this project from the start. (The fact that her performing alter ego Dicey Stewart, of Dicey and Paprika, has performed Rod's poetry onstage may have helped a bit.) Janet read various drafts of the book with sympathetic and discerning eyes, and her suggestions for improvement have always felt right. I must take slight issue with Rod—it *does* matter who you love and who loves you. Janet's love and guidance have been essential in making this book a reality.

NOTES

Introduction

"America's . . . poet" *The Dick Cavett Show*, ABC, March 30, 1972.

"I don't think . . . written" *A Man Alone*. YouTube. Directed by Arjan Vlakveld. Amsterdam: Netherlands Public Broadcasting System, 2006.

"McKuen's place . . . were remarkable" Michael Feinstein interview with author, August 2018.

"Over the years . . . used to say" Jack Goodwin, email message to author, April 22, 2018.

"There was a mystery . . . solve it" Rose Adkins interview with author. October 2017.

Chapter One

"very hard to please . . . long stove poker" Letter from Mrs. Jesse Woolever to R. E. Lee Steiner, Oregon State Hospital, Salem, Oregon, January 30, 1936. I am grateful to "Jean" for providing me with scans of this and other Woolever family documents by email.

"The economic interest . . . dance hall" Paul Goalby Cressey, *The Taxi-Dance Hall: A Study in Commercialized Recreation & City Life*. Reprint, Chicago: University of Chicago Press, 2008. 94.

"romantic interest . . . sex game" Cressey, 50.

"the physical . . . motherhood" *Oakland Tribune*, August 7, 1933 and February 12, 1934.

"It didn't matter . . . or a week" Rod McKuen, *Finding My Father*. Second edition, New York: Berkley Publishing, 1977. 178.

"Nobody really . . . rumpus inside" McKuen, *Finding My Father*. 34.

"If my stepfather . . . several times" *Santa Cruz Sentinel*, May 7, 1982. 7; *People*, August 16, 1982. 233.

"We were friends . . . loved him" McKuen, *Finding My Father*. 65.

"Innocence . . . world" McKuen, *Finding My Father*. 66.

Chapter Two

"The Nevada School of Industry: An Appraisal," Nevada Legislative Counsel Bureau report. Bulletin 34. December 1958. https://www.leg.state.nv.us/Division/Research/Publications/InterimReports/1959/Bulletin034.pdf (accessed June 23, 2018).

"At times . . . was happening" McKuen, *Finding My Father*. 68]

"I was just pretending . . . something happened" McKuen, *Finding My Father*. 73.

"horsing around . . . worth mentioning" McKuen, *Finding My Father*, 80-81.

"I felt unhappy . . . at once" McKuen, *Finding My Father*. 83.

"It was almost . . . was illegitimate" McKuen, *Finding My Father*. 95.

"somewhat of a misfit . . . extrovert" "Flight Plan," A Safe Place to Land, April 16, 2001. http://www.rodmckuen.org/flights/160401.htm (accessed March 1, 2018).

"who possessed him . . . as well" *Inside Stanyan*. Vol. 1, No. 3. Summer 1975. 50.

"a leader . . . broadcasters" Gordon Greb interview with author, July 2015.

"Professor . . . yesterday" *Rendezvous with Rod*. Unpublished radio script. August 5, 1950.

"Let me explain . . . up to you" *Rendezvous with Rod.* Unpublished radio script. December 9, 1950.

"that madcap meddler . . . I want you" *Rendezvous with Rod.* Unpublished radio script. December 6, 1952.

"Sweetie, no matter . . . whole world" Jack French, "Lonesome Gal Wasn't So Lonesome." http://www.otr.com/lonesome_gal.html (accessed November 10, 2017).

"You're very close . . . Yours and mine" *Rendezvous with Rod.* 1953 air check.

"The kid fascinated . . . a long time" *San Francisco Examiner*, May 29, 1951.

"Oldsters haven't heard . . . sick cat" *Oakland Tribune*, August 15, 1952.

"This is for the poor . . . for the wishless" *Rendezvous with Rod.* Unpublished radio script. January 10, 1953.

"Even a rumor . . . Communist party" David K. Johnson, *The Lavender Scare: The Cold War Persecution of Gays and Lesbians in the Federal Government.* Chicago: University of Chicago Press, 2009. 169

"a bunch of homosexuals . . . better than bars" San Francisco Alpha Chapter #109 meeting minutes. ONE Archives, University of Southern California.

"homosexual integration . . . young boys, anything" Kevin Killlian, "Spicer and the Mattachine," in *After Spicer: Critical Essays*, ed. John Emil Vincent. Middletown, Connecticut: Wesleyan University Press, 2011. 130.

"Rod McKuen set the whole thing . . . no one seemed to like" Gerard Brissette interview by John D'Emilio, November 1, 1976. International Gay Information Center Collection, Special Collections, New York Public Library.

Chapter Three

"Everybody else . . . going to learn" McKuen interview with Ben Vaughn, 2008.

"Wonder if you . . . Sure hope so" *Reno* (NV) *Gazette-Journal*, August 8, 1953, 5; *Inside Stanyan.* Early Spring, 1976. 5.

"the girl . . . down with" *Inside Stanyan.* Early Spring, 1976. 5.

"One of my creations was Moran . . . war criminal." McKuen interview with Ben Vaughn, 2008; "Flight Plan," A Safe Place to Land, February 22, 1999 and October 23, 2000. http://www.rodmckuen.org/flights/220299.htm and http://www.rodmckuen.org/flights/231000.htm (accessed June 23, 2018).

"We were headquartered . . . back to entertaining" McKuen interview with Ben Vaughn, 2008.

"loud and sensual . . . ape-like stance" Inside Stanyan, Early Spring, 1976. 5.

[Rod's boyish vigor . . . In addition to these live performances, Rod may have appeared in up to five Japanese movies released by Toho Films, a famous studio responsible for such blockbusters as Seven Samurai and Godzilla. One of these films, The Boy and the General, was supposedly scheduled for American as well as Japanese release. McKuen talked about these films in interviews and in press releases; no further confirmation of their existence has been discovered.]

"Until I was in a situation . . . myself" Inside Stanyan. Early Spring, 1976. 8.

"you laugh . . . male prostitute" Rod McKuen, . . . and autumn came. New York: Pageant Press, 1954. 12, 20, 31, 53.

"Rod had a bio . . . amazing" Randy Sparks interview with author, January 6, 2016 and January 5, 2018 email. Rod made it a point of being photographed with celebrities all through his career. The photo Sparks referred to is apparently lost.

"Life as a protégé . . . parties" McKuen, Finding My Father, 194.

"I got my first acting job . . . you've been here all day" McKuen interview with Ben Vaughn, 2008.

"All you had to do . . . publicity circuit" Val Holley interview with author, November 2017.

"One agent would promise . . . pass him on" Robert Hofler, The Man Who Invented Rock Hudson: The Pretty Boys and Dirty Deals of Henry Willson, New York: Carroll & Graf, 2005. 213.

"Rod McKuen broke his act . . . rocked the room" Mike Connolly column, February 21, 1956. Quote sent to author by Connolly biographer Val Holley, November 2, 2017.

Overall, the album . . . .eager to please According to Rod, his first LP was *Lonely Summer*, recorded before *Lazy Afternoon* and released on the small Bond Records label. Its tracks were a mix of standards and original tunes, several of which appeared on later McKuen albums. It may have remained in the can for a year of two—several sources give early 1958 as its release date.

"Chuck Weedn . . . all it took" Randy Sparks interview, January 6, 2016. The episode of Jack Benny's *Shower of Stars* featuring Rod aired January 10, 1957 on CBS-TV. Bob Crosby, Jayne Mansfield, Vincent Price, and Liberace were among the other guests.

"I was standing on a corner . . . ran off" *Lincoln* (Nebraska) *Star*, October 21, 1956, 2.

"it wouldn't lead . . . most of all" *Oakland Tribune*, January 31, 1957, 31.

"we'd go to . . . lovely guy" Corky Hale interview with author, March 23, 2015.

"There was no place . . . Rock Hudson" Sparks email to author, January 5, 2018. Story confirmed by Bob Weedn, Chuck Weedn's nephew.

"Life wasn't all . . . me on that" McKuen interview with Ben Vaughn, 2008.

Chapter Four

"The story goes . . . looking at Edward" Charlie Hallam interview with author, May 24, 2018.

"We hit it off . . . start of it" Ellen Ehrlich Mimran interview with author, April 11, 2016.

"We were . . . dyed his hair" Ellen Ehrlich Mimran interview with author, April 11, 2016.

"Rod was . . . wanted to go" Ellen Ehrlich Mimran interview with author. April 11, 2016.

"I think he might . . . that milieu" Ellen Ehrlich Mimran interview with author, April 11, 2016.

"I was at a party . . . totally agreed" Ben Shecter interview with author, January 19, 2018.

"He was a sweet, gentle . . . commitment" Ben Shecter interview with author, January 19, 2018.

"I think when . . . never really had" Ben Shecter interview, January 19, 2018.

"I didn't make . . . the fish, period" Rod McKuen interview with Ben Vaughn, 2008.

None of these LPs . . . Among McKuen's many compositions from this period was "Saturday Night and Sunday Morning Too." For whatever reason, Rod copyrighted the song in June 1961 under the pseudonym "Big Bill Hooper"—the name of his hated stepfather.

"sound like . . . next song" Benson Green, *Stranger in Town*. Kapp Records 3226. 1961. Liner notes.

"Though not dwelling . . . catch up" "Flight Plan," A Safe Place to Land, July 15, 2003. http://www.rodmckuen.org/flights/150703.htm (accessed June 23, 2018).

"Ronnie was . . . Danny Rose" Chuck Herman interview with author, July 28, 2015.

"Trudy was . . . getting into it" Chuck Herman interview with author, July 28, 2015.

"She required rockers . . . fuckin' twist" Genya Raven interview with author, December 31, 2015.

"I didn't understand . . . always a surprise" Connie de Nave interview with author, January 26, 2016.

"Every place . . . in trouble" Connie de Nave interview with author, January 26, 2016.

"You have to understand . . . would've done it" de Nave interview, January 26, 2016.

"Folk music . . . good folk stuff" Chuck Herman interview, July 28, 2015.

"We were . . . somebody's arm" Rod McKuen interviewed by Jim Pierson, 2011.

"Rod was not . . . as a singer" Chuck Herman interview, July 28, 2015.

"He had a little . . . these little notes" Ellen Ehrlich Mimran interview, April 11, 2016.

"We drifted . . . my own path" Ben Shecter interview, January 19, 2017.

Chapter Five

"Rod was the most . . . miles in them" Barry McGuire interview with author, April 27, 2015.

"Rod's mom . . . her family" Barry McGuire interview with author, April 27, 2015.

"He didn't seem morbid . . . though his words" Barry McGuire interview with author, April 27, 2015.

"Rod seemed to . . . over his poems" Art Podell interview with author, April 21, 2015.

"The folk community . . . responded differently" Art Podell interview with author, April 21, 2015.

"He was accepted . . . few folk songs" Art Podell interview with author, April 21, 2015.

"I think Rod . . . nobody discussed it" Art Podell interview with author, April 21, 2015.

"The folk world . . . who he was" Art Podell interview with author, April 21, 2015.

"I never knew . . . good input" Barry McGuire interview with author, April 27, 2015.

"the sensible loners . . . $500 fine" John Carlyle, *Under the Rainbow: An Intimate Memoir of Judy Garland, Rock Hudson & My Life in Old Hollywood*. New York: Carroll & Graf, 2006. 160.

"We were together . . . he didn't" Ellen Ehrlich Mimran interview with author, April 11, 2016.

"Goodbye Antoine . . . still so alive" "Le Moribond" translation found on Genius. com, https://genius.com/Jacques-brel-le-moribond-english-translation-lyrics (accessed June 21, 2018).

"I asked him . . . 'The Lovers'" "Flight Plan," A Safe Place to Land, April 7 and 8, 2007. http://www.rodmckuen.org/flights/070407.htm (accessed June 23, 2018).

"Brel didn't . . . English-speaking world" Alan Clayson, *Jacques Brel: La Vie Bohème*. New Malden, Surrey: Chrome Dreams, 2010; email from Clayson to author, April 21, 2015.

"When I first saw . . . saying" Rod McKuen interview with Jim Pierson, 2011.

"We don't have . . . do vicariously" Edwin Newman interview with Rod McKuen, ASCAP Today, June 1969. 16.

"I'd recorded . . . on my property" Glenn Yarbrough interview with Todd Everett for *If You Go Away: The RCA Years*. Bear Family Records BCD 16122. 2007. Liner notes.

"Rod finally talked . . . work for you" Charlie Hallam interview with author, May 24, 2018.

"Rod was really . . . loved his work" Annie Yarbrough Graves interview, with author May 18, 2015.

"Rod and Glenn . . . they weren't" Paula Bailey interview with author, May 20, 2015.

"I was going . . . I'd ever made" Glenn Yarbrough interview with Todd Everett for *If You Go Away: The RCA Years*. Liner notes.

"Glenn was recording . . . and more" "Flight Plan," A Safe Place to Land, April 7 and 8, 2007. http://www.rodmckuen.org/flights/070407.htm (accessed June 23, 2018).

"I'd go through . . . sixty-five thousand copies" Edward Habib interview with Jim Pierson, 2006.

"Ed would go . . . nothing about this" Rod McKuen interview with Jim Pierson, 2011.

"I'd pick up a book . . . my poems by heart" Rod McKuen interview with Jim Pierson, 2011.

"I knew the hills . . . rape of time" Rod McKuen, *Stanyan Street & Other Sorrows.* Reprint, New York: Random House. 1966. 13, 15, 81.

"Rod came to me . . . happening to him" Paula Bailey interview with author, May 20, 2015.

Chapter Six

"communicate with people" David Allyn, *Make Love, Not War: The Sexual Revolution: An Unfettered History.* Boston: Little, Brown. 2000. 29.

"I checked his figures . . . he accepted" Nan Talese interview with author, June 30, 2016.

"I introduced him . . . standing ovation" Nan Talese interview with author, June 30, 2016.

"Bob Bernstein . . . new Mercedes" Rod McKuen interview with Jim Pierson, 2011.

"I gave her some ideas . . . started all over again," Interview with Anita Kerr and Rod McKuen, Warner Bros. promotional single PRO 262, 1967. In a 2003 interview with journalist Todd Everett, Glenn Yarbrough recalled the origins of *The Sea* a bit differently: "I had always wanted to do a spoken-word album about the sea and felt that Rod was the person to write it. I took it to RCA, where I had a contract at the time. They said, 'What do we want that for—you're a singer.' So I took it over to [Elektra Records founder] Jac Holzman, who'd been my roommate in college, and he put up the money. In the meantime, Rod had disappeared. Finally, I heard from him—he'd cut a version of the album with [arranger] Arthur Greenslade. I had to pay Jac Holzman the hundred grand. Neely Plumb told me that RCA had turned down the project because Rod had told them that if I made the record, he wouldn't record for the label anymore. This was a guy who hadn't had any hits and owed the company money on the project . . . "

The name doesn't matter . . . said here" Rod McKuen, The San Sebastian Strings, *The Sea*, Warner Bros. WS 1670, 1967. Liner notes. Jesse Pearson also narrated the 1968 San Sebastian Strings LP *Home to the Sea*, as well as two volumes of *The Body Electric*, recordings of erotic Walt Whitman poems released on Rod's Stanyan label in the early seventies.

"Really, (Sloopy) . . . very nice to me" *The Mike Douglas Show*. Group W Productions. December 30, 1969.

"skips prettily . . . stay warm" Jack Fincher, "What? A Best-Selling Poet?" *Life*. February 9, 1968, 35

"fanatically dedicated . . . outlet for people" Fincher, "What? A Best-Selling Poet?" *Life*. February 9, 1968, 36.

"I had a tip . . . help pay Glenn" Rod McKuen interview with Todd Everett for *If You Go Away: The RCA Years*. Liner notes. 2003.

"I told Rod . . . out of my life" Glenn Yarbrough interview with Todd Everett for *If You Go Away: The RCA Years*. Liner notes. 2003.

Chapter Seven

"Nevertheless . . . more Rod McKuens" Bennett Cerf interview, Columbia University Libraries oral history project transcript. 889. http://www.columbia.edu/cu/lweb/digital/collections/nny///////cerfb/transcripts/cerfb_1_19_899.html (accessed June 23, 2018).

"I am concerned . . . too thin" Nan Talese to Rod McKuen, February 9, 1968.

"In one year . . . good businessman" Selma Shapiro to Ann Schumacher, October 10, 1968.

"Rod McKuen is part . . . Robert Burns" Byron Dobrell to Nan Talese, March 7, 1967.

"because here . . . buy your poetry" Nan Talese to Rod McKuen, March 5, 1968.

"It was single women . . . on the plane" Joe Smith interview with author, May 5, 2015.

"Rod was a scam . . . with the signs" Joe Smith interview with author, May 5, 2015.

"I tried for years . . . incredible" James Kaplan, *Sinatra: The Chairman*. New York: Doubleday. 2015. 790.

"The Beatles . . . his next move" Tina Sinatra, *My Father's Daughter: A Memoir*. New York: Simon & Schuster. 2000. 124.

"My vocals weren't as good . . . wouldn't like it" "Flight Plan," A Safe Place to Land, June 30 and July 1, 2012. http://www.rodmckuen.org/flights/300612. htm (accessed June 23, 2018).

"He would be . . . up to Sinatra" Lee Hirschberg interview with author, April 13, 2015.

"A chief complaint . . . in their stead" "Flight Plan," A Safe Place to Land, June 30 and July 1, 2012. http://www.rodmckuen.org/flights/300612.htm (accessed June 23, 2018).

"I acted as . . . around the piano" "Flight Plan," A Safe Place to Land, May 23 and 24, 2005. http://www.rodmckuen.org/flights/230505.htm (accessed June 23, 2018).

'Rock was very . . . dance man" Mark Griffin interview with author. October 11, 2017.

"A young man . . . so silly" David Nutter interview with author, February 22, 2016.

"Rock was thrilled . . . like that" Tom Clark with Dick Kleiner. *Rock Hudson: Friend of Mine*. New York: Pharos Books. 1989. 98.

"Ninety-nine percent . . . beauty" Carl Sterland, *Chuck: An Experience*. New York: Bantam. 1970. Author's note. The information about Roy Newquist comes from my interviews with his son Karl and daughter Karen Newquist, October 3, 2017.

"What Chuck and I . . . your affections" Sterland, *Chuck*. 213. According to his longtime correspondent Allen Weitzel, Rod claimed *he* was the author of Chuck. However, the book is copyrighted in Newquist's name. Allen F. Weitzel interview with author, May 2, 2017.

"If [Rock] . . . forgive him. Clark with Kleiner, *Rock Hudson: Friend of Mine.*
98.

"Rock was . . . good guys." "Flight Plan," A Safe Place to Land, May 23 and
24, 2005. http://www.rodmckuen.org/flights/230505.htm (accessed June
23, 2018).

Chapter Eight

"carve out . . . market" Unsigned Random House memo to Rod McKuen,
November 14, 1969.

"a typical . . . smart and funny" Susan A. Schwartz interview with author,
March 6, 2018.

"I'm concerned . . . things to do" Jane Wilkie to Nan Talese, 1970.

If Random House . . . feel better McKuen told *Saturday Review* that Stanyan
Books was "now considered the most successful line of gift books in the
world" and that Bennett Cerf had insisted that Random House take on the
venture. *Saturday Review*, December 2, 1972. 48.

"He said . . . it was worth" Morgan Ames interview with author, July 8, 2016.

"When I did . . . success I've had" Rod McKuen interview with Ben Vaughn,
2011.

"The average age . . . Rod McKuen" *McCall's*, February 1972. 22.

"He knows about love . . . like Rod" *McCall's*, February 1972. 22-23.

"I don't know . . . honest answer" *New York Times Magazine*. April 4, 1971. 33.

"He loved to talk . . . contact me" Allen F. Weitzel interview with author, May
2, 2017.

"a social plague" *New York Times*, April 17, 1971. 3.

"There is no other . . . his nonfans" *McCall's*, February 1972. 14.

'bored, hysterical . . . everyone concerned" *Book World*, November 24, 1968. 4.

"The greed and cynicism . . . can concoct" Karl Shapiro, *The Poetry Wreck:
Selected Essays: 1950–1970*. New York: Random House. 1975. 362-363.

"People who . . . the broker's" *The New Republic*, January 3, 1971. 32.

"Pure treacle . . . smallest vocabulary" Nora Ephron, "Mush," *Esquire*, June 1971. 89.

"How can it be . . . magnificently" *Anniston* [Alabama] *Star*, February 14, 1970. 4.

"in this violent . . . decay of it" *Cincinnati Enquirer*, June 27, 1970. 44.

"He wrote sincerely . . . identified with that" Aram Saroyan "Rod's Lonely Night," The Nervous Breakdown, June 20, 2013. http://thenervousbreakdown.com/asaroyan/2013/06/rods-lonely-night/ ; Saroyan email to author, April 10, 2018.

"The hypocrisy . . . must be bad" Robert Peters, *Where the Bee Sucks: Workers, Drones and Queens of Contemporary American Poetry*. Santa Maria, California: Asylum Arts. 1994.171-178.

Rod McKuen, "Driving Through Davis," *Fields of Wonder*. New York: Random House. 1971. 79-83.

"He accused me . . . responsible for it" *Saturday Review*, December 2, 1972. 48.

"I do consider . . . millions of people" Rod McKuen interview with Aram Saroyan, Coldspring Journal No. 10, April 1976.

"When I started . . . brilliant poetry of" *Saturday Review*, January 8, 1972. 18.

"I felt that . . . otherwise significant" Robert Sherman email to author, August 28, 2015.

"Stan Freeman . . . did his job" Michael Feinstein interview with author, August 2018. Stan Freeman was an in-demand studio pianist for artists like Frank Sinatra, Ella Fitzgerald, Charlie Parker, and Rosemary Clooney, as well as the composer of several lesser-known Broadway musicals.

"He has won . . . rid of him" Dick Krinsley to Nan Talese, February 21, 1973.

"No man . . . himself to himself" Jane Wilkie, "Seven Years on the Road Results in the Emergence of Rod McKuen's Musical Empire." Rod McKuen supplement in *Billboard*, May 5, 1973. RM-3.

"a full clothing line . . . wardrobe style" Rod McKuen supplement in *Billboard*, May 5, 1973. RM-14.

Chapter Nine

"The only reason . . . run around in" *McCall's*, February 1972, 12.

"Edward was . . . Rod McKuen" Charlie Hallam interview with author, May 24, 2018.

"Rod never stopped . . . he stayed" Charlie Hallam interview with author, May 24, 2018.

"He is my brother . . . be incest" "Flight Plan," A Safe Place to Land, June 28 and 29, 2004. http://www.rodmckuen.org/flights/280604.htm (accessed June 23, 2018).

"There are as many . . . by people" *Saturday Review*, December 2, 1972. 47.

"I think the straights . . . intellectual needs" *The Advocate*, September 8, 1976. 20. Gillian Frank wrote an intriguing blog article about how McKuen's press obituaries dealt with his sexual identity. See: "Straight After Death: Misremembering the Queer Life and Times of Rod McKuen," Notches, February 19, 2015. http://notchesblog.com/2015/02/19/not-by-my-definition-remembering-rod-mckuens-queer-life-and-times/ (accessed June 23, 2018).

"It's very difficult . . . my work" *ASCAP Today*, June 1969. 17.

"When I got . . . great time together" *Asbury Park Sunday Press*, December 21, 1972. 26.

"We just couldn't . . . thing to do" *Des Moines Register*, May 4, 1969. 56.

"My kids . . . good news" "Flight Plan," A Safe Place to Land, November 5, 2002. http://www.rodmckuen.org/flights/051102.htm (accessed, June 23, 2018).

"We were filming . . . stuff like that" David Nutter interview with author, February 22, 2016.

"My girlfriend . . . he did too" Lee Schaller interview with author, September 15, 2017. Rod also went to Dr. Schaller for dental work. He was reportedly "very good, very stoic" as a patient.

"I thought Rod . . . a kick out of" Henry Edwards interview with author, June 11, 2017.

"She wouldn't have . . . was worse" Henry Edwards interview with author, June 11, 2017.

"Tom used to brag . . . Rod was famous" Alan Eichler interview with author, May 25, 2017.

Rod and Tom . . . ten years later Among Eyen's papers archived at Ohio State University is a folder labeled "Rod McKuen collaboration." The file contains two newspaper clippings about Rod but is otherwise empty.

"There was a couple . . . Rod's life" Charlie Hallam interview with author, May 5, 2018.

"Wade filled a lot . . . he only gave them" Charlie Hallam interview with author, May 5, 2018.

James Sullivan, "Goodbye, Papa, It's Hard to Die," Slate, March 16, 2005. http://www.slate.com/articles/arts/music_box/2005/03/goodbye_papa_its_hard_to_die.html (accessed June 23, 2018).

"This is a vow . . . the other ends" Rod McKuen, "The Rod McKuen Marriage Ceremony," in An Outstretched Hand, New York: Harper & Row. 1980. 91-95.

"I had suddenly begun . . . it isn't enough'" The Advocate, September 8, 1976. 19-20.

Chapter Ten

"If he's a skid row . . . I'm grateful" Los Angeles Times, January 30, 1976. 83.

"Michael's reports . . . the reports" Richard Carlson interview with author, May 11, 2018. Carlson went on to become the director of the Voice of America, U.S. ambassador to the Seychelles, and the CEO of the Corporation for Public Broadcasting. Rod recorded a campaign commercial for him when he ran for mayor of San Diego in 1983.

"a hundred half-truths . . . single fact" McKuen, Finding My Father, 212.

"a poignant . . . meaningful" Los Angeles Times, September 19, 1976. 218.

"his private life . . . commercial persona" Kirkus Review, August 16, 1976.

https://www.kirkusreviews.com/book-reviews/rod-mckuen/finding-my-father/ (accessed June 23, 2018).

"[McKuen] pads . . . without 'meaning' to" *Democrat and Chronicle*, November 28, 1976. 79.

"I have a very . . . circumstances" McKuen, *Finding My Father*, 252.

"I was very . . . about this" Jerry Heleva interview with author, May 15, 2018.

"I found Ford . . . good times" Rod McKuen, "How Legitimate is Illegitimate?" *The Robesonian* (Lumberton, North Carolina), September 25, 1977. 7.

'I must say . . . men running it" Rod McKuen interview with Aram Saroyan, *Coldspring Journal*, No. 10, April 1976.

"A kind of Ginny . . . American citizens" *Florida Today*, May 3, 1977. 6B.

"An out-of-town . . . our business" *Florida Today*, May 3, 1977. 6B.

"If he can . . . label on me" *Tampa Tribune*, May 8, 1977. 31.

"That wasn't why . . . one of them" *The Journal Herald* (Dayton, Ohio), June 8, 1979. 27.

Set to a jaunty . . . leave in protest "Flight Plan," A Safe Place to Land, June 9 and 10, 2012. http://www.rodmckuen.org/flights/090612.htm (accessed June 30, 2018).

"Bureaucracy is busy . . . kind mankind" Rod McKuen, *The Power Bright & Shining*, New York: Simon & Schuster, 1980. 44, 46, 49, 132.

"We'd played . . . limited market" Joe Smith interview with author, May 5, 2015.

"I'll probably . . . I'm fifty." *Newsweek*, November 4, 1968. 114.

Chapter Eleven

"We were only . . . people in danger" Ray Gallagher interview with author, October 29, 2017.

"I had a terrific . . . can one man eat" "Flight Plan," A Safe Place to Land, August 2 and 3, 2004. http://www.rodmckuen.org/flights/030804.htm (accessed June 30, 2018).

"I was playing . . . about himself" Michael Feinstein interview with author, August 2018.

"Edward had been . . . back to Angelo Drive" Charlie Hallam interview with author, May 24, 2018.

"God-loving . . . practicing Christian" McKuen, *An Outstretched Hand*, 4, 51.

"Poetry is not . . . goes for Rod McKuen" *Writer's Digest*, February 1984. 26, 28, 29.

"Are you sure . . . felt I shouldn't" Rose Adkins interview with author, October 17, 2017.

"He was upstairs . . . until it was completed" Rose Adkins interview with author, October 17, 2017.

"He could get melancholy . . . nasty that Christmas" Rose Adkins interview with author, October 17, 2017.

"there was a joy . . . hurt in his poetry" Rose Adkins interview with author, May 16, 2018.

"All my life . . . good as everybody else" *People*, August 16, 1982. 233.

"He said, 'I don't . . . couldn't even talk" Rose Adkins interview with author, October 17, 2017.

"Halfway through . . . had to go home" *Philadelphia Inquirer*, July 13. 1982. 33.

"a secret . . . watch and wait" Rod McKuen, *Suspension Bridge*, New York: Harper & Row, 1984. 77.

"there are times . . . they are hell" *Writer's Digest*, February 1984. 30.

"I felt that the road . . . showed it to anyone" Rod McKuen interview with Jim Pierson, 2011.

"He seemed to enjoy . . . wouldn't respond" Charlie Hallam interview with author, June 2, 2018.

"I do know . . . Warhols and Picassos" Robyn Whitney interview, September 12, 2015.

"Fighting between them . . . checks coming in" Charlie Hallam interview with author, June 2, 2018.

"An extremely shy . . . he laughed" Robyn Whitney interview with author, September 12, 2015.

"They were codependent . . . for many lifetimes" Charlie Hallam interview with author, June 2, 2018.

"has little to say . . . hard rock" This quote from a review of Nirvana's *Nevermind* album by *Boston Globe* critic Steve Morse is found in such books as *Nirvana FAQ* by John D. Luerssen and *Classic Rock Albums: Nirvana–Nevermind* by Charles R. Cross and Jim Berkenstadt, as well as on blogs like Music Weird. http://musicweird.blogspot.com/2014/ (accessed June 23, 2018).

According to Rod . . . writing a song together "Flight Plan," A Safe Place to Land, June 21, 2001. http://www.rodmckuen.org/flights/210601.htm (accessed June 23, 2018).

"Overcoming it was . . . to be depressed" Rod McKuen interview with Jim Pierson, 2011.

"When he'd get blue . . . he still was" Robyn Whitney interview with author, March 12, 2015.

Chapter Twelve

"Rod had 'donated' . . . without him" "Flight Plan," A Safe Place to Land, December 27, 1999. http://www.rodmckuen.org/flights/271299.htm (accessed June 23, 2018).

"I always felt . . . good times even better" "Somewhere along . . . every step" "I was fifteen . . . gave me the will to live" "Flight Plan," A Safe Place to Land, December 29, 1999. http://www.rodmckuen.org/flights/291299.htm (accessed June 23, 2018).

"one of the great . . . it deserved" Kim Cooper, *Beatsville*, P22 Records P22-006, 1998. Liner notes.

"We were in Rod's . . . little awkward" Charlie Hallam interview with author, June 2, 2018.

"a great guy . . . disappointed with people" Robyn Whitney interview with author, September 12, 2015.

"Maybe it was . . . that song sung" David Galligan interview with author, June 5, 2015.

"He would stop . . . say no to" Robyn Whitney interview with author, September 12, 2015.

"My job was . . . so much fun" Ben McMillan interview with author, June 16, 2016.

"He was magnetic . . . commanded the room" Ben McMillan interview with author, June 16, 2016.

"They were genuinely . . . requested one" Jim McMillan interview with author, June 16, 2016.

"Apart from one track . . . with him again" Petula Clark email to author, May 17, 2015.

"Doing that album . . . with Mr. Magoo" Jim Pierson interview with author, June 10, 2018.

"It was like pulling teeth . . . ballot box" Jim Pierson interview with author, June 10, 2018.

"For the years I knew . . . get things done" Jim Pierson interview with author, June 10, 2018.

"That house . . . Sunset Boulevard" Jim Pierson interview with author, June 12, 2018.

"We were going . . . decided against it" Robyn Whitney interview with author, September 12, 2015.

"The funniest thing . . . in the house" Tom Truhe interview with author, August 2018.

"They asked me . . . people to get in" Charlie Hallam interview with author, June 2, 2018.

"the closest thing . . . grows longer" Rod McKuen to A. D. Winans, May 2007. Copy of letter sent by Winans to author via email, April 30, 2017.

"Rod said that he'd . . . never used to for himself" Robyn Whitney interview with author, September 12, 2015.

"With your own story . . . write a best seller" Helen Brann email to Rod McKuen, July 18, 2012.

"He had this . . . famous as he had been" Ben Vaughn interview with author, January 2, 2016.

"Rod was struck . . . he was grateful" Robyn Whitney interview with author, September 12, 2015

Coda

"Ada Sands . . . pathetic and tragic" Jim Pierson interview with author, June 12, 2108.

"He just wanted . . . grief go away" Robyn Whitney interview with author, September 12, 2015.

"Edward wanted . . . bins worth" Charlie Hallam interview with author, June 2, 2018.

"We had ninety-four file drawers . . . store them" Charlie Hallam interview with author June 2, 2018.

"I said to him . . . back to Angelo with Rod" Hallam interview with author, June 2, 2018.

SELECTED BIBLIOGRAPHY

McKuen, Rod. *A Safe Place to Land.* Los Angeles: Stanyan Book & Discs, 2001.

_____*An Outstretched Hand.* New York: Harper & Row, 1980.

_____*. . . . and autumn came.* New York: Pageant Press, 1954.

_____*And to Each Season . . .* New York: Simon & Schuster, 1972.

_____*Beyond the Boardwalk.* Los Angeles: Cheval Books, 1975.

_____*Caught in the Quiet.* Los Angeles: Stanyan Books, 1970.

_____*Celebrations of the Heart.* New York: Simon & Schuster, 1975.

_____*Come to Me in Silence.* New York: Simon & Schuster, 1973.

_____*Coming Close to the Earth.* New York: Simon & Schuster, 1978.

_____*Fields of Wonder.* New York: Random House, 1971.

_____*Finding My Father.* 2nd ed. New York: Berkley Publishing, 1977.

_____*In Someone's Shadow.* New York: Random House, 1969.

_____*Intervals.* New York: Harper & Row, 1986.

_____*Listen to the Warm.* New York: Random House, 1967.

_____*Lonesome Cities.* New York: Random House, 1968.

_____*Moment to Moment.* New York: Simon & Schuster, 1974.

_____*Rusting in the Rain.* Los Angeles: Stanyan Books, 2004.

_____ *Stanyan Street & Other Sorrows*. Los Angeles: Stanyan Music, 1966.

_____ *Suspension Bridge*. New York: Harper & Row, 1984.

_____ *The Beautiful Strangers*. New York: Simon & Schuster, 1981.

_____ *The Carols of Christmas*. New York: Random House, 1971.

_____ *The Power Bright & Shining*. New York: Simon & Schuster, 1979.

_____ *The Sea Around Me*. New York: Simon & Schuster, 1975.

_____ *The Songs of Rod McKuen*. Los Angeles: Cheval Books, 1969.

_____ *Twelve Years of Christmas*. New York: Random House, 1969.

_____ *Valentines*. New York: Harper & Row, 1986.

_____ *We Touch the Sky*. New York: Simon & Schuster, 1979.

SELECTED DISCOGRAPHY

Aaron Freeman

Marvelous Clouds. Partisan Records PTKF2101, 2012. LP. CD.

Rod McKuen

After Midnight. Stanyan Records STZ 105-2, 1988. CD.

Alone After Dark. Decca Records DL 78946, 1960. LP.

Anywhere I Wander. Decca Records 8882, 1959. LP.

Beatsville. HiFi Records R 419, 1959, LP.

Beatsville (enhanced reissue). Stanyan/P22 Records 006, 1998. CD.

Goodtime Music. Warner Bros. Records BS 2861, 1975. LP.

Grand Tour. Warner Bros. Records WB 1947, 1971. LP.

In Concert. Stanyan Records SR 5001, 1965. LP.

In Search of Eros. Epic Records LN 3814, 1961. LP.

In Search of Eros (reissue with added tracks). Stanyan/P22 Records 017,
   2003. CD.

Lazy Afternoon. Liberty Records LRP 3011, 1956, LP.

Listen to the Warm. RCA Victor LSP 3863, 1967. LP.

Listen to the Warm (deluxe edition). Real Gone Music RGM 0125, 2013. CD.

Lonesome Cities. Warner Bros. Records WS 1758, 1968. LP.

Mr. Oliver Twist. Jubilee Records 5803, 1962. LP.

Mr. Oliver Twist (reissue). Collector's Choice CCM-114-12, 1999. CD.

New Ballads. Warner Bros. Records 1837, 1970. LP.

New Carols for Christmas: The Rod McKuen Christmas Album.
    Stanyan Records SR 5045, 1971. LP.

New Carols for Christmas: The Rod McKuen Christmas Album
    (expanded edition). Real Gone RGM-0817, 2018. CD.

New Sounds in Folk Music. Horizon Records 1612, 1963. LP.

Odyssey. Warner Bros. Records BS 2638, 1972. LP.

Other Kinds of Songs. RCA Victor Records LSP 3635, 1966. LP.

Pastorale. Warner Bros. Records 2WS 1894, 1971. LP.

Prolific Composer Rod McKuen Sings His Own. RCA Victor Records
    LSP-3424, 1965. LP.

Rod McKuen '77. Stanyan Records SR 5093, 1977. LP.

Rod McKuen Sings McKuen/Brel. Stanyan Records 5022, 1972. LP.

Rod McKuen's The Black Eagle. Stanyan Records 2SR 5087, 1978. LP.

Seasons in the Sun, 2. Stanyan Records SR 5004, 1967. LP.

Slide . . . Easy In. Discus Records 7017, 1977. LP.

Sold Out at Carnegie Hall. Warner Bros. Records 2WS 1749, 1969. LP.

Sold Out at Carnegie Hall (deluxe edition). Real Gone Music RGM 1024,
    2013. CD.

Stranger in Town. Kapp Records KS-3226 1961. LP.

The Beautiful Strangers. Warner Bros. Records WS 1722, 1968. LP.

The Loner. RCA Victor Records LSP 3508, 1966. LP.

The Love Movement. Capitol Records ST 2838, 1967. LP.

The Single Man. RCA Victor LSP 4010, 1968. LP.

Through European Windows. RCA Victor Records LSP 3785, 1967.
    LP.

Time of Desire. HiFi Records R 407, 1958, LP.

Turntable. Stanyan Records SR 5100, 1980. LP.

The Word. Discus Records DS 7000, 1971. LP.

The San Sebastian Strings

For Lovers. Warner Bros. Records WS 1795, 1969. LP.

Home to the Sea. Warner Bros. Records WS 1764, 1969. LP.

The Earth. Warner Bros. Records WS 1705, 1967. LP.

The Sea. Warner Bros. Records WS 1670, 1967. LP. CD.

The Sky. Warner Bros. Records WS 1720, 1968. LP.

The Soft Sea. Warner Bros. Records WS 1839, 1970. LP.

Soundtracks

A Boy Named Charlie Brown. Columbia Records OS 3500, 1970. LP.

A Boy Named Charlie Brown (expanded edition). Varese Sarabande Records,
   302 067 222 8, 2015. CD.

Joanna. 20th Century Fox Records S 4202, 1968. LP.

The Prime of Miss Jean Brodie. Warner Bros. Records WS 1787, 1969. LP.

Frank Sinatra

A Man Alone. Reprise Records FS 1030, 1969. LP. CD.

Various Artists

Love's Been Good to Me: The Songs of Rod McKuen. Ace Records CDTOP
   1481, 2017. CD.

Glenn Yarbrough

The Lonely Things. RCA Victor Records LSP 3539, 1966. LP. CD.